The People's Duty

Can we talk about "the people" as an agent with its own morally important integrity? How should we understand ownership of public property by "the people"? Shmuel Nili develops philosophical answers to both of these questions, arguing that we should see the core project of a liberal legal system – realizing equal rights – as an identity-grounding project of the sovereign people, and thus as essential to the people's integrity. He also suggests that there are proprietary claims that are intertwined in the sovereign people's moral power to create property rights through the legal system. The practical value of these ideas is illustrated through a variety of real-world policy problems, ranging from the domestic and international dimensions of corruption and abuse of power, through transitional justice issues, to the ethnic and religious divides that threaten liberal democracy. This book will appeal to political theorists as well as readers in public policy, area studies, law, and across the social sciences.

SHMUEL NILI is Assistant Professor of Political Science at Northwestern University, Evanston, Illinois, and a research fellow at the School of Philosophy at the Australian National University, Canberra. He has published widely in leading journals, including *Ethics, The American Political Science Review, The Journal of Politics,* and *The American Journal of Political Science.*

The People's Duty

Collective Agency and the Morality of Public Policy

SHMUEL NILI
Northwestern University and the Australian National University

CAMBRIDGE
UNIVERSITY PRESS

CAMBRIDGE
UNIVERSITY PRESS

University Printing House, Cambridge CB2 8BS, United Kingdom

One Liberty Plaza, 20th Floor, New York, NY 10006, USA

477 Williamstown Road, Port Melbourne, VIC 3207, Australia

314–321, 3rd Floor, Plot 3, Splendor Forum, Jasola District Centre, New Delhi – 110025, India

79 Anson Road, #06–04/06, Singapore 079906

Cambridge University Press is part of the University of Cambridge.

It furthers the University's mission by disseminating knowledge in the pursuit of education, learning, and research at the highest international levels of excellence.

www.cambridge.org
Information on this title: www.cambridge.org/9781108480925
DOI: 10.1017/9781108691680

© Shmuel Nili 2019

This publication is in copyright. Subject to statutory exception and to the provisions of relevant collective licensing agreements no reproduction of any part may take place without the written permission of Cambridge University Press.

First published 2019

Printed in the United Kingdom by TJ International Ltd. Padstow Cornwall

A catalog record for this publication is available from the British Library.

Library of Congress Cataloging-in-Publication Data
Names: Nili, Shmuel, author.
Title: The people's duty : collective agency and the morality of public policy / Shmuel Nili.
Description: Cambridge, United Kingdom ; New York, NY : Cambridge University Press, 2019. | Includes bibliographical references and index.
Identifiers: LCCN 2018061493 | ISBN 9781108480925 (hardback)
Subjects: LCSH: Political participation – Moral and ethical aspects. | Abuse of administrative power. | Political corruption. | Political ethics. | Government property.
Classification: LCC JF799 .N55 2019 | DDC 172/.1–dc23
LC record available at https://lccn.loc.gov/2018061493

ISBN 978-1-108-48092-5 Hardback

Cambridge University Press has no responsibility for the persistence or accuracy of URLs for external or third-party internet websites referred to in this publication and does not guarantee that any content on such websites is, or will remain, accurate or appropriate.

לאבא משה,
שניכש מילים תועות רבות כל כך לאורך הדרך
לאמא מיכל,
שידעה לאן הדרך תוביל עוד בראשיתה
ולשניהם,
יחדיו

Contents

Acknowledgments		*page* viii
	Introduction	1
1	The People's Integrity	20
2	The People's Property	70
3	The People's Integrity, the People's Property, and the Abuse of Political Power	102
4	Their Property, Our Integrity: The Democratic Response to the Problem of Odious Debt	154
5	Policy Priorities for a Divided People: Israel as a Case Study	190
	Conclusion	233
Index		240

Acknowledgments

Academic writing is simultaneously a solitary and a collective endeavor. Since collectivist ideas form the core of this book, it is especially appropriate to start by acknowledging several institutions and individuals who helped to make this work much better than it would have been had I been left to my own devices. I presented different themes out of the book in conferences and colloquia at the Australian National University, the Free University of Berlin, The University of Birmingham, University of Canberra, Griffith University, Harvard University, The Hebrew University of Jerusalem, Northwestern University, Nuffield College Oxford, Princeton University, Queen's University, University of Toronto, University of Vermont, and Yale University. I am very grateful to the organizers and participants in these events – especially Eric Beerbohm, Luis Cabrera, Simon Caney, Joe Carens, Emilee Chapman, Avner De-Shalit, John Dryzek, David Enoch, Cécile Fabre, Jensen Sass, Will Kymlica, Stefan Gospath, Tori McGeer, Robert Lepenies, David Miller, Tom Parr, Lucia Rafanelli, Shlomi Segall, Duncan Snidal, and Alex Zakaras. I have also benefited greatly from exchanges with Elizabeth Anderson, Chris Armstrong, Samuel Freeman, Jeff Howard, Aaron James, Alex Kirshner, Ron Levy, Avia Pasternak, Bo Rothstein, Jeff Spinner-Halev, Annie Stilz, Kok-Chor Tan, Leif Wenar, and Lea Ypi.

The book's opening chapter updates, revises and extends a discussion of collective integrity I first offered in "Liberal Integrity and Foreign Entanglement," *American Political Science Review* 110.1 (2016): 148–159. A few paragraphs from Chapters 2 and 3 are borrowed from my "Rawlzickian Global Politics," *Journal of Political Philosophy* 21.4 (2013): 473–495, and "The Idea of Public Property," *Ethics* 129 (January 2019): 344–369. I am grateful to the editors and publishers of these journals for permission to reprint parts of those essays here.

I was a graduate student at Notre Dame when I was first trying to work through some of the ideas that would inform this book. Ruth

Abbey, Michael Desch, Vitorio Hosle, Dan Philpott, Ernesto Verdeja, Dana Villa, and Michael Zuckert were all kind enough to allow an overly excited student, unfamiliar with the mores of American academia, to inflict too many ideas upon them for too long. After I left South Bend, Michael wryly observed to me that he misses our exchanges, though he now finds that he has more time in his life. The latter part, at least, must have been true as well for Paul Weithman, whose quiet wit, pedagogical patience, analytical acumen, and mentorship were all extraordinary.

Transferring from Notre Dame to complete my PhD at Yale, I was equally fortunate to have extremely supportive faculty advisors across different disciplines. Paulina Ochoa made me feel welcome in the political science department from the very beginning, even while disagreeing – often vehemently – with virtually everything I wanted to say. My dissertation committee members – Ian Shapiro, Thomas Pogge, Seyla Benhabib, and Helene Landemore – were full of insights about many different elements of the project that would eventually yield this book. Insofar as the book engages with various core themes of empirical social science, this is partly due to much appreciated encouragement from Susan Rose-Ackerman, Alan Dafoe, Greg Huber, Niki Marinov, Nuno Monteiro, John Roemer, Frances Rosenbluth, Susan Stokes, and Elisabeth Wood. Many of the book's discussions of moral and legal philosophy have been improved through conversations with Shelly Kagan, Andrew March, Daniel Markovits, Andy Sabl, and Gideon Yaffe.

My fellow students at Yale also offered much social and intellectual inspiration, as did visitors and post-doctoral fellows whom I was lucky to get to know. For their friendship and for numerous helpful conversations, I am deeply grateful to Richard Adams, Consuelo Amat-Matus, Tom Andreassen, Tomasso Bardelli, Danielle Botti, Natasha Chichilnisky-Heal, Stephen Eich, Blake Emerson, Lucas Entel, David Ewert, David Froomkin, Adom Getachew, Henning Hann, Justin Hawkins, Pablo Kalmanovitz, Leora Katz, William Kwok, Paul Linden-Retek, Max Krahe, Markus Labude, Ed Limmer, Matt Lindauer, Tumi Makgetla, Florian Ostmann, Travis Pantin, Erin Pineda, Daniel Putnam, Anurag Sinha, Dan Smith, Jiewuh Song, Gilad Tanay, Becca Traber, Daniel Viehoff, and Becky Wolitz. This wonderful group was accompanied by two unique housemates in New Haven – Matthew Vermaire and James Dunn. Matt and Jamie indulged my philosophical ruminations about integrity and property over many more house meals, ping-pong matches, and game console competitions than these ideas deserved. It did not take long to discover that they are remarkable human beings to just the same extent that they are remarkable philosophers.

I completed this book as a faculty member at Northwestern's department of political science and a research fellow at the Australian National University's school of philosophy. I am indebted to friends and (present and former) colleagues at both institutions for much wisdom and good cheer, including Ana Arjona, Renee Bolinger, Devon Cass, Dylan Clements, Lauren Dickson, Loubna El-Amine, Jim Farr, Jordan Gans-Morse, Al Hayek, Josef Holden, Dan Krcmaric, Seth Lazar, Chad Lee-Stronach, Shang Long Yeo, Steven Nelson, Susan Pennings, Andrew Roberts, Jay Seawright, Hezkie Simmonds, Lachlan Umbers, Steve White, and James Willoughby.

The penultimate version of the manuscript was read with considerable care by three anonymous reviewers for Cambridge. I am grateful to them, and to my editor John Haslam, for extremely productive advice and encouragement. As the manuscript was nearing completion, I discussed some of its main claims with the students in my "global injustice" graduate seminar at Northwestern (Spring 2018). My thanks to all of them for a wonderful set of exchanges. Abby Bruxworth, Lior Erez, Andy Koppelman, and Jim Wilson read through the entire final manuscript and offered many probing comments. The seven consecutive hours that Jim and I spent in a Chicago café, each delving into the details of the other's forthcoming manuscript, come quite close to the nerdy ideal of pure intellectual joy.

Alongside all of these individuals, I owe special thanks to a few more people scattered in different parts of the world. In the midwest, Mary Dietz and Sara Monoson have been especially kind and helpful ever since I joined Northwestern and began learning the ropes of the institution. In Oregon, Burke Hendrix became – quite a while ago – a deeply valued source of informal advice, without having any institutional obligation to offer such advice. Notwithstanding the deep friendship we have formed over the years, Burke could still be relied upon to constructively disagree with almost every thought I have, and to review my work with more critical bite than even the most ferocious anonymous referee. Whether at Princeton, Stanford, or

Frankfurt, Ted Lechterman has similarly offered the benefits of his philosophical skill and sensitivity on many more occasions than one could reasonably expect. In Connecticut, Lizzie Krontiris saved my faith in the species in ways that only she knows, and has served as a model of integrity in many more ways than I know how to express.

In Australia, Christian Barry, Geoff Brennan, Jesse Hambly, Philip Pettit, and Nic Southwood have all shown an uncanny ability, not only to express my own philosophical ideas better than I could myself, but also to make Canberra and the ANU feel like more of a home. I am also grateful to Catherine Waldby, the director of ANU's Research School of the Social Sciences, for making multiple stays in Australia possible, and for her firm support during especially demanding periods.

In Brazil, a key inspiration for the themes of this work, Nara Pavao, Tiago Peterlevitz, and Clarissa Gross have taught me about a world very different from anything I knew before. Nara and Tiago, dear friends from different stages of my PhD work, took the time to read different parts of the manuscript, and to make many shrewd observations about the politics of corruption. Clarissa added to their observations many philosophical insights and many unique lessons about Brazilian joy and sorrow.

The final location of my debts is in my native Israel, the subject of the last chapter of this book. My Israeli thanks extend, in part, to Ram Ben Ari, Guy Ben Porat, Alex Bligh, Yossi Dahan, Tamar Hermann, Ilana Kaufman, Yagil Levi, Benny Neuberger, and Rafi Ventura. All of these scholars – some of them among my earliest teachers – prodded me, at different points in time, to pursue my scholarly interests, and without their prodding I am quite confident this book would not exist.

My most important debt, however, is to my family. With unparalleled warmth and all possible forms of intelligence, my sister Einav, and my brothers Uri and Yehonatan, have always encouraged my work in general, and my work on this book in particular. This was not surprising, since they somehow seemed to skip that part of life where the older siblings make things miserable for the youngest one (notwithstanding that ignoble incident, featuring Irish cream presented to my especially gullible eight-year-old self as "cocoa"). More seriously, their children – my extraordinary nieces and nephews Maya, Itamar, Shahar, Yarden, Shaked, Yuval, Avigail, and Uriah – are all the reason one needs to keep dreaming, even against the background of increasingly bleak realities, that our country can someday, somehow, step back from the abyss, and reclaim the universal ideals on which it was founded.

Though it took me a long time to understand this, the final chapter of this book, and much more generally, my determination to study political philosophy, can be traced all the way to that dreadful morning of November 5, 1995, in which I learned that Prime Minister Rabin was assassinated by a fanatic who wanted to end the Israeli–Palestinian peace process. The state of the nation in that moment seemed to me heartbreakingly encapsulated in the state of my parents, Michal and Moshe, who woke me to say what had happened during the night. Much has changed in our country, in its politics, and in our family, ever since that traumatic event. Yet through it all, my parents have always remained not just my most fundamental and loving support, but also the most striking exemplars of sheer humanity that I know. This book is dedicated to them.

Introduction

A memorable episode of the classic British satire *Yes, Prime Minister* provides a useful entry point into the themes of this book. This episode, titled "A Conflict of Interest," revolves around the government response to a brewing scandal in London's financial sector ("the City"). A major bank, "Phillips Berenson," is on the brink of insolvency due to its directors' misdeeds. These misdeeds range from tax evasion, through insider trading and embezzlement, to bribery and other corrupt dealings with foreign officials. Against this background, the prime minister is considering whom to appoint as the new governor of the Bank of England. The prime minister is initially keen on appointing Alexander Jameson, who is known for his professionalism and firm ethical principles, and who is bound to order an inquiry into Phillips Berenson. But Sir Humphrey Appleby, the cabinet secretary, is determined to change the prime minister's mind. Sir Humphrey notes in his diary that "It's not just the Phillips Berenson case that will be affected if Jameson gets the job and starts all his confounded amateur Sherlock Holmesing":

All sorts of other little matters could emerge. He could uncover a major scandal. Followed by collapse of confidence. Sterling crises. The pound could fall through the floor. It would, of course, be best for all of us if all those City fiddles could be cleared up. But that's just naïve optimism, I fully realise. Pie in the sky. The bottom line (as our American cousins like to say) is that the City earns this country 6 billion a year. We can't hazard all that just because a few chaps do a few favours for a few other chaps, who happen to be their friends, without telling the shareholders. It might be *right* to put a stop to it. But it simply wouldn't be reasonable. The repercussions would be too great. The time is not ripe.[1]

---

[1] Jonathan Lynn and Anthony Jay, *The Complete Yes Prime Minister* (London: BBC Books, 1989), 362. Italics in the original. Even when adjusting for inflation, the relevant figures in more recent years have actually been vastly higher than six billion pounds. See, e.g., Anjuli Davies, "Britain's Financial Sector Paid Record 71.4 Billion

Driven by this reasoning, Sir Humphrey seeks to paint Jameson to the prime minister as a man who is so fanatic in his principles, that his virtues are in fact a political liability. With typical guile, Sir Humphrey does this by appearing to praise and defend Jameson in response to the prime minister's questions. In his own diary, the prime minister reports his exchange with Sir Humphrey as follows:

> Humphrey, do you think he's good? 'Good is exactly the word,' replied Humphrey. 'A really *good* man... Extremely honest. Honest with absolutely everyone...' Humphrey obviously likes him a lot. And yet... there's something about his enthusiasm that worries me. 'It's good, isn't it, to be honest with everyone?' I asked... He was unequivocal. 'Of course it's good. If he finds a scandal anywhere, even here in Number Ten, he'll tell everybody. No doubt about that.' 'You mean... he's indiscreet?' Humphrey looked uneasy. 'Oh dear,' he replied with a sigh, 'that's such a pejorative word. I prefer merely to say that he's obsessively honest.'
>
> I was becoming concerned. I am all for honesty, God knows, but there is a time and place for everything. And we are discussing politics. Handling people, that sort of thing. 'Do you think, quite candidly, that he's the right man to bring the City into line?' 'Absolutely,' said Humphrey without hesitation. 'If you want a Saint. Of course, there are those who say he doesn't live in the real world. He *is* extremely puritanical... a bit of an Ayatollah, in fact. The only question is, do you want to risk a Samson who might bring the whole edifice crashing down?'[2]

This conversation begins to push the prime minister away from appointing Jameson. Later on, the prime minister's own short-term calculations, and the threat of a diplomatic crisis if Phillips Berenson's massive loans to corrupt foreign leaders are revealed, settle the issue, and produce the result that Sir Humphrey desires. The prime minister appoints as governor not Jameson, but rather the intellectually underwhelming chairman of a huge bank that lent heavily to Phillips Berenson.[3] This pick will make sure that the Bank of England bails

---

Pounds in Taxes Last Year before Brexit," *Reuters*, Dec. 5, 2016, at https://uk.reuters.com/article/uk-financial-services-tax/britains-financial-sector-paid-record-71-4-billion-pounds-in-taxes-last-year-before-brexit-idUKKBN13V005.

[2] Lynn and Jay, *The Complete Yes Prime Minister*, 365–366. Italics in the original.

[3] The Prime Minister's senior political advisor points out: "It's easy to see how he became Chairman. He never has any original ideas, he speaks slowly, and because he doesn't understand anything he always agrees with whoever he's talking to. So obviously people think he's sound... but he's a bumbling buffoon." Lynn and Jay, *The Complete Yes Prime Minister*, 372–373.

out Phillips Berenson with minimal publicity. Consequently, business will continue as usual for all involved – from the criminal directors to the foreign leaders who have been abusing Phillips Berenson's loans.

Now, in this particular instance, Sir Humphrey's (genuine) concern seems overstated – he appears to be exaggerating the costs of reform, and underestimating its benefits. Nonetheless, we recognize the intuitive pull of his desire to maintain stability, even if doing so means allowing various criminals to "get away with it." It would be wonderful, of course, if we lived in a world in which there was never any moral reason to behave in this way – to accommodate, turn a blind eye to, or otherwise compromise with wrongdoers. But fictional plot lines such as those of *Yes, Prime Minister* resonate with us precisely because of the degree to which they track sad realities. In many actual political cases, there clearly *are* moral reasons to compromise with the perpetrators of serious wrongs: the question is how to balance these reasons against countervailing moral considerations.

Here are some real-world examples, all of which will feature prominently in this book. What compromises, if any, are appropriate when considering kleptocrats who are effectively holding their people hostage – for instance, rulers who systematically abuse loans from foreign creditors, as in the *Yes, Prime Minister* tale, but who rely on the fact that their vulnerable population will suffer if loans are cut off entirely? What compromises, if any, are morally appropriate when dealing with dictators who threaten to unleash further violence unless they are guaranteed an amnesty by the democratic forces trying to replace them? If virtually all seasoned politicians in a developing country with a fragile democracy are implicated in wide-scale corruption, but if the country is facing an acute economic crisis that clearly requires experience at the helm, what should be done about the corrupt, and who should decide?

Within political theory, such questions have often been the purview of the "dirty hands" literature, which has been preoccupied with the question of whether one can – or should – "govern innocently."[4] This literature, much like *Yes, Prime Minister*, has been heavily focused on

---

[4] The phrase is famously due to Jean-Paul Sartre's play "Dirty Hands." See, e.g., Sartre's *No Exit and Three Other Plays* (New York: Vintage, 1989). The most influential treatment of the topic in contemporary political theory remains Michael Walzer's "The Problem of Dirty Hands," *Philosophy & Public Affairs* 2 (1973): 160–180.

individual political actors, and particularly on individuals at the apex of political power.[5] Yet, although I believe that such individual-level discussions contain valuable insights, I pursue a different approach here.

My main goal in this book is to develop two *collectivist* philosophical frameworks. Both of these frameworks focus not on individual political actors, but rather on *the people*, as the collective agent in whose name modern political power is exercised. The practical value of these frameworks, I argue, is especially evident when reflecting on intricate policy problems concerning corruption and other abuses of political power. But I also try to show that the two frameworks ultimately help us tackle further – related but distinct – public policy dilemmas.[6]

The first framework revolves around a collectivist version of a much debated individual virtue – integrity, understood as fidelity to one's identity-grounding commitments or projects.[7] Within the dirty hands literature, invocations of "integrity" have often been met with suspicion, especially by consequentialists of various stripes. Many in this camp have long argued that integrity can be a political vice rather than a virtue: if the public good requires public officials to sully their hands when making political decisions, then it is objectionable of them to appeal to their "identity-grounding commitments" as a justification for keeping their hands clean.[8] Such critiques, once again, have intuitive

---

[5] For a partial exception see Dennis Thompson, "Responsibility for Failures of Government: The Problem of Many Hands," *The American Review of Public Administration* 44 (2014): 259–273.

[6] Whenever speaking of "dilemmas," I will have in mind morally complex choices. This usage of "dilemma" is different from the technical sense sometimes employed by philosophers, to refer to a situation where all possible choices involve moral wrongs.

[7] As I note in Chapter 1, this understanding of integrity is most famously associated with Bernard Williams, though many of the ideas I will develop with regard to integrity depart quite substantially from Williams's views.

[8] "It is in the nature of public officials' role responsibilities that they are morally obliged to 'dirty their hands' – make hard choices, do things that are wrong (or would ordinarily be wrong, or would ordinarily be wrong for private individuals) in the service of some greater public good. It would be simply irresponsible of public officials (in any broadly secular society, at least) to adhere mindlessly to moral precepts read off some sacred list, literally 'whatever the consequences. ' Doing right though the heavens may fall is not (nowadays, anyway) a particularly attractive posture for public officials to adopt," Robert Goodin, *Utilitarianism as Public Philosophy* (Cambridge: Cambridge University Press, 1995), 10. In the same book (69), Goodin seems to simply equate "integrity" reasoning with "clean hands" reasoning, following, for example, Brian Barry, *Democracy,*

appeal: they are, for example, a key reason why Sir Humphrey, who portrays Jameson as "Mister Clean," succeeds in labeling him to the prime minister as dangerously rigorist.[9]

However, we can recognize that it is irresponsible of public officials to prioritize their own integrity when making political decisions that often have dramatic effects on millions of lives, without removing integrity from political morality altogether. We can avoid this path partly by shifting our attention from the individual to the collective level. It is in this spirit that I explore here a notion of *collective integrity*: I discuss how, in a liberal democracy at least, a sovereign people as a collective agent might have morally important integrity, in a sense that parallels the integrity of an individual person.

The basic reason for drawing this parallel, which I elaborate in Chapter 1, is that taking seriously the moral integrity of the people as a collective agent helps us to organize and clarify important moral intuitions concerning the policies of liberal democracies. For one thing, once we think about the people in a liberal democracy in integrity terms – as an agent with its own identity-grounding projects that unfold over time – we can capture important moral intuitions as to how a liberal democracy's particular history should bear on its current conduct. Furthermore, this framework also elucidates distinctive reasons for liberal democracies to prioritize certain policy reforms over others. And, last but far from least, the integrity framework helps liberal democracies in confronting myriad moral dilemmas – dilemmas concerning corruption being only one key example.

The second collectivist framework that I develop in this book has to do with the people's *property*. Ideas regarding public property form a key – if often only implicit – element of our moral reflection about fundamental

---

Power and Justice (Oxford: Clarendon Press, 1989), 340. I actually believe that this equation is misleading, partly for reasons that should become clear in the course of this book.

[9] Sir Humphrey is not alone, of course. Another *Yes, Prime Minister* scene, featuring Treasury opposition to a proposed plan to combat smoking that will cause tax revenue loses, captures a similar thought through the remarks of the Treasury's Permanent Secretary: "It must be admitted that there is a moral principle involved. And we at the Treasury ... earnestly believe in the moral principle. But when four billion pounds of revenue is at stake I think that we have to consider very seriously how far we are entitled to indulge ourselves in the rather selfish luxury of pursuing moral principles." Lynn and Jay, "Chapter 7: The Smokescreen," in *Yes, Prime Minister*, 201.

political issues. Here, too, issues of corruption and abuse of political power are paradigmatic examples, as our opening *Yes, Prime Minister* story again demonstrates. Our instinctive concerns about this story are clearly not exhausted by individualist considerations – for instance, by considerations of individual desert and reward. As I already pointed out, we are of course worried about the criminal directors of Phillips Berenson, for example, being rewarded by the government rather than punished. But another part of our unease with this story has to do with the people's property that provides the source of these directors' individual rewards. A key part of what alarms us about the government cover-up of Phillips Berenson's dealings is that this cover-up requires the use of public property to save the bank, with minimal public exposure.

However, in order to know just how morally significant this concern really is, we need to have a systematic account of public property. Given the centrality of public property to any functioning state and economy, one would expect political philosophers to have such an account on offer. Yet despite the many pages that philosophers have written on the idea of private property, contemporary political philosophy has had very little to say on public property. Starting in Chapter 2, I tackle this gap. In the process, I hope to show how ideas concerning public property can help our moral analysis even in policy areas where we do not expect them to do so – once again, organizing and clarifying a broad set of moral values.

There are at least four reasons why the collective integrity and collective property frameworks are fruitful companions. First, both of these frameworks provide an alternative to a purely consequentialist analysis of concrete policy problems. Few deny that consequences are a significant factor in the morality of public policy.[10] But many think that consequences are not the only significant factor. A public policy that is completely blind to any other moral consideration apart from consequences – that refuses, for example, to recognize any genuinely moral constraint on the attainment of good consequences – is (arguably) as morally lopsided as a policy that is completely oblivious to consequences.[11] The challenge, then, is to figure out how to combine

[10] As Rawls noted with uncharacteristic directness: "All ethical doctrines worth our attention take consequences into account in judging rightness. One which did not would simply be irrational, crazy." See John Rawls, *A Theory of Justice* (Cambridge, MA: Harvard University Press, revised edition, 1999, hereafter *TJ*), 26.
[11] If one interprets the tradition of "political realism" in this light – as a tradition that holds that our entire analysis of political decision making has to be purely

consequentialist and non-consequentialist moral considerations in a stable, coherent way. I will try to show that the collective integrity and collective property frameworks can both rise to this challenge.

Second, the two frameworks inform in complementary ways our thinking about the relationship between the sovereign people and the law of a liberal democracy. Thus for example, I will begin my analysis of the people's integrity from the appeal of seeing the sovereign people as the creator of a liberal democracy's legal system. I will argue that we should understand the core project of a liberal legal system – realizing equal rights – as the identity-grounding project of the collective agent that is the sovereign people, and thus as essential to the people's integrity. I will then pursue a parallel move when discussing the sovereign people as the owner of public property. I will seek to establish that the most compelling philosophical account of public property is one that focuses on the proprietary claims that are intertwined in the sovereign people's moral power to create property rights through the legal system.

A third, related reason for discussing the people's property alongside the people's integrity is that doing so allows us to capture multiple moral judgments concerning the responsibilities of a liberal democracy's legal system. The collective integrity framework insists that a liberal legal system – and ultimately the sovereign people as the creator of that system – carries responsibility even for those wrongs that it does not officially support but merely allows private actors to pursue: dodging this responsibility is a form of collective hypocrisy that is antithetical to the idea of integrity. Along parallel lines, the collective property framework rejects a sharp divide between private and public property, and, as a result, insists that wrongful private discrimination associated with private property can, and often should, be the business of the law, no less than discrimination associated more directly with public property.

> consequentialist – then of course the complaint I am making here would apply to this tradition as well. Part of the problem with assessing political realism, however, is that it is hard to specify the exact contours of this position, or indeed to distinguish it, in the political arena, from a thoroughly consequentialist outlook. For discussion of some of these concerns, see William Galston, "Realism in Political Theory," *European Journal of Political Theory* 9 (2000): 385–411; Jonathan Leader Maynard and Alex Worsnip, "Is There a Distinct Political Normativity?" *Ethics* 128 (2018): 756–787.

A final reason for combining the collective integrity and collective property frameworks is that, in different ways, each of these frameworks illuminates fundamental democratic convictions. Thus for example, by providing us with a clear and coherent way to think about the people's property, the collective property framework pushes us – as I will go on to argue – to consider specific cases in which it would be morally important for the people as a collective agent to exercise direct democratic control over policy decisions pertaining to its property. Similarly, by casting the legal system's core task of realizing equal rights as the people's identity-grounding project, the collective integrity framework captures the democratic conviction that the people ought not to leave this task exclusively to de facto leaders – especially when these leaders have clearly been abusing their power.[12]

"The People": Core Assumptions

These claims are inevitably compressed. Their full meaning and significance can become clear only against the background of the particular policy problems that I will try to address. But before I specify these problems further, some more introductory remarks are in order, first with regard to the basic concept of "the people."

In the following pages, I will often be speaking about "the people," "the public," "the body politic," or (especially in the international context) about "the polity." Whenever I use any of these terms, I will have in mind the sovereign people. In turn, I am going to assume that all of the individuals who permanently reside within each of the world's stable territorial jurisdictions comprise – at least on first approximation – different sovereign peoples.[13] A key thought underlying this assumption is that stable territorial borders accrue normative

---

[12] One might ask a more general question about the relationship between the two frameworks – namely, whether the ideas associated with collective property can ultimately be subsumed under the heading of collective integrity. I wish to remain agnostic on this question, in order to enable even readers who are skeptical of my integrity claims to adopt (at least) some of my arguments with regard to collective ownership.

[13] This understanding of "the people" is often thought to be threatened by what is known as the "democratic boundary problem." Elsewhere, however, I have argued at length that this problem is illusory. See my "Democratic Theory, the Boundary Problem, and Global Reform," *The Review of Politics* 79 (2017): 99–123.

significance over time. Stable borders delineate a (fairly) stable group of individuals as the polity's citizens. And the fact that these individuals (and their descendants) share a political community generates the moral expectation that they will work together to enact a political conception of justice to regulate their common affairs, consequently forming, over time, valuable "bonds of civic friendship."[14]

Note, moreover, that the moral expectation of such civic bonds obtains even when different co-citizens can trace their origins to distinct ethnic groups. Even in such circumstances, there are moral reasons to hope that the very experience of sharing a political community with its attendant tasks, will foster a unifying collective identity, which will make it plausible to focus on a single people – even if a multi-ethnic people – that resides within each state territory. Indeed, the idea that a shared civic identity can eventually replace different ethnic roots as the core of collective identification clearly has considerable moral appeal. This is especially true when thinking of joint civic struggles affirming the basic equality of all citizens and contesting discrimination of various kinds of minorities. Although I shall say more about these kinds of struggles in multiple chapters, we can note already here that it seems intuitive to think that co-citizens can and should take pride in achievements that "the people" together have been making in such struggles. Hence these struggles, and the particular way in which they unfold in each political community, form the core of a particular history around which civic "common sympathies" can emerge and can unite the members of the sovereign people.[15] This is true even when these members do not share (for instance) any pre-political ethnic, linguistic, or religious ties.[16]

---

[14] *TJ*, 5. Anna Stilz similarly emphasizes such civic bonds in her account of territorial rights, arguing that "over time, political cooperation can constitute a group of citizens into a collective agent with important ties binding them together." See her "Nations, States, and Territory," *Ethics* 121 (2011): 572–601, at 592–593.

[15] In turn, one important implication of understanding the sovereign people in civic rather than ethnic terms is the possibility of an inclusive position on the question of who may become a member of the people – as Chapters 1 and 2 will make clear.

[16] This point obtains even for polities struggling to overcome the most extreme types of internal ethnic conflict. For a sustained normative argument along these lines see Ernesto Verdeja, *Unchopping a Tree: Reconciliation in the Aftermath of Political Violence* (Philadelphia, PA: Temple University Press, 2009). At the empirical level, as two influential development scholars note, "the very act of

Now, as I already indicated, both the collective integrity framework and the collective property framework rely on an understanding of the sovereign people as a group agent. Both frameworks thus presuppose that we can meaningfully speak about group agents in a way that is not merely metaphorical. It might be helpful, then, to explain briefly why I think this presupposition is sensible.

The idea that group agency does not have to be purely metaphorical – a mere shorthand for the aggregation of individual agents – has become somewhat less controversial in recent years. Specifically, in this book I will follow a non-metaphorical view of group agency associated with Christian List and Philip Pettit's work.[17] Their key claim is that group agents supervene on individual agents, but are not readily reducible into the mere sum of individual agents. One important reason for holding this view is that there is often no easy way to translate the judgments of a group agent into any single collection of individual judgments, and in fact there might be cases where the group agent's judgments conflict with the judgments of each of its individual members.[18] Another, more general reason, is that an account that refuses to treat group agency as a mere

---

working together on a collective project may help communities rebuild their social ties after a major civil conflict. The so-called Community Driven Development Projects, in which the communities choose and manage collective projects, are quite the rage in post-conflict environments like those in Sierra Leone, Rwanda, Liberia, and Indonesia." See Abhijit Banerjee and Esther Duflo, *Poor Economics* (New York, NY: Public Affairs, 2011), 248.

[17] Christian List and Philip Pettit, *Group Agency: The Possibility, Design, and Status of Corporate Agents* (Oxford: Oxford University Press, 2011).

[18] The core issue here concerns the distinction between (on the one hand) a particular proposition on which individual members of a group agent may form a judgment, and (on the other hand) each individual's complete profile of judgments regarding *all* of the propositions on which the group has to decide. "A group's judgment on a particular proposition," List and Pettit insist, "cannot generally be a function of the group members' individual judgments on that proposition. Rather, it must be a function of the group members' inputs in their entirety. The upshot is that knowing what the group members individually think about some proposition does not generally tell us how the group as a whole adjudicates that proposition." List and Pettit, "Group Agency and Supervenience," *Southern Journal of Philosophy* 44 (2005): 85–105, at 76. See also List, "The Discursive Dilemma and Public Reason," *Ethics* 116 (2006): 362–402; List and Pettit, "On the Many as One: A Reply to Kornhauser and Sager," *Philosophy and Public Affairs* 33 (2005): 377–390 (replying to Lewis Kornhauser and Lawrence Sager, "The Many as One: Integrity and Group Choice in Paradoxical Cases," *Philosophy & Public Affairs* 32 [2004]: 249–276).

shorthand for the aggregation of individual agents provides us with a much more holistic picture – causally and normatively – of the social world.[19]

This last point seems especially clear when reflecting on corporate responsibility.[20] Consider, for instance, the responsibility of British Petroleum (BP) for the calamitous Gulf of Mexico oil spill that occurred in 2010.[21] The question "who is responsible for the BP oil spill?" clearly cannot be answered in an adequate manner by focusing only on the precise causal relationship that each BP employee had to the occurrence of the spill. This is true, moreover, not only for causal analysis or legal liability, but also for moral responsibility. It seems extremely intuitive to think that, whatever special responsibility particular individuals may have had for the oil spill, the oil corporation as a group agent also has to feature in any plausible normative account of the oil spill: it has to feature in a way that goes beyond the mere aggregation of individual BP employees. A view that conceives of group agents as supervening upon, but not as readily reducible to, individual agents, comports well with this intuition. And this is the view that I shall be assuming when discussing the sovereign people as a group agent.[22]

---

[19] Fixating on individual rather than group action, as List and Pettit emphasize, will often cause us to "fail to see the wood for the trees" in thinking about the social world ("Group Agency," 76 and passim).

[20] See Pettit, "Responsibility Incorporated," *Ethics* 117 (2007): 171–201.

[21] See Campbell Robertson and Clifford Grauss, "Gulf Spill Is the Largest of Its Kind, Scientists Say," *New York Times*, Aug. 2, 2010, at http://nytimes.com/2010/08/03/us/03spill.html?_r=2&fta=y

[22] I do not want to entirely close the possibility that certain alternative accounts of shared activity – including even some more reductionist accounts – may also align with the arguments I develop (see, e.g., Michael Bratman, *Shared Agency* [New York: Oxford University Press, 2014]). Whether this is in fact the case depends on whether there actually is any philosophical cost, for my purposes here, in "readily" reducing a group agent into a set of individual agents engaged in joint action. If one could show that such an immediate reduction can still produce all of the intuitive results on which I will rely, and if one could further show that such immediate reduction still allows us to systematize all of the moral intuitions that I will invoke, yielding the same reflective equilibrium, then I would have no opposition to such an alternative. I am doubtful that an alternative of this sort can succeed in all of these tasks, but I will not try to show this here. For a discussion of the complex relationship between joint action and group agency, see List and Pettit, *Group Agency*, 215–216; Philip Pettit and David Schweikard, "Joint Actions and Group Agents," *Philosophy of the Social Sciences* 36 (2006): 18–39.

The Functions of a Moral Framework

The preceding remarks should help to clarify the nature of the collective agent that is at the heart of the collective integrity and collective property frameworks. But it would also be useful at this point to offer some clarifications about the term "framework" itself, which I have already employed multiple times, and which will recur throughout this book.

A moral "framework," on my usage, is a set of moral values, each of which has a (more or less close) affinity to the others. A compelling moral framework, in turn, connects moral values in a way that yields distinct dividends: the framework organizes the multiple values in such a way that we are able to do more with them than we could by simply invoking each of the relevant values taken separately. A cogent moral framework, in other words, arranges our values in such a way that their sum is greater than its parts.

Such an arrangement can be important – can advance our moral thinking – in at least three ways, all of which will play a role in my argument. First, a moral framework can advance our moral reflection by unifying our values. In some cases, such unity might be attained by showing that certain conflicts among our values are only apparent rather than real.[23] One example, which I elaborate when constructing the collective property framework, has to do with the moral obstacles that individual property rights seem to place in the way of anti-discriminatory government action. If the owner of a private apartment complex, for instance, is unwilling to accept people of color as tenants, then it may appear as if we have a conflict between upholding his property rights and upholding the value of anti-discrimination. The collective property framework, however, shows why such conflicts are illusory: why private property rights are not a genuine moral factor in such situations.

In other cases, a framework can increase the unity of our moral outlook by tying together multiple moral intuitions that, while not necessarily in conflict with one another, simply relate to distinct issues. In Chapter 1, for instance, I argue that the collective integrity framework ties together our intuitions regarding multiple elements of liberal democracy that may appear quite disparate. Themes such as civic

---

[23] This was a central aim of Ronald Dworkin's philosophical framework, for example. See especially Dworkin's *Justice for Hedgehogs* (Cambridge, MA: Harvard University Press, 2011).

engagement in a liberal democracy, the moral authority of liberal law, and the place of struggles to realize equal rights in a liberal democracy's collective identity, are all widely agreed to be morally significant. But we rarely try to see how our intuitions regarding each of these distinct themes can be brought together to form a unified view. The collective integrity framework fills this gap.

This type of unifying function arguably warrants attention in and of itself: it is philosophically worthwhile to see how as many of our values as possible can be joined to form a coherent whole. But there is a further reason why this unifying role is important. By unifying distinct moral values – by deepening our understanding of how each of the relevant values fits together with the others – a compelling moral framework buttresses our confidence in all of them. And this added confidence, in turn, should make us more willing to insist that these values, as a set, should be prioritized when they truly conflict with countervailing moral considerations. Thus for example, I will suggest that we can use the collective integrity framework in order to unify our moral expectations concerning steadfastness, honesty, and decency on the part of a liberal people. But if my argument will be cogent, then bringing those different expectations under the umbrella of the integrity framework will amount to more than merely citing these expectations. Rather, this unifying exercise will make us more willing to insist that the values of steadfastness, honesty, and decency are not only genuine, but that in many cases, at least, they should take precedence when conflicting with opposing moral considerations.

This example, in turn, suggests that a moral framework's unifying function is closely related to a second, adjudicating function. A compelling moral framework will not only show us how multiple values can be coherently brought together, nor will it only show that some conflicts among our values are illusory. Such a framework would also prove useful in situations where conflicts among our values are genuine, and where we accordingly need guidance as to how to balance them vis-à-vis one another. Examining many such situations throughout this book, I will try to show that the integrity and property frameworks can provide the requisite guidance.[24]

[24] There are, of course, philosophers who insist that we have no systematic way to adjudicate such conflicts. See, for example, Joel Feinberg, "Duty and Obligation in the Non-Ideal World," *in Rights, Justice, and the Bounds of Liberty* (Princeton, NJ: Princeton University Press, 1980), 252–264; G. A. Cohen,

The third and final function of a moral framework that will feature in my analysis is once again related. A compelling moral framework can help us to better organize our moral values by showing us when we ought to make special efforts to realize certain moral duties, and when it would be especially wrong of us not to fulfill these duties. Knowing that we (or others) have especially stringent and weighty moral duties to take certain actions is of course important in and of itself. But this amplifying function is important also because it helps us address conflicts of a different sort from the ones emphasized above. A moral framework that has an amplifying function will help us to figure out what to do not only in cases where we are unsure which is the right thing to do. Such a framework will also offer some help in assigning priorities in those cases where the relevant conflicts are more indirect: cases where we are sure about which is the right thing do, but find ourselves unsure as to which of the many things that are right for us to do ought to be done first. This kind of priority problem, as I note in the final chapter, features far too rarely on political philosophy's radar, even though it is pervasive in political life. I hope to show how the collective integrity framework in particular can help us address this gap as well.

Before moving on, I should make one more remark about how I understand collective integrity and collective property to relate to more familiar values of liberal democracy. As I will emphasize several times in the course of the book, I do not intend to argue that collective integrity or collective property are more fundamental than core values of liberal democracy. Rather, what I intend to show is that the two collectivist frameworks can organize familiar values of liberal democracy so as to make the practical implications of these values more determinate.[25] I mention this point here to anticipate an intuitive but mistaken thought: that because the two collectivist frameworks are not morally fundamental, they cannot really provide any independent practical guidance. The following chapters should demonstrate otherwise.

Rescuing Justice and Equality (Cambridge, MA: Harvard University Press, 2008), e.g., at 4. Like Rawls, however, I think we have ample reason to oppose the intuitionism to which such a view leads. See *TJ*, Section 7.

[25] This is again a Rawlsian idea in many ways, though applied to much more concrete political problems than those on which Rawls typically focused. I say more on the Rawlsian parallel here in Chapter 1, Section 3.

Integrity and Property, Unity and Division

Having clarified in what sense I intend to construct moral "frameworks" that revolve around the people's integrity and property, I should now say more about the particular policy problems to which these two frameworks will be applied.

The best way to introduce the policy problems on which I focus is to consider an apparent puzzle. Given the central place of "the people" in modern political thought, why has there been remarkably little by way of sustained normative discussion, either of the people as a collective agent with its own integrity, or of the people as a collective agent with its own property? It is impossible to know for sure. After all, when scholars are silent about a certain topic, they also tend to be silent about the reasons for their silence. Yet we can nonetheless speculate that the reason here has to do with a view that pervades much of contemporary political theory. According to this view, it makes little sense to pivot our analysis of political affairs on a concept of "the people" as a unified collective agent, because real-world politics revolves around intense friction and division.[26]

Because I believe this kind of skepticism is deeply ingrained in the field, I aim to preempt it. This aim, in turn, underlies the particular policy problems that I take up in the applied chapters of this book. The overarching goal of these chapters is to show that ideas regarding the people's integrity and property can guide concrete policy decisions even in circumstances where key political divides take center stage.

In Chapter 3, I take up the real-world divide between ordinary citizens and leaders who hold de facto political power – a divide that is particularly manifest in special legal protections of those who wield power. In the chapter's first part, I discuss the practice of formally shielding senior members of an elected government from the ordinary reach of the law. I argue that this practice cannot be justified in normal circumstances. I then turn to morally abnormal circumstances, where the abuse of elected office for private gain has been pervasive, and where all-out battles against such corruption might pose real risks to

---

[26] For a few examples from this decade alone, see John McCormick, *Machiavellian Democracy* (Cambridge University Press, 2011); Robert Martin, *Government by Dissent* (New York: New York University Press, 2013); Jeffrey Green, *The Shadow of Unfairness: A Plebeian theory of Liberal Democracy* (Oxford: Oxford University Press, 2016).

political and economic stability. Examining cases such as Brazil's ongoing political and economic crisis, I argue that the collective property and integrity frameworks can guide our thinking about some of the main moral dilemmas triggered by endemic corruption.

The chapter's second part considers pardons and amnesties. I begin with the general practice of presidential pardons, and explain why collective integrity and collective property ideas militate strongly in favor of abolishing this practice. I then show (using the example of Watergate) how these ideas militate especially strongly against pardoning former democratic leaders. I end the chapter with a sustained discussion of amnesty grants to former leaders of repressive regimes, as a strategy for facilitating a transition to democracy. Using multiple historical examples, I show how the property and integrity frameworks advance the moral analysis of such amnesties.

In Chapter 4, I turn from the divide between "the people" and its rulers to another divide that has long been of interest to political theory – namely, the divide between "the people" and outsiders. I delve into the latter divide by examining some international dimensions of the corruption problems which Chapter 3 explores in the domestic realm. More specifically, I examine how the integrity and property frameworks bear on de facto-ist international practices concerning sovereign debt. With very few exceptions, current practice allows every de facto government – no matter how undemocratic or corrupt – to borrow funds internationally in its people's name, and every de facto government inherits the sovereign debt incurred by previous de facto governments. This ongoing state of affairs means that the dubious loans to corrupt foreign rulers depicted in *Yes, Prime Minister* are very much real rather than merely satirical.

This real problem, in turn, challenges us to think about another sort of philosophically salient division – one where the integrity and property frameworks apply to different peoples. This division arises because, by taking loans in their people's name, corrupt and manifestly undemocratic rulers are committing a portion of their people's property to future payment of these loans.[27] At the same time, by facilitating and benefiting from these loans, each affluent liberal democracy – and ultimately the sovereign people in each affluent liberal democracy –

---

[27] As noted, for example, in Christian Barry, "Sovereign Debt, Human Rights, and Policy Conditionality," *Journal of Political Philosophy* 19 (2011): 282–305.

might be compromising their own integrity. Accordingly, I employ both the property and the integrity frameworks to challenge de facto-ist practices governing sovereign debt. These frameworks, I contend, not only condemn the status quo, but also support specific promising proposals for its reform.

Finally, in Chapter 5, I consider another political divide that often explains the hesitation to speak about "the people" as a unified collective agent: the divide that stems from ethnic and religious cleavages separating different groups within "the people." I seek to establish that my collectivist frameworks can be of use even in stark circumstances where the effects of such cleavages have been acute, and even when these cleavages feed into extremely fraught divides between "the people" and outsiders. To this end, I zero in on one of the most fractured societies in the Western world: Israel. I argue that the collective property and collective integrity frameworks can cast a distinctive light on Israel's ethnic and religious divisions, which have been largely overlooked by political theorists. I then explain why progress with regard to these internal divisions might be a useful gradualist strategy for achieving positive change in the context that is much more familiar to political theorists – that of the Israeli-Palestinian conflict. Finally, I use the historical emphases of the integrity framework to discuss issues related to Israel's refugee policy, and reflect, through the same lens, on how prevalent demographic, political, and economic dynamics shape the prospects for progressive civic engagement in Israel going forward.

Political Theory and the Real World

Before I turn to developing the book's substantive arguments, I want to note one more general thought that animates them. The thought is that normative political theory ought to take seriously more of the characteristics of political decision making that we observe in the real world – including characteristics that accompany, but extend beyond, the basic concern with political stability, so sharply exemplified in Sir Humphrey.

One such characteristic is the uncertainty inherent to many fundamental political decisions.[28] Many mainstream political philosophers

---

[28] Following Keynes and Knight, economists have long distinguished between decision making under "risk" and under "uncertainty." (See John

either fail to recognize the practical weight of this uncertainty, or treat it as a technical issue best left for social scientists to address while philosophy contemplates visions of perfect justice.[29] In my view, however, this mainstream approach exaggerates not only the practical role that such visions can play. There are also numerous contexts where this mainstream approach exaggerates the ability of social science to settle our uncertainty about the macro-level implications of specific political decisions.[30] This kind of uncertainty will be prominent already in Chapter 1, but will become especially salient in Chapters 3 and 4, when we discuss domestic decisions about political and economic crises in developing countries and the effects of international reforms to sovereign borrowing.

Another cause of uncertainty to which I will pay considerable attention is the fundamental opacity of micro-level calculations by "veto players." In Chapters 3 and 4, I discuss calculations and threats made by repressive or corrupt leaders; in Chapter 5, I examine threats made by politically powerful religious minorities. I will be especially interested in how to respond to such players' proclaimed willingness to

---

Maynard Keynes, *A Treatise on Probability* [London: Macmillan, 1921]; Frank Knight, *Risk, Uncertainty, and Profit* [New York: Houghton Mifflin, 1921].) Agents who make decisions under risk are able to assign probabilities to different outcomes materializing. Agents making decisions under uncertainty do not have this luxury. I will be discussing both kinds of situations in this book, and will use the two terms interchangeably, although, as will become clear, I shall be especially interested in uncertainty in the narrower sense, where probabilities cannot be assigned.

[29] See for example A. John Simmons, "Ideal and Nonideal Theory," *Philosophy & Public Affairs* 38 (2010): 5–36; Joshua Cohen, "Philosophy, Social Science, Global Poverty," in Alison Jaggar (ed.), *Thomas Pogge and His Critics* (London: Polity, 2010), 18–45.

[30] One does not have to fully endorse the extreme skepticism of leading scholars such as Jon Elster, for instance, who asserts that "a non-negligible part of empirical social science consists of *half-understood statistical theory applied to half-assimilated empirical material*," to accept his claim that we should beware of "excessive ambitions" and excessive confidence of social science – whether in political science, sociology, or economics. President Truman, seeking to retain and expand New Deal reforms, and tired of hearing "on the one hand but on the other hand" from his economic advisors regarding virtually every macro policy choice, famously yearned for a "one-handed economist." But he never found this fantastical breed, nor is it clear that we should trust this breed if we ever find it. See Jon Elster, "Excessive Ambitions," *Capitalism and Society* 4 (2009): 1–30, at 17 (italics in the original). For Truman's remark, see Niel Johnson, *Words to the Wise from Harry S. Truman* (Overland Park, Kansas: Leathers Publishers, 2007), 57.

violently oppose reforms that set back their interests. Explicit threats of this sort always involve uncertainty because we can never be confident about the probability that violence will actually be used, or about the magnitude of the violence that can be expected. But it is nonetheless important to try to devise principled responses to such threats. I will try to do so here.

Alongside these types of uncertainty, another feature of real-world politics that I will try to capture is the character that normative rhetoric often assumes in actual politics. When political actors – be they office holders, opposition members, or grassroots activists – try to create political momentum for or against certain decisions, they often do so by appealing to relatively concrete moral ideas. Thus, for example, political actors often condemn corrupt rivals by appealing not to a highly abstract standard of economic distribution, but simply to the idea that these rivals are stealing the people's property. Similarly – and more generally – when political actors wish to mobilize public opinion against various policies, they rarely appeal to abstract theories. Much more frequently, they appeal to concrete history – arguing that the particular history of a particular people should push it to reject certain policies as antithetical to its long-held, fundamental commitments.

To be sure, we should not always take such political invocations of "the people's history" (nor, for that matter, political accusations of theft from the people) at face value. But we should be interested in normative frameworks that systematize such real-world political arguments – that explain when these arguments might have actual moral force, and that trace out their actual policy implications. This is another important contribution that the collective integrity and collective property frameworks can make to our thinking about the morality of public policy. Or so, at least, I will argue in the pages that follow.

1 The People's Integrity

"America's relationship with South Africa in the second half of the twentieth century . . . forced citizens to ponder their personal values and national identity."

Robert Massie[1]

This quotation from Massie may seem like an odd way to begin a book dealing with moral dilemmas in public policy. It was clearly morally wrong for the United States to be entangled in South Africa's apartheid. We may disagree on whether this entanglement amounted to material American complicity in apartheid – complicity, after all, comes in many shapes and forms.[2] We can, however, say that it was clearly morally right for the United States to extricate itself from its entanglement in apartheid. It was clearly right for the US Congress to enact the Comprehensive Anti-Apartheid Act "to prohibit loans to, other investments in, and certain other activities with respect to South Africa."[3] But if divestment from apartheid was clearly morally right, then, morally speaking, what is there to "ponder" here?

To see the answer, consider the following scenario. Imagine that black South Africans, even while seeing themselves as victims of the apartheid regime, would have publicly opposed foreign divestment from this regime out of uncertainty about divestment's economic consequences.[4] I assume that, even under such circumstances, customary ties between

---

[1] Robert Massie, *Loosing the Bonds: The United States and South Africa in the Apartheid Years* (New York: Doubleday, 1997), xxvii.
[2] See, for example, Chiara Lepora and Robert Goodin, *On Complicity and Compromise* (Oxford: Oxford University Press, 2013).
[3] See US Public Law 99–440, www.gpo.gov/fdsys/pkg/STATUTE-100/pdf/STATUTE-100-Pg1086.pdf
[4] Note that, after apartheid's demise, economists have disagreed on divestment's actual effects. See, for example, Philip Levy, "*Sanctions on South Africa: What Did They Do*," Economic Growth Center, Yale University Discussion Paper, No. 796, Feb. 1999, and the references therein.

the United States and South Africa would not have been morally care-free. These ties would not have been morally on a par with customary ties between the United States and, say, Norway. But why? What exactly could explain this enduring compunction regarding ties with apartheid?

It is tempting to respond simply by appealing to reasons related to apartheid's victims – for example, by appealing to their rights, autonomy, or equal standing. Yet it is not clear how such reasons will work. For one thing, we can imagine these victims responding to such an appeal as follows: *Precisely because of our rights, autonomy, and equal standing, our voice should matter when we say to outsiders that we fear the economic repercussions of divestment, and that we therefore do not want them to divest from the regime.* Along the same lines, if one argued simply that the racist regime is unjust, apartheid's victims could emphasize that there is no assurance that foreign divestment from the regime will lead to reforms mitigating its injustice: "constructive engagement," of the kind preached by the Reagan administration,[5] might do better. Finally, it will not do to say that the victims' relevant rights are inalienable. Even if one could establish that the South African regime violated inalienable rights of its victims, under the scenario in question these victims are not trying to waive any rights vis-à-vis the regime. The victims are merely asking third parties to retain customary ties with the perpetrators who violate their rights. So it is far from obvious that victim-related reasons can address the question at stake here.

There is, however, another option, which runs as follows. It is true that, even in the scenario we are considering, it would have been morally risky for the United States to retain customary ties with the apartheid regime. But the moral risks here would have been first and foremost risks to the identity of American society itself – the same identity to which our opening quote refers.

I am going to assume that this identity intuition is morally significant, and that it is important to find a systematic way to account for it. This is not to suggest that this intuition is always decisive when it conflicts with opposing moral reasons. I am only going to assume that it is not morally negligible, and that it merits attention.[6] My aim here is to ask

---

[5] See, for example, Patti Waldmeir, *Anatomy of a Miracle: The End of Apartheid* (New York: W. W. Norton, 1997).
[6] Indeed, I believe this identity intuition warrants attention independently of what we think about the victim-related reasons just noted. Yet seeing why these

what is the best way to ground this intuition – what is the deeper normative idea to which it leads.

I wish to suggest that this deeper normative idea is that of integrity. More specifically, my goal in this opening chapter is to show that there is distinctive normative value to thinking about a liberal democracy as an agent with integrity that can be threatened, paralleling the integrity of an individual person. I will argue that the idea of liberal political integrity organizes and clarifies important moral intuitions concerning the policies of liberal democracies, domestically as well as globally.[7] In the course of the chapter, I will sometimes demonstrate the appeal of the idea of liberal integrity through specific cases. But at this stage I will use these cases primarily in order to advance a more general philosophical thesis: that we can and should take the idea of liberal political integrity seriously in our moral reflection. This idea, I will argue, gives moral weight to the frequent references – both popular and scholarly – to liberal democracies' "identity"[8] and "sense of self."[9]

I advance this thesis as follows. In 1.1, I consider Bernard Williams's claim that an agent's integrity consists in the pursuit of identity-

---

reasons may not operate in a straightforward manner nonetheless helps bring this intuition to the fore.

[7] I am going to assume, with much of mainstream contemporary theory, that any viable vision of liberal individual rights will make room for basic democratic convictions regarding majority rule and the sovereignty of the people, just as any viable vision of democratic sovereignty and majority rule will make room for liberal protections of individual rights. I shall further assume that a key shared task of (domestic) liberal and democratic theory is to explore different aspects of a bedrock commitment to the equality of citizens – and eventually to bring these different aspects into alignment. For different variants of this view see
Ronald Dworkin, *Sovereign Virtue* (Cambridge, MA: Harvard University Press, 2000); Joshua Cohen, "A More Democratic Liberalism," *Michigan Law Review* 92 (1994): 1503–1546; Jürgen Habermas, "Constitutional Democracy:
A Paradoxical Union of Contradictory Principles?" *Political Theory* 29 (2001): 766–781. This view of liberal and democratic theory as intertwined will lead me to use "the liberal people" and "the liberal society" interchangeably with "the democratic people" or "the democratic society." I will also refer here to "the integrity of a liberal polity" (or simply to "liberal integrity," for terminological ease) as a shorthand for "the integrity of a liberal-democratic people."

[8] See, for example, Alexander Wendt, *Social Theory of International Politics* (Cambridge: Cambridge University Press, 1999); "The State as Person in International Theory," *Review of International Studies* (2004): 289–316.

[9] See John Ruggie, "What Makes the World Hang Together: Neo-Utilitarianism and the Social Constructivist Challenge," *International Organization* 52 (1998): 855–885.

grounding projects, and offer additional framing remarks. I then elaborate the sense in which a liberal polity ought to see the realization of its citizens' equal rights as an identity-grounding project, explain how this project underlies what I term identity-grounding institutions, and show why threats – domestic and global – to the coherence of these institutions constitute morally important threats to a liberal polity's integrity (1.2–1.4). In 1.5, I build on these foundations to show how the idea of liberal integrity can elucidate not only hypothetical entanglement cases such as the apartheid scenario, but also an actual ongoing case: the entanglement of liberal democracies in dictators' violations of their peoples' ownership over state-owned natural resources. I then turn to explore the relationship between liberal integrity and the values of hypocrisy (1.6), public honesty (1.7), and decency (1.8). In 1.9 I examine consequentialist concerns about the role that liberal integrity might play under extreme political conditions.

In 1.10, discuss how the liberal integrity framework bears on disagreements regarding liberal identity. I close by anticipating some final objections relating to individual integrity, to morality's overall requirements, and to the integrity of illiberal polities.

1.1 Setting the Stage

The first step in constructing the idea of liberal integrity is to provide a working account of the concept of integrity and its moral significance.

Following Bernard Williams, I will presume that an agent's integrity consists in fidelity to the projects or commitments that the agent considers constitutive of its identity.[10] One reason why this pursuit can be morally significant has to do with alienation. It can often be crucial that agents avoid deep conflict between their actions and their constitutive projects. In extreme cases, such conflict might generate a situation where the agent is unable to make sense of itself – unable to give an account of how the actions it takes in the world cohere with the commitments essential to its identity. Like Williams, I will assume

---

[10] See Bernard Williams, "A Critique of Utilitarianism," in Williams and J. J. C. Smart, *Utilitarianism – For and Against* (Cambridge: Cambridge University Press, 1973). I will use "commitments" and "projects" interchangeably.

that "psychological fragmentation"[11] of this kind should be at least potentially worrisome from a normative viewpoint.[12]

A second reason for integrity's significance has to do with purposefulness. Constitutive projects or commitments – as the core of an agent's identity – provide the agent with reasons for existing. Having "identity-conferring commitments," as Williams writes, is "the condition of my existence, in the sense that unless I am propelled forward by the conatus of desire, project, and interest, it is unclear why I should go on at all."[13] When an agent's actions conflict with its identity-grounding projects, in other words, this can undermine the very reason for the agent being in the world. Like Williams, I will assume that any normative theory should be concerned about a world of such despairing – and potentially disappearing – agents.

With this basic view of integrity's importance in the background, I want to make three brief remarks about what a successful account of integrity should be able to do. First, such an account should be able to overcome a difficulty posed by a familiar distinction. This is the distinction between what the agent may deem important to its identity and integrity, and what morality deems important simpliciter. This distinction might cause problems even when we focus (as I will here) solely on liberal agents – that is, agents whose identity is compatible with the idea of the equal moral worth of all human beings. After all, we can imagine even a liberal individual, who obeys the moral constraints generated by others' equal rights and standing but who does not see morality as an identity-grounding project.[14] However, fortunately for our purposes, this difficulty should not even arise in the case of a liberal polity. Insofar as we can talk of a liberal polity as an agent with an identity (and I will contend below that we can and should talk this way), I will argue that

---

[11] Elizabeth Ashford, "Utilitarianism, Integrity, and Partiality," *The Journal of Philosophy* 97 (2000): 421–439, at 422.

[12] I am speaking in qualified form here ("potentially worrisome") in light of natural concerns about alienation associated with action that contradicts objectively repugnant commitments. Throughout this chapter, and especially in 1.8, I shall try to explain why we can coherently put such commitments aside when reflecting on moral integrity.

[13] Bernard Williams, "Persons, Character and Morality," in *Moral Luck* (Cambridge: Cambridge University Press, 1981), 12.

[14] Though later I will suggest that the language of identity-grounding projects or commitments can capture normative requirements that extend beyond respect for such constraints.

1.1 Setting the Stage

all liberal peoples must see a morally crucial task – the realization of their citizens' equal rights – as an identity-grounding project. Thus the distinction between what is deemed important by the agent and by morality will not undermine the discussion of a liberal people's integrity.

Second, a successful account of integrity should capture the intuitive relationship between integrity and sacrifice. Arguably, integrity is most visible to us in others in the context of sacrifice. A person who is steadfast in her adherence to moral principles – who not only tries to act in accordance with certain principles, but is also clearly willing to incur nontrivial costs for the sake of these principles – is far more likely to strike us as a person of integrity.[15] By way of contrast, when we encounter a person who claims to be committed to certain moral principles, but who repeatedly tries to exempt himself from the hold of these principles whenever following them requires real sacrifices, we may reasonably ask whether he is committed to these principles at all. So, just as integrity involves steadfastness in acting on moral principles, it goes against the pursuit of self-seeking exemptions from moral requirements.[16] A compelling account of political integrity should be able to capture this intuition, and I will try to show that my account of liberal integrity can do so.

Third, a persuasive account of integrity should also relate the idea of integrity to values on which integrity is typically thought to bear. One such value is *decency*, which I understand to bear primarily on how agents – especially powerful, well-off agents – treat vulnerable others.[17] I assume that a person who consistently behaves toward vulnerable others in repugnant ways is unlikely to strike us as a decent human being, nor, indeed, as a person of integrity.[18] I will therefore try to construct here an account of

---

[15] I borrow this emphasis on "steadfastness" from Stephen Carter's *Integrity* (New York: Harper, 1996), although my aims here, especially at the political level, are quite distinct from Carter's.

[16] This is not to say that such pursuit is rare. On the contrary. "We all know," as Jed Rubenfeld notes "... what it is to be judge in one's own case. This is why individual morality is so consistently feeble. We all imagine ourselves committed to doing right, or at least to doing no wrong, and we all find ways to tell ourselves that what we want to do here and now conforms to this commitment." See Jed Rubenfeld, *Freedom and Time* (New Haven: Yale University Press, 2001), 172.

[17] In this I partly follow Avishai Margalit, *The Decent Society* (Cambridge, MA: Harvard University Press, 1996).

[18] I am aware that this link between decency (and its substantive demands) and integrity (often understood as a purely formal notion) is bound to be

liberal political integrity that reflects a view of decency as a necessary condition for integrity.[19] In a similar spirit, I assume that an account of integrity that had nothing to say about deception and truthfulness would be deficient. I shall accordingly try to show how my account of liberal political integrity supports the thought that agents acting with integrity are highly concerned with truth and highly averse to deceptive behavior – whether deception of others or, equally importantly, self-deception.

Before I turn to actually advancing these tasks, let me offer, as last framing remarks, a pair of clarifications about what I will and what I will not be trying to do here. The identity-based conception of liberal integrity that I will offer here is not meant to be a sociological depiction of the identity of actual liberal democracies. My main focus will be on what the identity and conduct of a liberal democracy ought to be when conceived ideally, from a purely normative perspective. I will suggest that the language of liberal integrity casts in the best possible light actual practices of existing liberal polities, including, crucially, their actual efforts to overcome manifestly illiberal elements of their histories. But the significance of this point will ultimately be normative rather than empirical.

Another thing that I will *not* try do is to argue that the idea of liberal integrity is entirely distinct from, or more foundational than, familiar liberal values. Nor, for that matter, will I argue that liberal integrity exhausts the universe of liberal political morality (which, if true, would render the concept far too broad to be of interest). Rather, in the first instance, I want to buttress the thought with which I began: that the notion of liberal integrity allows us to explain, in a way that a simple appeal to familiar liberal values arguably cannot, exactly why it is that liberal polities have identity-based moral reasons not to entangle themselves in manifestly illiberal practices beyond their borders. In turn, while elaborating and strengthening this claim, we shall also come to

---

controversial to some extent; I accordingly try to motivate this link in the following discussion.

[19] Necessary but not sufficient, if nothing else because an agent may behave decently toward others, not out of any deep principled commitment to doing so but simply out of prudential calculations or conformity to broader social norms. This is especially clear at the individual level. It would be odd, I assume, to see a person who just "does what everyone else does," and who would change his conduct completely if social norms around him changed, as exhibiting the kind of "self-authorship" often associated with integrity. (See, for example, Daniel Markovits, "The Architecture of Integrity," in Daniel Culcutt [ed.], *Reading Bernard Williams* [London: Routledge, 2009]: 110–138.)

see how the notion of liberal integrity distinctively captures important moral intuitions as to how the tainted histories of actual liberal societies should bear on their present policies.

Finally, as part of the same process, we shall reach a more general contribution of the idea of liberal integrity – namely, the novel, unifying framework it provides for liberal values.[20] Clarifying and organizing our moral outlook, this framework will ultimately yield important policy prescriptions. In certain cases, the integrity framework will boost the attractiveness of specific, familiar answers to concrete policy dilemmas at the expense of competing familiar answers. In other cases, it will push us to explore new answers.

Yet, for the most part, these policy benefits will await later chapters. In order to get to these benefits, we first need philosophical foundations. Let us turn, then, to some fundamental ideas regarding the identity – and integrity – of a liberal people.

1.2 The Integrity of a Liberal Polity

In order to gain traction on the integrity of a liberal people, we need to start with the sense in which one can speak of a liberal people as having an identity. We speak of the "identity" of a liberal people when we treat the people, at least in some normative contexts, as a unitary agent. One such central context is liberal law. From a normative perspective, we often consider the laws of a liberal democracy to be the creation of "the sovereign people," conceived in turn as a unitary group agent.

One way to evince the normative significance of this group agency is through the sovereign people's moral responsibility for the shape of the laws. Consider, for instance, the moral responsibility that the American body politic had for the legal institution of slavery in the United States. It would be misleading to simply disaggregate this responsibility, so as to focus solely on the particular actions of each individual American citizen toward each particular slave. It is clearly more apt to understand this responsibility as lying with the American

---

[20] In emphasizing this unifying framework, I am partly following the lead of philosophers who are inclined to view integrity as a "cluster concept" or "master virtue" combining multiple virtues. See, respectively, Damian Cox, Marguerite La Caze, and Michael Levine, *Integrity and the Fragile Self* (Aldershot: Ashgate, 2003); Cheshire Calhoun, "Standing for Something," *Journal of Philosophy* XCII (1995): 235–260.

body politic as a group agent – an agent that imposed and retained the laws of slavery.[21] Indeed, this normative thought obtains even if, as an empirical matter, only some American citizens actually owned slaves, or took part in slave trade.[22] And as long as we endorse this thought, we already endorse a basic moral sense in which collectively sovereign citizens form a group agent when enacting law. To borrow a term from Dworkin's conception of "law as integrity," we already accept, at least for the sake of normative reflection, the assumption that the legal order they establish turns collectively sovereign citizens into a "community personified."[23]

Now, if we assume that the law of a liberal polity makes it a single agent in some morally salient sense, then the commitments that underlie this law can be described as the core of this agent's identity. No legal system, in turn, can be liberal unless it is committed to the realization of the equal rights of all citizens: that is the fundamental project of liberal law. One way to see this is to note that the law cannot revolve around a collectivist project: a polity cannot be liberal if, for example, it takes "the glory of the nation," not reducible to individual citizens and their rights, as its ultimate goal. At the same time, the law can only aim at the realization of the equal rights of all citizens, unless it is to embody a conception of natural moral hierarchy among individuals that is

---

[21] For an emphasis on the centrality of the sovereign body politic to the liberal tradition, and a useful contrast with the libertarian picture of individual political power, see Samuel Freeman, "Illiberal Libertarians: Why Libertarianism Is Not a Liberal View," *Philosophy & Public Affairs* 30 (2001): 105–151.

[22] Note that if we were to focus only on such individuals, at the expense of thinking about the responsibility of the American body politic, then we would have no principled way to distinguish between Americans' responsibility for the institution of US slavery, and the responsibility of any foreigner who could have influenced this institution from outside the United States. But this is a distinction that we clearly want to make. For general discussions along these lines see Christopher Kutz, *Complicity: Ethics and Law for a Collective Age* (Cambridge: Cambridge University Press, 2000); Eric Beerbohm, *In Our Name* (Princeton, NJ: Princeton University Press, 2012); Alex Zakaras, "Complicity and Coercion: Toward an Ethics of Political Participation," in David Sobel, Peter Vallentyne, and Steven Wall (eds.), *Oxford Studies in Political Philosophy* 4 (2018): 192–218. I borrow the discussion of the specific case of US slavery from Thomas Pogge, *Realizing Rawls* (Ithaca, NY: Cornell University Press, 1989), 35.

[23] Ronald Dworkin, *Law's Empire* (Cambridge, MA: Harvard University Press, 1986), 167. Dworkin, it should be noted, writes that "integrity holds within political communities, not among them." Yet he offers no sustained argument for why this must be the case.

1.2 The Integrity of a Liberal Polity

inimical to liberalism. Therefore, insofar as the commitments that underlie the law can be seen as the core of a liberal people's identity, we can say that any liberal people must understand the realization of its citizens' equal rights as an identity-grounding project.

How does this point lead to a picture of a liberal people's integrity, and how might this integrity be threatened? We can begin to see the answer by noting that, to have a liberal identity, a people must formally and effectively instantiate equal rights through its legal system. One can accordingly say that from a liberal people's identity-grounding commitment to equal rights follows a certain set of identity-grounding institutions that guarantee equal rights for all citizens. Admittedly, it can be difficult to define with perfect precision exactly which institutions are necessary instantiations of equal rights and thus fall under the rubric of "identity-grounding."[24] Yet for our purposes, a fairly intuitive list should suffice, including core liberal institutions such as legal protections of bodily integrity, freedom of speech, equality before the law, and a ban on racial, religious, and gender discrimination. These institutions are necessary corollaries of a liberal commitment to citizens' equal rights, under any plausible account of liberalism.

In turn, if in order to have a liberal identity at all a people must have specific effective legal institutions, then there is a fairly direct sense in which a people with a liberal self-conception would not truly be able to live up to its self-professed identity if these legal institutions did not exist, existed formally only and were ineffective, or were removed or distorted. Just as a person's integrity is threatened when her identity-grounding commitments fundamentally conflict with her actions, the integrity of a people with a liberal self-conception is threatened when the institutions that its law enacts conflict with or fail to take seriously its own grounding commitment to equal rights.

Examples abound. If the law of a people with a liberal self-conception professes a commitment to respect the rights of all citizens equally, but denies the vote to women, or refuses to recognize marital rape as a crime, this people suffers from a failure of liberal integrity. If the law declares respect for the life and property of all citizens, but law enforcement authorities never enter the poorest parts of a polity and knowingly leave

---

[24] Though this is not an issue unique to the concept of liberal integrity. It is just as – if not more – difficult to define with perfect precision which institutions fall within Rawls' concept of a polity's "basic structure," for instance.

them segregated and mired in de facto anarchy, this is a failure of liberal integrity. If the supreme law of a purportedly liberal land prohibits racial discrimination, yet gives policy discretion to subordinate governmental units dominated by racists, knowing that many of these units will make provisions of racial equality a dead letter, this too is a failure of liberal integrity. In all of these cases, by flatly contradicting its own core commitment to equal rights, the law of a people that professes a liberal identity fails, to borrow another phrase from Dworkin, to "speak with one voice."[25] Indeed, just as when a liberal person loses her integrity she cannot make sense of herself due to the deep conflict between her actions and her identity-grounding commitments, when liberal law does not speak with one voice we can say that the polity it governs also, in losing its integrity, cannot make sense of its liberal identity.[26]

Yet these remarks are only a first step. They may make the language of liberal integrity somewhat more intelligible, but they do not yet make it useful. For it is not clear yet what are the philosophical benefits of describing political failures to realize liberal equal rights – or successes in advancing liberal equal rights – in terms of liberal integrity.

We can start with four benefits. First, by highlighting the thought that the realization of liberal equal rights is an identity-grounding *project*, the language of liberal integrity captures a key element of liberal societies' actual practices. This language captures the myriad official ways in which actual liberal societies mark both their failures and their achievements, with regard to fundamental liberal values, as failures and achievements that are constitutive of the national identity –

---

[25] Dworkin, *Law's Empire,* 165. There are, of course, challenges that one could raise against this image of the law – not least, whether it really captures what liberal law is (as Dworkin would have it), rather than only what liberal law ought to be. In fact, there are theorists who believe that even the latter ambition is too grand, since political bargaining and compromise, inescapable in a liberal democracy, will inevitably prevent the kind of coherence that is needed for the law to exhibit Dworkinian integrity. (See, e.g., Andrei Marmor, *Law in the Age of Pluralism* [Oxford: Oxford University Press, 2007], Chapter 2.) This criticism, I think, has force, but only up to a point: presumably Dworkin's critics too would concede that there are some elements of the rule of law and protection of liberal rights that we normally refuse to subject to political bargain and compromise (even if in morally abnormal circumstances we may have no choice). Part of my aim here is to show the dividends of thinking about this (normally) non-negotiable space in terms of collective integrity.

[26] This claim is of course compatible with thinking that the magnitude of the threat to integrity may vary from case to case – indeed, it is sensible to think of integrity as a scalar rather than a binary concept. Thanks to Jeff Green for stressing this point.

1.2 The Integrity of a Liberal Polity

of "who we are as a people."[27] The idea of liberal political integrity thus provides a ready way to think about official traditions (national holidays, official ceremonies) commemorating iconic figures who played a key role in the struggle to realize liberal values in the polity, and about official traditions marking the polity's past grave violations of liberal norms. The idea of liberal integrity similarly makes sense of the emblematic public monuments that celebrate successes in affirming liberal equal rights, as well as of other emblematic monuments that display public memory of victims of past rights violations. And the idea of integrity makes sense of the fact that both these successes and failures play an important role in the educational system of many liberal societies, as an essential part of the national history and national ethos.

However, second, the idea of liberal integrity is not only a way to make theoretical sense of ongoing practices, which officially recognize successes and failures in realizing liberal values as constitutive of national identity. This idea also provides a way to ground the thought that it would be morally wrong if such official recognition did not exist. It seems plausible to hold that a liberal people must officially recognize, as constitutive of its identity, profound historical failures, and achievements tied to the realization of liberal values. Such recognition is not only necessary as a way to properly respect in the present those whose equal rights were violated in the past. Nor is it only a proper way to give their due to admirable figures who have sacrificed much to advance the struggle to realize equal rights. This official recognition is morally necessary also because of the enormity of the moral stakes involved in the ongoing struggles to realize equal rights within liberal polities – from the efforts to end racial discrimination, through an end to religious discrimination, to the realization of the equal rights of women. The sheer scope of these moral struggles is such that officially integrating them into the national identity, making them a part of "who we are" as a people, is a way of respecting morality itself – giving morality itself its due.[28]

---

[27] This is not meant to suggest that the identities of all liberal polities ought to be indistinguishable. I am *not* arguing that the only identity-grounding project a liberal polity can have is the realization of familiar liberal values. Liberal polities may have additional projects. And they may differ when it comes to these projects – for instance, in the degree to which they see it as important to their identity to protect a certain national language.

[28] These claims naturally ally with accounts of liberal nationalism, although my claims are more focused on group agency than are many of these accounts, and are ultimately meant to elucidate moral conundrums that are more concrete

With these claims in view, we can turn to a third benefit of thinking about political failures to realize equal rights – especially failures of the law – in terms of failure of liberal integrity. When we understand a manifest failure to realize equal rights as a "disintegration" of a liberal polity's law, we can see more immediately how this failure undermines citizens' reasons to respect the law – to obey it "for the sake of duty" rather than out of mere fear of punishment. The internal coherence of the law, at least in matters that clearly bear on its grounding moral principles, is essential to its moral claim to obedience. When this coherence is deeply undermined, the demand that citizens obey the law is significantly weakened. The more the law of a self-professed liberal people contradicts its own grounding moral principles, the more, we might say, the law fails to take itself seriously; and if the law does not take itself seriously, it is not clear why any citizen should.[29]

This thought, in turn, leads to a final, related, yet broader notion. When we understand the realization of equal rights as an identity-grounding project, we get an immediate way to capture the fact that relevant political institutions are not easily created nor maintained – that, like all significant projects, they require continuous effort and sacrifices. Obedience to the law frequently requires individual citizens to sacrifice various things (autonomy, resources, and so on). But there will be many contexts in which broader sacrifices and efforts are needed – especially through various forms of civic engagement – in order to achieve reform of the law and to make sure it fulfills more of the liberal promise of equal rights.[30] The idea of liberal integrity,

---

than those that liberal nationalists typically analyze. See, for instance, Yael Tamir, *Liberal Nationalism* (Princeton: Princeton University Press, 1993); Jan-Werner Muller, *Constitutional Patriotism* (Princeton: Princeton University Press, 2007); Anna Stilz, *Liberal Loyalty* (Princeton, NJ: Princeton University Press, 2009). See also Avishay Margalit, *The Ethics of Memory* (Cambridge, MA: Harvard University Press, 2002).

[29] Philosophical anarchists might not be troubled by this. Yet I believe they are mistaken, for reasons neatly captured in Thomas Christiano, "The Authority of Democracy," *Journal of Political Philosophy* 12 (2004): 266–290.

[30] In this I take myself to be presenting a more active conception of the people's direct role in the collective project of liberal democracy than is often proposed by liberal theorists, many of whom are content with rare political engagement by ordinary citizens. Bruce Ackerman might be the most well-known defender of such a view. (See, for instance, Ackerman's *We the People: Foundations* [Cambridge, MA: Harvard University Press, 1991].)

casting the realization of rights as a collective project, brings these potential sacrifices to the fore. Yet at the same time, the aforementioned suggestion that identity-grounding projects provide agents with their reason to exist also alerts us to the opposite possibility. A people's failure to realize equal rights might in extreme cases be so pronounced, and so entrenched by widespread societal attitudes, that one might consider oneself relieved from the duty to make sacrifices for the sake of reform, given others' manifest failure to do their part and the extraordinarily high hurdles facing reform. In such extreme situations, the polity's failure to fulfill its constitutive project can be so profound that a conscientious citizen could actually give up and lose a moral stake in the polity's existence – whether this loss is translated into emigration, into indifference as to how the polity fares against existential threats, or into a principled refusal to make sacrifices to combat these threats.

If what I have said in the last four paragraphs is plausible, then the idea of liberal integrity provides important theoretical gains already at the domestic level. This idea expands our moral thinking, by highlighting the broader moral implications of successes and failures to realize equal rights, going beyond the obvious implications for the rights-bearers. At the same time, by tying together these implications, which might otherwise seem disparate, the idea of liberal integrity increases the unity of our moral outlook. With these domestic contributions in the background, we can turn to the global context that triggered our inquiry.

1.3 Liberal Integrity in a Global Context

Reflection on the roots of liberal law's commitment to the equal rights of all citizens immediately suggests that liberal integrity must have some kind of a global dimension. If nothing else, this is because the effort of liberal law to realize the equal rights of all citizens must be at least partly grounded in the deeper notion of universal human equality. One way to see this point is to note that a people that realized the equal rights of its citizens through blatant violations of non-citizens' most basic rights (through conquest and colonial exploitation, for example), could not coherently claim to be liberal. Another way to see why universal human equality must be an underlying principle of liberal law is to consider who may become a citizen of a liberal polity: a polity that professes a liberal identity ought (arguably) to allow at least those outsiders who are willing to immerse themselves in its political culture, language(s) and traditions to (eventually) acquire citizenship, meaning that it must see all of the world's individuals as potential citizens.[31] What both of these thoughts suggest is that liberal integrity cannot end at the border. The question is therefore not whether liberal integrity has global implications, but rather what these implications are.

I believe we can make progress on this question through the following test, which we might term simply the *global integrity test*. When assessing a foreign political or economic practice, a polity with a liberal self-conception ought to ask itself whether it would still be able to retain its identity-grounding commitment to equally respect the rights of all of its citizens, if the same foreign practice were institutionalized through its own legal system, *within* its borders. Where the answer is clearly negative – where the practice in question is incompatible with any plausible interpretation of what it means for a government to equally respect the rights of all of its citizens – perpetuating, legitimating, or reaping benefits from this practice through its own law threatens the polity's liberal integrity. If the polity perpetuates, legitimates, or reaps benefits from a manifestly illiberal foreign practice through its own law, then, when set against its constitutive domestic elements, its law is self-contradictory in much the same way as described in the domestic context.[32]

I defer to the next section the question of what applied conclusions result from this test. Here I wish to take a preparatory step toward these conclusions, by addressing explicitly a general objection that was implicit in some of the previous questions I confronted. This objection holds that the real heart of liberal integrity is not the concept of integrity at all, but simply standard liberal values. The attractions of liberal integrity derive from liberalism rather than integrity: familiar

---

[31] I say more about this point in Chapter 2.
[32] Note that the complicated cases that the global integrity test is meant to elucidate are cases where we assume (as I did regarding the apartheid scenario) that those living under manifestly illiberal foreign practices do see these practices as violating their rights. Hence the key issue here is *not* the one familiar from discussions of toleration and diversity, of people who autonomously choose to live under illiberal political Institutions. I am in fact skeptical of arguments that appeal to diversity to justify customary liberal ties with what Rawls calls "decent" illiberal regimes (see Rawls, *The Law of Peoples* [Cambridge, MA: Harvard University Press, 1999]). But elaborating on this skepticism here will take me too far afield.

1.3 Liberal Integrity in a Global Context

liberal values are doing all the philosophical work, with "integrity" doing none.

I believe that this charge misses the mark. For one thing, even if we temporarily grant, *arguendo*, that the idea of liberal integrity only reflects more fundamental liberal values, it is not clear why this should be a fatal objection. Consider, for the sake of comparison, a famous criticism against Rawls' theory of justice, according to which Rawls argues for his two principles of justice through the original position, yet what Rawls is really arguing from is the deeper liberal value of equal respect.[33] Even if one grants this claim, this does not mean that the original position is insignificant: one may still consider it a useful device in capturing and elucidating a way in which liberal values can coherently fit together.[34] A parallel point applies to the idea of liberal integrity and the global integrity test. Even if one thinks that the "deep concept" here is not really integrity – that I am really arguing *through* rather than *from* integrity – it does not follow that the idea of liberal integrity is insignificant. Liberal integrity may still be considered a useful device for organizing moral intuitions regarding the conduct of liberal democracies.

Moreover, there is in fact no reason to accept the claim that the idea of liberal integrity merely reflects familiar liberal values, which are doing all the practical work. For this claim to hold, it would have to be the case that even without the machinery of integrity, liberal values would generate, in straightforward fashion, determinate duties for liberal peoples in all cases of liberal entanglement in foreign rights violations. Yet the trigger for our exploration of liberal integrity has been precisely the worry that such obvious, determinate duties might be absent: it is precisely because liberal values do not generate obvious conclusions regarding the kind of entanglement that has been our concern that we have been prompted to examine the idea of liberal integrity as a tool that will help us adjudicate our conflicting moral impulses. Or, to put the same point through another parallel to Rawlsian reasoning: we need a global procedure that resolves the indeterminacy of liberal values regarding concrete foreign policy

---

[33] See Dworkin, *Taking Rights Seriously* (Cambridge, MA: Harvard University Press, 1978), Chapter 6.

[34] See Joshua Cohen, "Democratic Equality," *Ethics* 99 (1989): 727–51; Paul Weithman, *Why Political Liberalism: On John Rawls's Political Turn* (Oxford: Oxford University Press, 2010), 352.

choices, just as we need a domestic procedure to render the practical requirements of liberal values more determinate with regard to the basic structure of a liberal polity. The global integrity test is meant to serve as this global procedure: by rendering liberal global duties more determinate, the test, just like Rawls' original position, seeks to provide "guidance where guidance is needed."[35]

1.4 Integrity in Global Action

I do not, however, want to proceed immediately to discussing the integrity solution to the liberal indeterminacy I have highlighted. It will be better to make our way to this solution more gradually, by examining broader benefits of thinking about liberal entanglement in manifestly illiberal practices as a threat to the integrity of a liberal polity. I want to start with the general way in which the language of liberal integrity extends our moral reflection on entanglement in foreign rights violations. This language, I wish to suggest, highlights how the effects of such entanglement go beyond the obvious victims, and involve moral repercussions for the liberal polity itself.

One way to see this extension of our moral outlook is to note that, in the global as in the domestic case, the language of liberal integrity highlights how the entanglement of liberal law in manifestly illiberal practices threatens this law's claim to obedience. This is particularly true with regard to actors – especially corporations – whose global economic interests push them to transact with foreign elites in ways that would never be legal within the polity. If the laws of a polity that professes a liberal identity nonetheless condone such transactions, or even officially legitimize and incentivize their continuation, liberal law arguably fails once more to take itself seriously, since its elements concerning foreign dealings blatantly contradict its domestic foundations and principles. When we think of the result as the "disintegration" of the law, we can again see immediately why the moral claim of liberal law to deserve actors' allegiance – this time, corporations' allegiance – is substantially weakened.

---

[35] *TJ*, 18. That said, it is at the very least an open question, as I noted in the introduction, whether the apparatus of Rawls' theory can actually provide this guidance with regard to many concrete policy problems.

1.4 Integrity in Global Action

This problem is particularly evident where the laws of a liberal polity formally legitimate and incentivize the violation of foreign laws whose domestic parallels are essential to liberal government. Consider for example the decades during which the laws of many liberal democracies considered corporate bribery of foreign officials, formally prohibited in the relevant foreign countries, not only legal but even tax deductible.[36] During this period, liberal lawmakers would have obvious difficulties appealing to "the dignity of legislation"[37] to explain why the same corporations ought to obey domestic prohibitions on bribery. The same problem can remain, however, even if the manifestly illiberal foreign practices are declared legal by the relevant illiberal regime: even such circumstances would not necessarily preserve the integrity of liberal law, nor repair its damaged moral claim to obedience. To continue with the bribery example, suppose, for instance, that a democratically elected government abroad is overthrown in a coup, leading to the rise of a severely oppressive regime, which promptly cancels official prohibitions on bribery – or perhaps even announces formal regulations that require all foreign corporations that wish to conduct business in the state to transfer sizable sums to personal bank accounts associated with the ruling elite. The same transfers that would never be legal within a liberal polity are therefore now legal abroad. But does it really follow from this change that liberal law could retain its integrity and its claim to obedience unharmed, if it recognized such transfers as permissible and even tax deductible?

Bearing in mind this example of how the idea of liberal integrity extends our moral outlook, I now want to note how this idea also clarifies important moral intuitions regarding certain kinds of liberal foreign entanglement. This contribution parallels the domestic context as well. At the domestic level, I suggested that by framing the realization of equal rights as an identity-grounding project for any liberal polity, the idea of liberal integrity provides an immediate way to see the moral value of treating historical struggles to realize equal rights as constitutive of the polity's collective identity – of "who we are as

---

[36] See Pogge, *World Poverty and Human Rights* (Cambridge: Polity Press, 2002), 174.
[37] I borrow the term from Jeremy Waldron's *The Dignity of Legislation* (Cambridge: Cambridge University Press, 1999), although the broader position I develop here is much more sympathetic to judicial review of democratic legislation than is Waldron.

a people." I now want to suggest that, because it accounts well for the moral significance of these historical struggles, the idea of liberal integrity can also clarify some of our more elusive moral intuitions regarding liberal entanglement in illiberal foreign practices.

It will be helpful to give a specific example to illustrate these claims. Let us consider again, then, the example of customary ties between the United States and South Africa's apartheid regime. I suggested at the outset that even if apartheid's victims would have opposed American divestment from the South African regime, the United States would still have important identity-based moral reasons against ties with this regime. In turn, what arguably explains much of the instinctive force of these reasons is the particular history of the United States. This history underlies much of the instinctive moral unease that accompanies reflection on customary ties between the United States and the apartheid regime, even in a scenario in which apartheid's victims would have wanted these ties to continue. Even under such conditions, choosing to legitimate, perpetuate, or benefit from South Africa's racist regime would have profoundly conflicted with the American polity's own historical – and continuing – struggle against racism. What is less clear is how to explain the impact of this conflict on our moral thinking.

The idea of liberal integrity provides the needed explanation. By casting the realization of equal rights as an identity-grounding *project* – one that, like any other project, unfolds over time, requiring effort and sacrifice – the idea of liberal integrity can explain why the historical struggle of American society to overcome its racist heritage would have made continued ties with the South African regime particularly morally loaded. Such ties would have blunted the sense of American progress in the long march toward ending racial discrimination. These ties would have (arguably) conflicted with the acknowledgment of the tremendous sacrifices made through generations for the sake of ending racial discrimination within the United States. And such ties would have conflicted with the moral promise, both explicit and tacit, to treat racial discrimination as constitutive of what American society is *not* going to be, endorse, or condone.[38] The idea of liberal integrity captures these

---

[38] In similar spirit, List and Pettit write (*Group Agency*, 200): "Just as I [an individual] may say of my past self that he is no longer me, so a group agent may say of it in the past: 'That is no longer us', 'We are not the church that condemned Galileo', 'We are not the nation that dispossessed indigenous peoples', 'We are no longer the company that made contracts with the Nazis.'"

historically driven concerns, explaining how and why they have moral force.

I should clarify that this historical perspective is meant to be circumscribed in the following sense. It is perfectly compatible with my view to say that liberal polities have reasons of integrity that go against entanglement in illiberal foreign practices, even in contexts that do not bear in any way on their own historical struggles. So, to continue with our running apartheid scenario, it is perfectly compatible with my view to say that any liberal polity, even one that had no loaded racial history, would have had reasons of integrity going against customary ties with the South African regime. What I am suggesting is that such reasons would have been particularly strong for polities that did have the relevant history.

Since this is a somewhat unusual point, it might be helpful to demonstrate it further through an additional hypothetical example. Imagine a liberal democracy whose collective identity is constituted to a large degree by its successful effort to overcome a history of brutal dictatorship – an effort enshrined in its current constitution, education system, public monuments and ceremonies, and so on. Suppose, however, that this polity is now forced to fight a war in self-defense, and that as part of this war it is systematically employing the worst methods of the past dictatorship, including even systematic torture of enemies. Whether or not we think that morality, all things considered, treats such methods as permissible under the circumstances, and whether or not we think that the aggressors lose their moral immunity against such methods, it seems hard to deny that these methods threaten the polity's own identity-grounding historical achievement of breaking free from the shadow of dictatorship. These methods generate an acute sense of the polity going against its own identity-grounding moral journey. Hence it is not only the general moral question of "what are we fighting for" that clearly looms large here, and that ought to loom large for any liberal polity in such a situation, regardless of its history.[39] There is also a more specific conflict between the identity-grounding commitments of this particular liberal polity and its actions.

---

[39] Note that this question is arguably made more, not less, urgent when the enemy is particularly morally repugnant – when there is a fear that certain methods make the polity worryingly similar to those it is combating. I say more about such concerns in Chapter 3.

Accordingly, it may not be entirely implausible to see this polity as suffering from a kind of alienation from its actions, paralleling, perhaps, the kind of alienation that a reformed criminal might experience if circumstances forced him to go against his identity-grounding journey to break free from a life of violence. Both cases, we may think, feature a kind of self-betrayal. The actions of the reformed criminal pose an especially severe threat to his integrity, to "who he is" and to what his life is about, because these actions take him back to the kind of person he promised himself never again to be. But the same is also true for the liberal polity which undertakes actions that clearly conflict with its identity-grounding moral efforts – actions that take it back to "what we have decided never again to be."

1.5 Liberal Integrity and Natural Resource Trade with Dictatorships

I hope to have done enough by this point to show how the idea of liberal integrity elucidates the hypothetical apartheid scenario with which we began. In Chapter 4, I will delve into current problems surrounding liberal lending to odious regimes, which have important moral similarities to this scenario. But it might be helpful to give a sense, already here, of how such actual problems of liberal entanglement look, and why the integrity framework might be helpful in thinking about them.

Consider, then, the case of ongoing trade in state-owned natural resources between dictatorships and corporations based in liberal democracies. A prominent normative argument emphasizes that at least some dictators ought not to be recognized as legitimate vendors of natural resources because they cannot claim valid authorization to sell these resources from their people – the real owners of state property. In the lack of such authorization, at least some dictators should be seen as stealing state property from their people; corporations that are based in liberal democracies and that transact with these dictators should accordingly be seen as trafficking in stolen goods.[40]

---

[40] See, e.g., Pogge, "Achieving Democracy," *Ethics and International Affairs* 15 (2001): 3–23; Leif Wenar, "Property Rights and the Resource Curse," *Philosophy & Public Affairs* 36 (2008): 2–32; Leif Wenar, *Blood Oil* (Oxford: Oxford University Press, 2016). See also my "Rigorist Cosmopolitanism," *Politics, Philosophy & Economics* 12 (2013): 260–287 and "Democratic

1.5 Liberal Integrity and Natural Resource Trade with Dictatorships 41

Most philosophers who have discussed natural resource trade with dictators have taken it for granted that this trade ought to be reformed, and that the challenges involved concern institutional design, rather than any normative conundrums.[41] However, this widespread assumption ignores an important problem, one that remains even if we endorse the idea that dictators are violating their peoples' property rights over natural resources. There is no assurance that stopping natural resource trade with dictators will make the peoples living under them better off. And in the lack of such assurance, the peoples living under dictators might very well consent to the continuation of customary trade in their natural resources, even if these peoples do think that these dictators are violating their property rights.

Take just two important examples. First, many Russians might view Putin's dictatorship as a "third world kleptocracy" that is systematically stealing the Russian people's natural resource wealth.[42] But there is no certainty that disrupting customary ties with Putin's regime will make ordinary Russians better off. And so many Russians might very well consent to the continuation of customary transactions in their natural resources. Similarly, consider the claim that by purchasing oil from the Saudi royal family, and by making such purchases legal, the corporations and governments of liberal democracies are heavily implicated in this family's violations of the property rights of the Saudi people.[43] It is far from obvious that ordinary Saudis will be better off if the royal family could no longer sell oil to liberal democracies. And so, even if a growing number of Saudis complain that the royal family is

---

Disengagement: Toward Rousseauian Global Reform," *International Theory* 3 (2011): 355–389.

[41] For just a few examples of this conventional wisdom, see Stephen Macedo, "What Self-Governing Peoples Owe to One Another," *Fordham Law Review* 72 (2003–4): 1721–1738, at 1732; Joseph Heath, "Rawls on Global Distributive Justice: A Defence," *Canadian Journal of Philosophy* 35 (2005): 193–226, at 198; Samuel Freeman, "Distributive Justice and the Law of Peoples," in Rex Martin and David Reidy, eds., *Rawls' Law of Peoples: A Realistic Utopia?* (Malden, MA: Blackwell, 2006): 243–260, at 251.

[42] See the quotes from political analyst Stanislav Belkovsky, in Luke Harding, *Mafia State* (London: Guardian Books, 2012), 21–22. Belkovsky claims that the wealth of President Putin alone stands (on a conservative estimate), at forty *billion* dollars, the majority of which comes from natural resource revenues siphoned off the Russian state.

[43] See, e.g., Pogge, *World Poverty and Human Rights*, 2nd ed. (London: Polity, 2008), 148.

illicitly treating the vast oil riches that are public property as private "spoils,"[44] ordinary Saudis might nonetheless consent to liberal democracies continuing their customary dealings with the Saudi government.

Once we consider this possibility, the actual present case of natural resource trade with dictators becomes similar in important respects to the past hypothetical scenario we have considered regarding South Africa's apartheid. Just as in the apartheid scenario, we have a situation where the victims of a blatantly illiberal practice might very well consent to liberal democracies continuing their involvement in this practice, even if the victims *do* see the practice itself as violating their rights. And just as in the apartheid scenario, it seems difficult to appeal to victim-related reasons to justify why liberal democracies ought to disengage from the practice in question. Here as well there is no obvious reason why respect for either victims' rights or their equal moral standing straightforwardly requires that liberal societies stop practices that the victims might very well want to see continuing. Therefore, just as in the apartheid scenario, it seems that here as well, if we want to retain the intuition against liberal entanglement in a manifestly illiberal practice, we may have to look beyond familiar victim-related reasons. And once again, the idea of liberal integrity provides the needed expansion of our moral outlook.

The best way to see this contribution is to return to the global integrity test presented above. Could a polity that professes a liberal identity retain its claim to be a liberal society, if the practices of the House of Saud or of Putin's regime regarding state property were instantiated within any liberal polity? It seems safe to say that the answer is "no." As Allen Buchanan writes, the "gospel of liberalism, at least in its democratic variants [has involved] the message that the state ... is not the property of a dynasty, an aristocracy, or any political elite, but rather "belongs" to the people."[45] To accept that a state's de facto rulers are also the de facto owners of state property would be to accept a fundamentally illiberal doctrine.[46] And to formally enact this doctrine within the jurisdiction of a liberal polity would be to distort

---

[44] See "The Long Day Closes," *The Economist*, June 23, 2012, at http://economist.com/node/21557327
[45] Buchanan, "The Making and Unmaking of Boundaries: What Liberalism Has to Say," in Allen Buchanan and Margaret Moore (eds.), *States, Nations, and Borders* (Cambridge: Cambridge University Press, 2003), at 234.

1.5 Liberal Integrity and Natural Resource Trade with Dictatorships 43

beyond recognition a core element of its identity-grounding institutions. Hence it seems that, through the global integrity test, the idea of liberal integrity is able to capture the intuition that liberal polities have identity-based moral reasons against entanglement in dictators' violations of their victims' property rights – reasons that exist independently of whether the victims consent to third parties' dealings with the perpetrators.

There is, however, an added complication. It seems (or so at least I assume) that concerns regarding liberal entanglement would have been more pressing in the hypothetical apartheid scenario than they are in the actual present case of natural resource trade. This difference might be explained in several ways, but there is at least one explanation that the idea of liberal integrity again captures particularly well. According to this explanation, if liberal entanglement in dictators' control of their peoples' property is less immediately morally disturbing than entanglement in South Africa's apartheid, this is, at least in part, because of collective identity considerations. Simply put, the struggle against racism is a more fundamental component of the collective identity of contemporary liberal democracies than is the struggle against manifestly undemocratic forms of control over state property.

This difference might be due to the fact that, while the fight against racism in many liberal democracies is still ongoing, the struggle against manifestly undemocratic control over public property seems lodged too far in the past of many liberal democracies to really play a formative role in their present collective identity. Or it might be that this struggle is easily absorbed under the broader category of struggles against authoritarian rule, which have a more central role in the collective identity of many liberal democracies. But whatever the precise cause, the threat to the self-conception of liberal polities, to the coherence of the moral struggles and achievements constitutive of their contemporary identity, seems greater in the case of apartheid than it does in the case of natural resources. The idea of liberal integrity captures this comparative point and brings it to the fore as an element of our moral reasoning about complex forms of liberal entanglement.

[46] As we will see in Chapter 2, it is important to actually situate this conviction within a broader compelling account of state or public property. At this stage I am assuming – only temporarily and for the sake of simplicity – that we can treat this conviction as self-evident on its own, without further theoretical machinery.

1.6 Liberal Integrity and Hypocrisy

Let me now turn to values on which integrity is often thought to bear, starting with hypocrisy. A compelling account of integrity should be able to tell us something about the relationship between integrity and hypocrisy. On one attractive definition, a hypocrite is someone who pretends to be better than he actually is.[47] A moral hypocrite, in particular, preaches lofty moral principles to others but clearly fails to live up to these principles himself. Integrity, in contrast, centrally involves, as we have seen, fidelity to one's principles. Thus hypocrisy and integrity cannot – at least over time – reside side by side. A person of integrity avoids hypocrisy. Can our conception of liberal integrity capture this observation with regard to a liberal democracy?

I believe that it can. In particular, we can use the liberal integrity framework to capture a politically important phenomenon, which might be termed the "hypocrisy of distance." The problem of domestic racism discussed above provides a vivid illustration of this kind of hypocrisy. Earlier I mentioned, as a paradigmatic failure of liberal integrity, a case where the supreme law of a purportedly liberal land formally rejects racial discrimination, yet allows lower-level governmental units to wield their power in such a way that will foreseeably make a mockery of legal guarantees of racial equality. Such a moral failure can be characterized as a "hypocrisy of distance" insofar as it is hypocritical for the highest levels of government to claim an artificial distance from subordinate units. It is hypocritical of national leaders to say "our moral credentials are impeccable, it is they who are the racists": the highest levels of government cannot in good faith dodge responsibility for the power and discretion of subordinate units.[48]

The liberal integrity framework also captures another variant that the "hypocrisy of distance" often takes, and that may even be more ubiquitous in political life. This variant revolves around artificial distance of the legal system as a whole from glaring moral wrongs. Such distance is supposed to be manifest in the fact that the law does not officially call

---

[47] This definition follows Judith Shklar, *Ordinary Vices* (Cambridge, MA: Harvard University Press, 1984), Chapter 2, although Shklar is much more sympathetic toward hypocrisy than I will be here.

[48] For other kinds of "institutional hypocrisy" see the discussion in Dennis Thompson's "Hypocrisy and Democracy," in Bernard Yack (ed.) *Liberalism without Illusions* (Chicago: Chicago University Press, 1995): 173–190.

1.6 Liberal Integrity and Hypocrisy

for the relevant wrongs; rather, it is (formally or effectively) silent in the face of these wrongs. But on the account I am advancing here, even such silence can be – and usually will be – extremely distressing, and will typically constitute a serious failure of liberal integrity. To be clear, I do not mean to deny that for the law to officially defend or promote morally abhorrent actions or practices is usually worse than the law simply being silent in the face of such actions or practices. What I do deny is that the "mere" silence of the law suffices to make it compatible with liberal integrity.

By way of illustration, take again the example of women's rights discussed above. Imagine a society in which women are treated as the property of their husbands, enjoy little protection against sexual assault, and are generally viewed as manifestly subordinate to men anywhere from the workplace to the household. It would surely be a massive failure of integrity for a liberal democracy to formalize any such discrimination in the law. But it would be odd to think that there is no serious violation of collective integrity if the laws are simply silent (formally or in practice) in the face of such pervasive, and widely known, gender discrimination.

This point, in turn, has especially serious repercussions at the global level, where the entanglement of liberal law in morally disturbing practices often occurs through the silence of the law. The case of US ties with South Africa's apartheid regime is useful here as well. At no point in the history of these ties did US laws formally express any kind of support for the ideology of the South African regime. Yet the silence of these laws clearly did not suffice to distance the American legal system from entanglement in apartheid.

Nor is the case of apartheid unique. Take, for example, the contemporary problem of human trafficking. In June 2014, the US State Department, defining human trafficking as the "recruiting, harboring, transporting, providing, or obtaining a person for compelled labor or commercial sex acts through the use of force, fraud, or coercion," has estimated the number of victims of such practices to be *twenty million* men, women, and children. Yet despite this staggering number, many liberal democracies still feature at best limited efforts to enact or enforce meaningful legislation to combat human trafficking.[49] Now,

---

[49] See the US State Department's *Trafficking in Persons Report,* at http://state.gov /j/tip/rls/tiprpt/2014/index.htm.

it should be completely obvious that laws Which officially designate certain outsiders as slaves, and which protect the "property rights" of traders who "purchase" these outsiders, cannot align with the integrity of liberal democracy. But then should our judgment really be so different when faced with laws that are formally or effectively silent, even when global trade in human beings is known to be extremely prevalent?

With these claims in view, let me turn to a final form of hypocrisy captured by the liberal integrity framework. This form of hypocrisy might be termed "the hypocrisy of self-seeking rationalizations." Agents guilty of this kind of hypocrisy are engaging in bad-faith moral reasoning in order to rationalize why they do not act on demanding moral principles: they offer superficially moral justifications for why they may be exempted from the reach of the relevant principles, even though their pursuit of such exemptions is actually driven by amoral (if not immoral) motivations.

The hypocrisy of self-seeking rationalizations is often evident in discussions of global reform, where it feeds on the structural uncertainty of social science, and on the status quo bias associated with this uncertainty. The endemic limitations of social science in a global context, such as the inability to compare global institutions across "parallel worlds," mean that there is endemic social-scientific uncertainty concerning the effects of global reforms. This uncertainty buttresses a tendency toward "system justification," casting the status quo as "the least worst" feasible state of the world.[50] The predictable result is a breeding ground for self-seeking rationalizations of the status quo. As long as powerful actors can attach social-scientific uncertainty to almost every global reform proposal, we can predict a proliferation of self-serving moral justifications for why it is morally permissible to avoid reform. To employ our key examples again, just as the Reagan administration sought to explain how the aforementioned "constructive engagement" with apartheid was not meant only to maximize profits, so can powerful oil corporations, for instance, seek to explain

---

[50] A familiar definition of system justification sees it as "a form of motivated moral reasoning consciously or unconsciously aimed at defending, justifying, and bolstering aspects of the status quo, including existing social, economic, and political institutions and arrangements." See John Jost and Joanneke van der Toorn, "System Justification Theory," in Paul A. M. Van Lange, Arie W. Kruglanski and E. Tory Higgins, (eds.) *Handbook of Theories of Social Psychology*, Vol. 2 (Los Angeles: SAGE, 2012): 313–343.

1.6 Liberal Integrity and Hypocrisy

why oil trade with kleptocratic dictators actually has a chance of improving the condition of their victims,[51] accordingly emphasizing that these victims might very well be disposed to consent to the continuation of such trade, or that it might very well be in their rational interest to so consent.

It should be clear that this is not a morally desirable state of affairs. If agents may benefit from foreign violations of victims' rights as long as this could somehow be shown to be in line with the victims' interests, then we are bound to see many agents seeking "loopholes in morality."[52] It is therefore significant that the claims of liberal integrity combat such loopholes in at least three ways. First, the claims of integrity push each liberal polity to respond to foreign rights violations in certain ways, independently of questions about the rights-bearers' consent. Second, more generally, recall that integrity requires steadfastness in acting on one's commitments – it involves a willingness to make non-trivial sacrifices for the sake of the principles that one professes. Integrity does not align with agents seeking exemptions from the hold of principles they proclaim whenever these principles become costly.

Third, the claims of liberal integrity preempt hypocritical rationalizations of the status quo associated with global collective action.[53] As long as the reason to end entanglement in illiberal foreign practices is contingent on the ability of reform to realize the rights of the victims of these practices, each state will often exempt itself from any duty to initiate reform by claiming "ineffective sacrifice" – pointing out that since there is no overarching authority above states, there is no guarantee that other states will join the reform, and that without them doing so, the moral gains from solitary action will be minuscule (the level of pressure will not suffice to realize victims' rights) but the cost that the solitary polity will have to bear will be significant. Furthermore – the excuse will continue – were that state to act alone, it will only be the "sucker" incurring absolute and relative costs in relation to its competitors.[54] Yet collective-action excuses cannot affect integrity

---

[51] On such explanations from Exxon Mobil, for instance, see Steve Coll, *Private Empire* (New York: Penguin, 2012), e.g., at 521.

[52] Pogge, "Loopholes in Moralities," *Journal of Philosophy* 89 (1992): 79–98.

[53] This paragraph draws on my "Global Taxation, Global Reform, and Collective Action," *Moral Philosophy and Politics* 1 (2014): 83–103.

[54] For a discussion of this "sucker exemption" see Pogge, *World Poverty*, Chapter 5.

reasons to end entanglement in foreign rights violations. Consider the apartheid example again. If the United States had strong reasons of integrity to divest from South Africa's apartheid regime, independently of whether doing so would have precipitated apartheid's demise, then it would have been beside the point for the United States to invoke collective-action problems as excusing continued customary ties.

1.7 Integrity and Public Honesty

Having outlined some important connections between liberal integrity and aversion to hypocrisy, I now want to turn to an adjacent idea that the integrity framework similarly incorporates, and that I shall refer to as *public honesty*.[55] Three main aspects of this idea are worth highlighting here.

First, at least in some important cases, integrity requires of us to make both our principled conduct, and the reasons underlying it, public. A person who does not want to pay his taxes and who tells himself that this is because of the government's injustice is unlikely to strike us as a paragon of integrity if he is simply evading taxes secretly. In fact, he is more likely to strike us as engaged in self-deception – trying to convince himself that he is acting out of fidelity to lofty moral principles that "just happen" to coincide with his economic interests. By way of contrast, a person who, in Thoreauian fashion, publicly declares that he will not pay his taxes because of the government's injustice, and who is willing to incur the government sanctions that are bound to follow, is far more likely to strike us as a person of integrity.[56]

---

[55] I recognize that "honesty" may seem to overlap significantly with aversion to hypocrisy. But part of the honesty I have in mind – as will become clear in a moment – concerns honesty with oneself. And I take it that one can lack this kind of honesty – one can engage in systematic self-deception – without thereby becoming a hypocrite, seeing as we typically think of hypocrisy as an interpersonal rather than an intra-personal vice.

[56] As this example indicates, we can draw a fairly immediate link between public honesty and steadfastness. This link is prominent, for example, in Carter's *Integrity*, e.g., Chapter 2. In the same work, however (Chapter 4 – "The Insufficiency of Honesty") Carter is also keen to show that integrity properly understood sometimes requires that we hide certain wrongs that we have done, and incur various costs in the process, in order to spare others of even more serious costs. I believe that this view is mistaken, but I will not argue for this belief here.

1.7 Integrity and Public Honesty   49

An analogous point, I believe, obtains with regard to a liberal government's moral duties in general, and its egalitarian duties in particular. A liberal government acting with integrity will not only work to realize the equal rights of all of its citizens. It will also make it publicly clear that it is pursuing such equality, even when such honesty involves non-trivial political costs. Thus, for example, a government that is working to transfer resources away from politically powerful groups who have been unjustly privileged, to others who have been victims of discrimination, may be tempted to keep such transfers "under the radar," precisely in order to avoid backlash from the powerful. But a liberal government acting with integrity will (under anything but the most extreme circumstances) accept such a backlash as part of its job. Such a government would not only be willing to channel resources to those who have endured discrimination: it will also be willing to make it publicly known that the powerful will lose some of their privileges for the sake of those whose rights have long been marginalized.

A second aspect of public honesty that the integrity framework incorporates concerns honest confrontation with difficult policy choices. It is often too tempting for liberal societies to willfully ignore key policy problems that feature no easy solutions. Instead of coming to terms with a difficult reality, a society may choose to simply ignore this reality. Present-day examples include British attitudes toward Brexit, American attitudes toward the "war on drugs," and German attitudes with regard to the welfare state. In all of these cases, large portions of both the political class and the electorate opt for willful blindness rather than an honest confrontation with difficult realities. At the time of writing, many Britons seem extremely disinclined to face up to the fact that they have to choose between "freedom" from EU regulations and the economic benefits of EU membership;[57] many Americans are loath to concede that increasing the criminalization of drug use will not, by itself, curb (let alone halt) the drug epidemic, and that some form of wide-ranging legalization of drugs might be

---

[57] See, e.g., Charles Grant and John Springford, "The 10 Brexit Compromises Theresa May Won't Talk About," *The Guardian*, June 19, 2017, at https://theguardian.com/commentisfree/2017/jun/19/10-brexit-compromises-theresa-may-britain; "Theresa May Bows to Inevitable Hard Choices on Brexit," *Financial Times*, Mar. 3, 2018, at https://.ft.com/content/5bc2301e-1e0e-11e8-aaca-4574d7dabfb6

necessary.[58] Many Germans are reluctant to admit that they cannot sustain their current welfare state without falling behind in global economic competition, and certainly not without tackling the problem of a rapidly aging population.[59] These are all cases of a collective attempt to "bury heads in the sand." Insofar as such attempts amount to collective self-deception, they are incompatible with collective integrity.

A third and final aspect of public honesty is very much related. A liberal polity that acts with integrity avoids self-deception not only with regard to those problems that ostensibly lie in the distant future. Such a polity avoids self-deception also with regard to its past. A liberal polity acts with integrity when it does not flinch from taking a hard look at its own history, even if this means facing up to deeply distressing moral failures that – inconveniently – tarnish the collective self-image. The collective integrity framework can easily capture the thought that such an honest confrontation with the collective past should play an important part in a liberal democracy's collective identity.[60]

---

[58] See, e.g., "War on Drugs: Report of the Global Commission on Drug Policy," June 2011, at www.globalcommissionondrugs.org/wp-content/themes/gcdp_v1/pdf/Global_Commission_Report_English.pdf; Mona Chalabi, "The 'War on Drugs' in Numbers: A Systematic Failure of Policy," *The Guardian*, Apr. 19, 2016, at https://theguardian.com/world/2016/apr/19/war-on-drugs-statistics-systematic-policy-failure-united-nations; http://globalcommissionondrugs.org/2-april-2016-the-uns-war-on-drugs-is-a-failure-is-it-time-for-a-different-approach/.

[59] See, e.g., Iain Begg, "Can EU Countries Still Afford Their Welfare States?" *BBC News*, Sep. 17, 2015, at http://bbc.com/news/world-europe-34272111.

[60] In some cases, such confrontation can also serve to distinguish the relevant liberal democracy from other societies that refuse to acknowledge similar traumas. Thus, for example, Taiwan's president, Tsai Ing-wen, used her 2016 inauguration speech to call for a truth and reconciliation commission with regard to past political repression. As two transitional justice scholars put it, "Tsai's call for a TRC was in sharp contrast to the deafening quiet across the Taiwan Strait, where Chinese government officials and state media marked the 50th anniversary of the violence and depredations of the Cultural Revolution with muted, terse statements." Tsai's initiative can thus be interpreted as seeking "cultural and political distinction from the irredentism and authoritarianism of China," as well as demonstrating "adherence to international norms of democracy and human rights" Ian Rowen and Jamie Rowen, "Taiwan's Truth and Reconciliation Committee: The Geopolitics of Transitional Justice in a Contested State," *International Journal of Transitional Justice* 11 (2017): 92–112, at 92–93.

1.8 Integrity and Decency

1.8.1 Decency and Personal Integrity

With these points in mind, we can turn to one last value on which integrity is often thought to bear: decency. Many of us would be reluctant, I assume, to describe an agent who repeatedly displayed a lack of basic moral decency as an agent who acts with moral integrity. To say this is *not* to suggest that we are only willing (or should only be willing) to ascribe integrity to moral exemplars. Rather, the more modest suggestion is that we only ascribe integrity to people whose moral views we regard as passing some minimal threshold of substantive plausibility. And people who we believe to lack basic moral decency fail to meet even this very low threshold.

We can further spell out this suggestion by considering the indecent characters that have often absorbed moral philosophers contemplating integrity. Should we, for example, ascribe "integrity" to the committed Nazi, simply in virtue of his profound or "wholehearted"[61] attachment to Nazi principles?[62]

In my view, there are two key points to be made in response to this question. First, we may simply deny that the question is as significant as the integrity literature often assumes. This, at the very least, should be our conclusion if we avoid from the outset the thought that integrity is morally fundamental, and instead view integrity – as I do here – as an idea that comes into its own only in the presence of certain other, substantive values.[63] Once we proceed down this path, it becomes readily apparent that the Nazi's putative integrity – whether real or imaginary – is devoid of moral interest.[64] And so we can simply say that

---

[61] Harry Frankfurt presented an influential argument in favor of associating integrity with "wholeheartedness" in his "Freedom of the Will and the Concept of a Person," *Journal of Philosophy* LXVIII (1971): 5–20.

[62] For an extended discussion of such questions, see Mark Halfon, *Integrity: A Philosophical Inquiry* (Philadelphia: Temple University Press, 1989).

[63] Here I am again echoing Rawls (*TJ*, 456).

[64] More specifically, when considering such extreme cases, we can simply say that some fundamental commitments that agents may adopt as the core of their integrity exert their own independent moral weight once adopted, even though other commitments – such as those of the Nazi – are entirely devoid of such

fundamental commitments that meet the substantive requirements of decency are a necessary condition for having *moral* integrity.

The second response to the question of "the Nazi's integrity" is also worth mentioning here, since it also supports a link between integrity and decency. This response highlights our sheer incredulity when confronted with ostensibly "moral" views that are too abhorrent to count as decent. This is the kind of incredulity we convey by telling someone *"you can't possibly believe that."* Such incredulity, I assume, makes us reluctant to ascribe integrity to our interlocutor, and for good reason. Most obviously, when we say to someone "you can't possibly believe that," we are likely expressing the thought that our interlocutor is trying to deceive us, and/or himself – paradigmatically, by assuming away or simply ignoring inconvenient facts that would fatally undermine his "moral" views. Less obviously, we may be suggesting that our interlocutor is parroting the views handed to him by others – and so that his "commitments" are not truly his own. And of course, these two failures – to think about one's commitments for oneself, and to incorporate clearly pertinent facts into one's thinking – often come together.

In turn, it seems to me that these failures go a long way toward explaining why we are so hesitant to attribute moral integrity to those whose proclaimed "moral" views are too indecent to count as reasonable.[65] Someone who simply refuses to reflect either on the principles he is uttering, or on facts that plainly bear on these principles, is failing the most minimal, everyday understanding of what being "reasonable" means.[66] And it is counter-intuitive to insist that such

---

weight due to their substantive content. This, after all, is just how we normally think about the adjacent topic of promises, for example. Some promises clearly exert their own independent moral force once made (the sheer fact that we have promised to do X gives us a moral reason to do X), even though other promises exert no such force, precisely because their substantive content clearly lies beyond the moral pale. It would take a brave moral philosopher to insist that if one man promises another to help him rape a woman, for instance, this promise has even presumptive moral force.

[65] As Lynn McFall, for instance, observes, "when we grant integrity to a person we need not approve of his or her principles or commitments, but we must at least recognize them as ones a reasonable person might take to be of great importance ... " Lynn McFall, "Integrity," *Ethics* 98 (1987): 5–20, at 11.

[66] On this particular issue I am largely in agreement with David Enoch, "The Masses and the Elites: Political Philosophy for the Age of Brexit, Trump and Netanyahu," *Jurisprudence* (2017): 1–23, passim (especially 15).

1.8 Integrity and Decency

a person – merely in virtue of reciting certain commitments like an automaton, in complete disregard of the reasons that obviously apply to the views he is spouting – qualifies as a person of integrity. Thus for example, a person may very well be committed to certain supposed "facts" and "moral principles" concerning the "natural inferiority" of Jews, or blacks, or women. But to the extent that such a person refuses to check his alleged "facts" against reality, then his attachment to his distorted picture of the world, no matter how profound, cannot suffice to make him an example of integrity.[67]

Building on the claims I have just laid out, I shall go on to view moral decency as a necessary condition for having moral integrity. But, having briefly relied on an implicit, rough-and-ready understanding of what moral decency involves, I should now be a bit more specific about this concept.

1.8.2 Integrity, Decency, and the Vulnerable

I assume that decency is at least partly a function of how agents treat vulnerable others.[68] More specifically, we can connect decency to the vocabulary of integrity by saying the following: *Agents acting with moral integrity have an identity-grounding commitment to treat vulnerable others decently.*

---

[67] These remarks are partly inspired by Allen Buchanan's harrowing account of his upbringing in the American South, in the opening of his "Political Liberalism and Social Epistemology," *Philosophy & Public Affairs* 32 (2004): 95–130, especially at 96: "A person brought up in a racist society typically not only absorbs an interwoven set of false beliefs about the natural characteristics of blacks (or Jews, and so on), but also learns epistemic vices . . . For example, when a child, who has been taught that blacks are intellectually inferior, encounters an obviously highly intelligent black person, he may be told that the latter 'must have some white blood.' Along with substantive false beliefs, the racist (like the anti-Semite and the sexist) learns strategies for overcoming cognitive dissonance and for retaining those false beliefs in the face of disconfirming evidence."

[68] To take a well-known example from US history, the widespread sense that he is preying upon vulnerable individuals was arguably a key reason for Joseph McCarthy's eventual downfall. This sense was evident when an opposing counsel famously interrupted McCarthy's public shaming of a young lawyer, asking him directly: "Have you no sense of decency, sir?" See "Welch-McCarthy Exchange" at http://americanrhetoric.com/speeches/welch-mccarthy.html.

I do not intend to try to offer here an exhaustive account of what it means for an agent to have an identity-grounding commitment to treat vulnerable others decently. But I do want to offer some concrete moral requirements that I believe would have to feature in such an account. After introducing these requirements at the level of individual conduct, I will try to show that they can be usefully incorporated into the liberal integrity framework, and that they have important implications for the conduct of liberal peoples as collective agents.

Arguably the first requirement of decency with regard to vulnerable others is to avoid exploiting them in blatant ways. To exploit others is to use their vulnerability to one's own advantage in ways that are unfair.[69] To engage in blatant exploitation (on my proposed terminology) is to use others' vulnerability to one's own advantage in a way that is, beyond reasonable doubt, profoundly unfair. To take a famous example, a water vendor in a desert who sells a water bottle to a badly dehydrated man for a thousand dollars is engaging in blatant exploitation. He is using the vulnerability of the man whose life is at risk to make a profit that is manifestly unfair. This profit is manifestly unfair because it exceeds, by orders of magnitude, the profit that the vendor would make under normal conditions, where such exceptional vulnerability would not be present. And so the vendor who makes this profit is failing basic demands of decency.

Another demand of decency is not to ignore the severe plight of vulnerable others, when this plight is manifest and one is easily able to make the greatest difference for them. Consider Peter Singer's classic example of a man who witnesses a child drowning in a shallow pond right in front of him, yet chooses to walk past the child, even though he could easily save the child's life.[70] Some of us, at least, would be inclined not only to say that this man did the wrong thing in ignoring the drowning child but, more specifically and more damningly, would also say that this man lacks basic moral decency.

---

[69] See, e.g., Allen Wood, "Exploitation," *Social Philosophy and Policy* 12 (1995): 136–158; Allen Wertheimer, *Exploitation* (Princeton: Princeton University Press, 1996); Mikhail Valdman, "Exploitation and Injustice," *Social Theory and Practice* 34 (2008): 551–572.

[70] Peter Singer, "Famine, Affluence, and Morality," *Philosophy & Public Affairs* 1 (1972): 229–243.

1.8 Integrity and Decency

Alongside the requirement to avoid blatant exploitation of others, and to be willing to act when confronted with the obvious plight of others, we can also mention a demand of moral decency concerning the resolution of disputes. Decency constrains how a person – especially one who is well-off and powerful – should approach a potential or actual dispute with vulnerable others. In such a situation, a decent person would not fight to get every single advantage he can, in a way that is entirely oblivious to the condition of the vulnerable. This point should be especially clear where the benefits of victory would be marginal for the well-off person, while the costs of his winning would be disastrous for the vulnerable. Consider, for instance, a billionaire landlord who is determined to pursue a legal dispute against his impoverished tenants, even if there is no obvious moral case in his favor, even if the gains of victory would be trivial for him, and even if the resulting costs would be unbearable for the tenants. The landlord's obsession with forcing his tenants to pay every single cent he can get out of them is indecent.

Now, why think that these requirements of decency connect with the notion of integrity?[71] One reason has to do with the relationship between the requirements of decency that I have just described, and with the hostility toward self-seeking rationalizations that I have associated with the integrity framework. Take again the case of blatant exploitation in the desert. The vendor who sells the dehydrated man a bottle of water for a thousand dollars can be expected to rationalize his profit-seeking by appealing to the buyer's consent – and indeed to claim that he is making the buyer better off than he would be otherwise. But we have already seen how the integrity framework can be used to push against such consent-based rationalizations of profit-seeking. This is one key sense in which the claims of integrity and the claims of decency are mutually reinforcing.

Another key way in which the notions of integrity and decency are mutually reinforcing has to do with my emphasis above on a person of integrity having an identity-grounding commitment to treat vulnerable others decently. Having such a commitment means seeing it as essential

---

[71] This connection is not meant to suggest that integrity ideas are in any way necessary to derive claims about the moral importance of decency. Rather, part of my aim here is to show how these two independently appealing ideas can stand together. This will be important for practical cases, discussed later, where some "integrity impulses" seem to run counter to demands of decency.

to one's own self-conception to treat vulnerable others decently. And this particular motivation for decent behavior, in turn, has important practical implications. For one thing, agents who have such a motivation are more likely to actually behave decently toward the vulnerable.[72] But there is also a further, less obvious implication. A person who has reasons of integrity to treat the vulnerable decently will have those reasons independently (at least to some extent) of what the vulnerable may consent to or even actively want.

By way of illustration, consider a variant of the desert case. If our water vendor crossing the desert is a morally decent person, he will not only refrain from charging the dehydrated man an extortionist price for a water battle; our water vendor will be committed to helping the man escape the risk to his life, and will treat such help as far more important than the profits he might make in such a situation. But suppose further that, long after the emergency is resolved, the recipient of this help actually wants to give the water vendor a thousand dollars by way of gratitude for his simple but crucial help. Although it would obviously be the recipient's prerogative to offer this sum, we can expect the water vendor to decline the offer by appealing to his own integrity – saying that he helped not because he wanted the man's money, but simply because he was committed to doing the decent thing – and in fact accepting the money would go against his principles.

This example, in turn, points toward a final, closely related moral standard that combines the notions of decency and integrity. A person acting with moral integrity not only has a general identity-grounding commitment to treating vulnerable others decently. More specifically, such a person should be averse to accepting sacrifices from the vulnerable even when the vulnerable might have the prerogative of offering these sacrifices. Thus an affluent man of integrity touring a developing country, for instance, should be averse to accepting sexual favors from very young women who are clearly in dire circumstances, even if, at least in some circumstances, these women might have the moral prerogative of offering such favors. Rather than appealing to any kind of consent from the women as an excuse for accepting their "overtures," such a man should be steadfast in refusing, as a matter of his own

---

[72] Thus, for instance, a man who has an identity-grounding commitment to behave decently toward the vulnerable is much more likely to actually step in to save the child drowning in a shallow pond, than is a man who will only do so when failing to help will trigger sanctions (whether social or legal).

integrity, to reap sexual benefits from their vulnerability. And insofar as the man has good grounds to suspect that the vulnerable women are offering him such benefits out of the expectation of financial reward, then his own integrity should compel him to do the decent thing and offer the women money simply by way of help, with no strings attached.

1.8.3 Decency and Collective Integrity

The integrity of an individual person, then, has some important connections to the value of decency. And I believe that we can say the same about the integrity of a liberal democracy as a collective agent. I will offer multiple examples of this parallel later in the book, but a few brief illustrations, relating to liberal democracies' foreign conduct, might be helpful already here.

One example has to do with aid to those in dire need. Just as an individual person acting with integrity would have an identity-grounding commitment to do the decent thing and offer help to those in desperate need, so should an affluent liberal democracy acting with integrity offer help to impoverished foreign peoples, especially when such help can make a tremendous difference. Thus if no affluent democracy did the decent thing and offered support when natural disasters ravaged Haiti, for example, this would be a serious failure of collective integrity.

Another example has to with the avoidance of exploitation. An identity-grounding commitment to avoid exploitation would not only affect a liberal democracy's direct conduct – prohibiting it, as noted in the earlier example, from pursuit of colonial exploitation. An identity-grounding commitment to avoiding exploitation would also affect how a liberal government regulates the conduct of agents within its jurisdiction, corporations being once again the most notable example. Thus, for instance, it is a failure of integrity for a liberal democracy to allow corporations to systematically benefit from the vulnerability of some of the world's most impoverished people through systematic use of sweatshop labor.[73]

---

[73] See, for instance, the introduction in Yossi Dahan, Hanna Lerner, and Faina Milman-Sivan (eds.), *Global Justice and International Labor Standards* (Cambridge: Cambridge University Press, 2016)

Yet another example concerns aversion to accepting certain sacrifices from the vulnerable. A reasonably affluent liberal democracy should not only offer the vulnerable help, which it can clearly provide with ease and which will make a tremendous difference to their lives, but also be averse to accepting sacrifices on their part by way of response. An affluent liberal society that offers medical help to the victims of a civil war raging on the other side of the border, for instance, is acting decently.[74] But it would be indecent for such a society to accept – let alone to demand – any kind of payment that such victims might offer, even if their offer is genuine.

Now, some may worry that examples of this sort point at an important tension at the heart of the liberal integrity framework. On the one hand, integrity requires a liberal democracy to treat the vulnerable – including the vulnerable beyond its borders – decently. On the other hand, the global integrity test that I emphasized earlier seems to push liberal democracies to disentangle themselves from various kinds of customary ties, even when doing so might be deleterious for the vulnerable. But will there not be something callous – and in fact, indecent – about such disentanglement, if it might very well be harmful for the vulnerable? And if this is the case, is there not a self-contradiction at the core of the integrity framework?

This objection, however intuitive, is mistaken. The integrity framework can coherently push liberal democracies to reform their relationship to certain foreign practices, in line with the global integrity test, while also requiring of liberal democracies, as a matter of decency, not to abandon the vulnerable – including the vulnerable that might be adversely affected by such reform. To take an important example, suppose that a liberal democracy is considering its ongoing customary diplomatic, economic, and military ties with a repressive foreign regime that presides over a very poor population. There is nothing inconsistent about saying that this liberal democracy should seek to dissociate from the regime, in line with the global integrity test, while also showing decent concern for the situation of the vulnerable people living under this regime – for instance, by channeling direct aid to the vulnerable in a way that bypasses the regime as much as possible.

Skeptics, to be sure, may highlight situations in which there does seem to be a trade-off between associating with odious foreign

---

[74] Or, more precisely, it is satisfying some necessary conditions of decency, even if there are other things it ought to do. I say more about this issue in Chapter 5.

1.8 Integrity and Decency

practices or foreign regimes and caring for the vulnerable.[75] But, for one thing, there is no reason to believe that this is always the case, especially with regard to particular forms of customary ties with certain regimes. There is no automatic reason to think that every liberal democracy that refuses to sell arms to a brutal dictatorship, for example, is (even indirectly) harming the vulnerable population living under the regime. Moreover, it is crucial to note that even when disentanglement on liberal integrity grounds may harm vulnerable people, the integrity framework can still be useful in shifting the practical presumption. Instead of seeing liberal involvement in manifestly illiberal foreign practices as the moral default, the integrity framework turns such entanglement into a moral anomaly, which has to be justified on a case-by-case basis precisely by *proving* that reform will pose imminent, grave risks to the vulnerable.

This demand for detailed justification takes us back to the steadfastness I associated with the idea of integrity, and to integrity's resulting aversion toward self-seeking rationalizations. Thus, for example, a liberal democracy that is steadfast in its commitment to liberal principles will not allow natural resource corporations transacting with the most odious regimes to rationalize their profit-making by simply postulating that the only alternative to their customary dealings is severe, massive-scale threats to the most basic interests of the people living under these regimes. Instead of taking such self-seeking rationalizations at face value, a liberal democracy acting with integrity will demand that corporations show that such threats to the most vulnerable are indeed likely to materialize – including in cases where the gains of the vulnerable from customary commercial ties are vanishingly small. Additionally, a liberal democracy acting with integrity will demand that resource corporations show, on a case-by-case basis, that there is no realistic way of supporting the vulnerable through various kinds of foreign aid without transacting with the relevant regimes.

Along similar lines, powerful liberal democracies that are steadfast in their commitment to liberal values will demand that their corporations show, on a case-by-case basis, precisely why and how prohibiting the

---

[75] See, e.g., Scott Wisor, "Conditional Coercion versus Rights Diagnostics: Two Approaches to Human Rights Protection," *Politics, Philosophy & Economics* 15 (2016): 405–423.

employment of sweatshop workers will be harmful to the workers themselves. And they will also demand that corporations show why "business as usual" is the only realistic way to improve workers' conditions, instead of committing resources, for example, to work toward the establishment of a global minimum wage,[76] or instead of public-private partnerships incentivizing corporations to pursue meaningful improvements in the safety, health, and educational opportunities of sweatshop workers.

In such contexts, one can see how concerns about entanglement in manifestly illiberal practices can align rather than conflict with the demands of decency. These two strands of the integrity framework can together challenge the tendency to present policy choices in stark binary terms – to argue that liberal democracies' only options are either to participate even in the most appalling ongoing practices, or to risk the most basic interests of people who desperately need their support.[77]

1.9 Integrity in Extremis

I am aware that some readers, especially those of a more consequentialist bent, may feel a certain impatience with the arguments I have been making so far in this chapter, and especially in the last section. Such readers will be prone to emphasize that, at the end of the day, the main test of any moral framework lies in its practical verdicts, and particularly in its verdicts regarding the most dramatic questions. Such readers are unlikely to be satisfied, for example, with my suggestion that it is misleading to portray liberal democracies' policy choices in binary terms. For it is surely the case that sometimes such binary choices are real: liberal democracies genuinely have to choose between their own purity and a concern for the practical needs of the vulnerable. Liberal democracies can either refuse to commit – or even to support or condone – certain kinds of grave wrongs, or they can partake in such wrongs as the lesser evil, when there is no other way to save many human beings from calamities. When push comes to shove – the consequentialist critic will likely ask – which of these two does integrity call for?

---

[76] For a defense of this alternative see Ian Shapiro, *Politics against Domination* (Cambridge, MA: Harvard University Press, 2016).
[77] I will further explore such challenges to binary policy thinking in later chapters.

1.9 Integrity in Extremis

In my view, assuming we want to keep the idea of integrity sharply distinct from sheer fanaticism, the only responsible decision when faced with decisions of this sort is indeed to commit the lesser evil. This point is clear, at minimum, with regard to those truly cataclysmic situations that provide much of the intuitive pull of the consequentialist challenge. Any view that would have prohibited liberal democracies from cooperating with Stalin to beat Hitler, for example, even if this meant that Nazi Germany would conquer the world, is clearly untenable. When life and death is literally on the line (at least on a massive scale), the integrity framework steers away from a suicidal view that prioritizes fidelity to principles over survival.

Nonetheless, even such "supreme emergencies"[78] do not render liberal integrity irrelevant. For one thing, granting that consequences must take precedence in supreme emergencies is fully compatible with continuing to insist that consequences are not the only thing that is of moral significance – and, accordingly, persisting in trying to realize non-consequentialist values associated with integrity to the greatest extent possible. Put otherwise: when life and death are literally on the line, the integrity framework grants that we must live; but it continues to insist that, at the same time, we must do everything within our power to continue living by our deepest commitments.

The example of the Second World War is again useful in spelling out this balance. The Western Allies' decision to form a military alliance with Stalin to beat Hitler may have been morally obvious. But it was not at all obvious what stance the Allies ought to have taken toward Stalin's regime during the war. And here the integrity framework is helpful. Had they acted with full integrity, the Western Allies would have shied away, for example, from any attempt to portray Stalin as an innocuous "Uncle Joe." Instead, in line with the demands of public honesty emphasized above, the Allies would have assumed the stance that Churchill had assumed upon announcing the German invasion of the Soviet Union – namely, publicly refusing to retract previous criticism of the Soviet dictatorship, even while making clear that cooperating with this dictatorship is the necessary lesser evil.[79]

---

[78] This phrase is famously credited to Michael Walzer's *Just and Unjust Wars*, 3rd ed. (New York: Basic Books, 2000).

[79] "No one has been a more consistent opponent of Communism than I have for the last twenty-five years. I will unsay no words that I've spoken about it. But all this fades away before the spectacle which is now unfolding." "Winston

Moreover, the collective integrity framework – and specifically the value of public honesty I have associated with this framework – would have also required that the Western Allies take no pride in other "lesser evils" they had to pursue during the war. The British government, for example, complied with the demands of public honesty during the many decades in which (despite honoring many other military units) it refused to honor Bomber Command pilots, who repeatedly performed extremely morally fraught tasks, including the bombing of Dresden.[80] Even if it was true that such "dirty" tasks were, in fact, necessary to win the war, we may nonetheless think it sensible that the pilots serving in the Bomber Command were not given the same honors as those given to many other military units who fought in the war. The reason, presumably, is not that these particular pilots fought less bravely, or with less dedication to the cause. Rather, the reason is that it was inappropriate to take *collective pride* in their actions. The collective integrity framework neatly captures this powerful judgment.

1.10 Liberal Integrity and Contested Liberal Identity

I will further explore the kind of guidance that integrity may offer in extreme situations in Chapter 3. At this point, however, I want to turn to philosophical challenges that concern less dramatic circumstances, and particularly to eminently familiar circumstances featuring disagreements about the implications of liberal values and liberal identity. Some readers might wonder how the moralized notion of liberal identity that I have been developing here relates to such disagreements. My answer is that the view that I have presented is best seen as *constraining* these disagreements, rather than as intended to settle them completely. My account provides another way to see that citizens ought to put certain interpretations of liberal collective identity "beyond the pale."

Churchill: Broadcast on the Soviet-German War," Jewish Virtual Library athttp://jewishvirtuallibrary.org/churchill-broadcast-on-the-soviet-german-war-june-1941.

[80] See, e.g., "Campaign Medal Call for WWII Bomber Command Veterans," *BBC*, May 26, 2018, athttps://bbc.com/news/uk-england-lincolnshire-44255399. For similar concerns surrounding a statue of the head of Bomber Command in central London see, for example, Geoffrey Wheatcroft, "Firestorms Darken Our Past," *The Independent*, Aug. 7, 1994, at https://independent.co.uk/voices/firestorms-darken-our-past-those-who-defend-bomber-harriss-destruction-of-german-cities-are-wrong-1374893.html,

1.10 Liberal Integrity and Contested Liberal Identity 63

This point has important implications for collective decisions surrounding political symbols, especially symbols that clearly conflict with constitutive struggles to realize equal rights. Take another example from the struggle against racism in the United States: the 2015 decision by the South Carolina legislature to remove the Confederate flag from the capitol building.[81] The liberal integrity framework captures, in a forceful way, the thought that this was the only morally defensible decision for the legislature to take. Just as citizens ought to treat as illegitimate, for example, blatantly racist policies that seek to dismantle official recognition of struggles to realize racial equality, so they ought to treat as illegitimate political symbols that flatly contradict these struggles. This kind of stance, we might say, ought to be treated as a non-negotiable component of the identity of a liberal polity: political symbols such as that of the Confederacy flag cannot plausibly claim to reflect what a liberal political community stands for.

Yet political symbols, however important, are not the end of the story. The liberal integrity framework also provides a forceful way of capturing the conviction that certain substantive policies – including policies regarding outsiders – lie beyond the liberal pale. To take another recent example from US politics, consider the ban that the Trump administration has imposed on the entry of travelers from multiple Muslim countries into the United States. While any sensible political theory should condemn this policy, the integrity framework can do so with particular force. This framework alerts us to the fact that a ban that clearly targets Muslims as a group cannot align with the values of religious freedom and toleration that are an essential liberal creed in general, and have been essential to American collective identity in particular. The integrity framework further alerts us, in line with the requirements of decency noted previously, to the drastic effects of such a ban on extremely vulnerable refugees whom the United States could easily help. And through its historical emphases, the integrity framework also captures the powerful intuition that it is especially troubling for the United States as an immigrant society to engage in such exclusion. Considering the famous stanzas at the base of Lady Liberty,[82]

---

[81] See Jason Hanna and Ralph Ellis, "Confederate Flag's Half-Century at South Carolina Capitol Ends," *CNN*, Jul. 10, 2015, at http://edition.cnn.com/2015/07/10/us/south-carolina-confederate-battle-flag/

[82] "Give me your tired, your poor, your huddled masses yearning to breathe free, the wretched refuse of your teeming shore. Send these, the homeless, tempest-

critics of the ban may have been dramatic – but they were not wrong – when saying that it is "akin to President Trump taking a wrecking ball to the Statue of Liberty."[83]

Two other aspects of this particular example are worth mentioning. First, the liberal integrity framework, as I stressed above, captures the crucial moral significance of civic engagement in realizing liberal rights. And so the framework can readily explain why it was so significant that the Trump administration's travel ban was met with widespread public protest. It reminds us that the project of realizing liberal rights ultimately ought to be *the people's* project: elected leaders bear special responsibilities with regard to this project, but it does not follow that ordinary citizens are freed of responsibility for the shape of political institutions – especially when elected leaders clearly try to shape them in the wrong way (a theme that I will explore in more detail in Chapter 3).

Second, it should be plain that treating policies such as the Trump administration's travel ban as lying "beyond the pale" is fully compatible with leaving a very wide range of other policies within the scope of reasonable disagreement about liberal collective identity and its implications. But that is as it should be. We should be able to argue that our interlocutors' practical proposals do not represent in the best light either what we stand for as a political community—what our collective identity is about—or what we ought to stand for. However, not every policy that might be unjust or wrongheaded from a liberal perspective is also ipso facto a threat to liberal integrity. Some citizens may find unjust the policies that a majority enacts on a plethora of issues, from free speech through redistribution to multiculturalism. But as long as these policies are grounded in plausible (even if suboptimal) interpretations of the core liberal commitment to equality—both the equality of citizens and universal human equality—there is no reason to see them as a threat to liberal integrity. The idea of liberal integrity is thus compatible with enduring disagreements regarding liberal justice

---

tost to me, I lift my lamp beside the golden door!" Emma Lazarus, "The New Colossus (1883) at https://en.wikisource.org/wiki/The_New_Colossus.

[83] Quoted in Richard Pérez-Peña, "Trump's Immigration Ban Draws Deep Anger and Muted Praise," *New York Times*, Jan. 28, 2017, at https://nytimes.com/2017/01/28/us/trumps-immigration-ban-disapproval-applause.html?_r=0; see also Rick Rojas, "Statue of Liberty Climber Upends Holiday for Thousands," *New York Times,* Jul. 4, 2018 at https://nytimes.com/2018/07/04/nyregion/statue-of-liberty-protester-july-4.html?action=click&module=Ribbon&pgtype=Article.

and components of the collective identity of any particular liberal polity.

What happens, however, when non-trivial segments of the population come to abandon liberal values completely? What can the integrity framework contribute in such a context? Under distressing conditions of this kind, the integrity framework, like any other normative account, will primarily serve as a basis for moral criticism, emphasizing the gap between "where we are" as a society and where we ought to be. However, the integrity framework will have the added advantage of making this moral criticism an internal one – pointing to the way in which a society might be failing its own historical commitments. The struggle against racism in the United States again illustrates the force of such criticism. Consider the famous invocation by Martin Luther King Jr. of the "promissory note" of equality for all that he associated with the founders of the United States.[84] Or Muhammad Ali's trenchant refusal to fight abroad in the name of American ideals he was denied at home.[85] Or Langston Hughes's emblematic call, decades earlier, to "let America be America again – the land that never has been yet."[86] These were all different messages delivered by different voices in different contexts. But they can all be described as voices demanding collective integrity from American society.[87]

Instead of a Conclusion: Is the Integrity Argument Incomplete?

I want to close this chapter by considering a few final objections, each – in a different way – alleging that for all I have said here, the liberal integrity framework is somehow incomplete.

---

[84] See Martin Luther King, "I Have a Dream," in James M. Washington (ed.), *A Testament of Hope: The Essential Writings and Speeches of Martin Luther King Jr.* (New York: Harper One, 1986).

[85] See "Muhammad Ali on the Vietnam War-Draft," YouTube at https://youtube.com/watch?v=HeFMyrWlZ68

[86] Langston Hughes, "Let America Be America Again," in *The Collected Poems of Langston Hughes* (New York: Alfred A. Knopf., 1994).

[87] For an attempt to systematize these voices, very much in the spirit of my claims here, see Christopher Lebron, *The Color of Our Shame: Race and Justice in Our Time* (New York: Oxford University Press, 2013).

One form of this worry has to do with liberal normative individualism. Some might object that if the integrity of a liberal democracy is really going to have moral value, this will ultimately be because of the integrity of its individual citizens. But if that is the case, then collective integrity is a distraction from the real site of the normative action, and focusing on the collective level gives us a woefully incomplete moral picture.

The opening step in addressing this objection is to note that individual identity – and therefore integrity – can be in many ways intertwined with collective identity. One does not have to endorse communitarian critiques of liberalism in order to agree with Joseph Raz, for instance, that there are important "aspects of the personal sense of identity which are inextricably bound up with... communities and their common culture."[88] This is true, furthermore, not only as a matter of empirical observation but also as a matter of normative principle. Thus for example, it is commonly thought that there is moral value in citizens identifying with the constitutive moral achievements of their political community, including even past achievements for which they can claim no credit: there is moral value in citizens shaping their fundamental worldviews and aspirations in light of these moral achievements, and even in deriving pride from them. Along the same lines, there is arguably a moral need for citizens to integrate into their personal identity, at least to some degree and over some time span, their polity's constitutive moral failures, even when they carry no individual responsibility for these failures.[89]

All of this matters here, in turn, because if individual identity is often intertwined with collective identity as an empirical matter, and should (in some sense) be intertwined with collective identity as a normative

---

[88] Joseph Raz, *The Morality of Freedom* (Oxford: Oxford University Press, 1986), 209.

[89] For remarks in similar spirit, see David Miller, *National Responsibility and Global Justice* (Oxford: Oxford University Press, 2007), 161. Of course, we do not want people's identity to be overwhelmed with psychological burdens of massive political wrongs in which they did not partake. But it is precisely because of the scale of at least some political wrongs that the opposite response – completely shrugging off these wrongs, not incorporating them into one's identity at all – would be morally disturbing. If one's polity committed genocide before one was born, it could be dangerous and unreasonable for one to grow up feeling as if one were a perpetrator. But it would arguably not be a positive thing either, if one grew up entirely unencumbered, just as if the horror was brought about by a completely alien nation on the other end of the world.

matter, then it is mistaken to say that a focus on collective identity and integrity is a distraction from the truly significant individual level. We can see this point by considering Rawls' theory of justice again. Assuming Rawls is correct that a society's "basic structure" has "profound" effects on individual citizens that are "present from the start,"[90] there is no reason to think that Rawls' focus on fundamental collective institutions is a distraction from an individualist viewpoint. The same is true in the case of collective identity and integrity: insofar as collective identity has and ought to have a profound impact on individual citizens, there is no reason to think it is merely a distraction from an individualist perspective.

Let me turn, then, to the penultimate objection, which alleges a different kind of incompleteness. According to this objection, no account of integrity can be complete without an all-things-considered judgment of what a given moral situation requires. This is because the integrity of any agent – whether individual or collective – should be entirely derivative from such a judgment. But this means that focusing on integrity is once again a distraction. If agents do what morality ultimately requires of them, then there is no reason for them to feel that their integrity has been compromised at all.

I have postponed this objection up to now, because I believe that one of the best ways to meet it goes through the preceding arguments regarding the significance of agents' moral history. To see why, note first that a critic who espouses this objection necessarily denies that agents' identity-grounding moral projects can ever conflict with what morality, all things considered, requires. Therefore, the objection commits such a critic also to deny that the different moral histories of different agents – the histories that underlie their moral projects – should factor at all in their moral reflection. If someone said, for example, "I have struggled for years to break free from the Mafia, and doing business with the Mafia now will go against this identity-grounding struggle," our critic will have to respond: "Your moral situation is not different in any way from the situation of people who lack this kind of history. You are precisely in the same moral position as they are."

Such a response, however, reflects an impoverished understanding of actual moral experience. To demand of an agent to simply forget its

[90] *TJ*, 7.

particular moral history – to engage in moral reflection that entirely "subtracts" this history – is to demand to ignore what the agent cannot and arguably should not ignore. It is implausible, for example, to say to a man who has struggled throughout his adult life to combat his racist upbringing that he should simply forget this struggle if morality, all things considered, requires that he does business with racists. And it is similarly implausible to say to a polity struggling to combat centuries of racism, that it should simply forget about this struggle if morality, all things considered, permits its doing business with a racist regime. It is sensible to say that an agent might sometimes be permitted or even obliged to do things that conflict with its constitutive, identity-grounding moral struggles. But it strains credulity to say that the agent should not give any moral weight at all to this conflict.[91] Even when the claims of integrity are outweighed by opposing considerations, there is a genuine moral loss that should be kept in sight – and that the idea of liberal integrity brings into view.

Equipped with these remarks, we can turn to the final objection. According to this objection, a complete account of political integrity must say something not only about the integrity of liberal democracies, but also about the potential claims of integrity that might apply to illiberal polities.

There are three reasons why I did not discuss these claims. First, it is not clear that global concerns are relevant to the identity of an illiberal polity to the same degree as in the liberal case. Insofar as the identity of any liberal polity necessarily features universalist elements, the kinds of blatant contradictions between domestic and global practices that I have described above always pose a threat to the polity's integrity. Yet the identity of an illiberal polity may not feature universalist elements. Hence even a deep contradiction between domestic and global practices may not suffice to trigger a threat to the integrity of an illiberal polity.

---

[91] Lepora and Goodin (*On Complicity and Compromise*, 19-20), note a similar point when discussing "compromise" at the individual level: "It is only when the intra-personal conflict forces an agent to choose among items of principled concern . . . that a compromise is genuinely involved. That explains, in turn, the phenomenology of compromise – why one feels 'compromised' when engaging in a compromise, even when on balance she thinks it was the right thing to do. Something of principled concern to her had to be sacrificed, and she rightly regards that fact as a source of regret."

Instead of a Conclusion: Is the Integrity Argument Incomplete?

Second, there are at least some manifestly illiberal polities – at the limit, ones featuring clearly despotic regimes – where it seems normatively misleading to think of the sovereign body politic as a group agent, and therefore as an entity that might have integrity. "A group agent that is constructed around a dictator," as List and Pettit note, " . . . can be seen as just an extension of that individual's agency rather than as a group agent proper."[92] Hence, when it comes to at least some manifestly illiberal regimes, discussions of the integrity of the sovereign body politic might be fundamentally misconceived.[93]

The final, most important reason why I have not discussed the integrity of an illiberal polity is the following. We can imagine a manifestly illiberal polity that believes that its own integrity is undermined by support for certain practices beyond its borders. We may imagine, for instance, a racist polity that sees a threat to its integrity in support for other regimes that are committed to racial equality. But this kind of threat is clearly not morally disturbing. Hence this kind of scenario only reaffirms the point I have been stressing throughout this chapter: the moral importance of collective integrity should not be separated from familiar liberal-democratic values, or treated as more fundamental than these values. Rather, the aim of reflecting on the people's integrity is to construct a framework that improves our understanding of what the values of liberal democracy actually require. The same aim, I now turn to argue, should guide us when reflecting on the people's property.

---

[92] List and Pettit, *Group Agency*, 59.
[93] Rousseau suggests a similar thought in *The Social Contract*: "When scattered men, regardless of their number, are enslaved to a single man, I see in this nothing but a master and slaves, I do not see in it a people . . ." in Victor Gourevitch (ed.), *The Social Contract and Other Later Political Writings* (Cambridge: Cambridge University Press, 1997), Book 1, Chapter 5, Paragraph 1.

2 The People's Property

In late October 2014, the authoritarian Blaise Compaoré, having ruled Burkina Faso for twenty-seven years, fled the country to exile in the Ivory Coast. His departure was the result of a popular uprising, triggered in turn by a combination of ever-increasing government corruption and Compaoré's intent to change the constitution so as to allow himself yet another term as president.[1] At the height of the uprising, demonstrators converged on the luxurious villa of the president's brother and adviser. The villa, as one foreign journalist put it,

> had been a forbidding presence for many in the capital . . . Set back behind a high wall topped with bougainvillea, the blocky structure with its pillar-flanked entrance embodied the high life enjoyed by members of the president's inner circle – as well as their remove from the problems facing ordinary citizens in one of the world's poorest countries.[2]

With the regime's sudden and swift collapse, protests barged into the villa, where they discovered remarkable riches, including "a kennel for the Compaoré family's dogs . . . sturdier than many people's homes in Burkina Faso, with a floor plan that appeared to include two bedrooms as well as a sizeable salon."[3] Security forces that initially tried to block the villa off to visitors quickly gave up. As one local who became a tour guide in the villa explained, the security personnel "eventually acknowledged that from now on, this house belongs to the people."[4] One of the leaders of the popular protests, however, offered a more

---

[1] See, e.g., "'One Game Too Far': The Downfall of Burkina Faso's President," *Reuters*, Nov. 2, 2014, at https://reuters.com/article/us-burkina-politics-compaore/one-game-too-far-the-downfall-of-burkina-fasos-president-idUSKBN0IM0FL20141102.

[2] Robbie Corey-Boulet, "In Burkina Faso, a Mansion Offers a Glimpse into the Revolution," *Al-Jazeera America*, May 7, 2015, at http://america.aljazeera.com/multimedia/2015/5/In-Burkina-Faso-a-mansion-offers-glimpse-into-the-revolution.html.

[3] Corey-Boulet, "In Burkina Faso."   [4] Corey-Boulet, "In Burkina Faso."

radical view, describing the popular takeover of the villa as a form of *re-appropriation* – "a seizure by the people of what should have been theirs all along."[5]

In turn, one way to understand such claims is to see them as expressing a specific complaint against those who have wielded effective political power. The complaint is not merely that de facto leaders have ruled incompetently or unjustly, but rather that they have stolen from the people. One does not have to be Proudhon to think that this distinction matters. When we consider key political actors who enact unjust policies, or who are guilty of incompetence, we are often inclined to think that they should simply be removed from office. But when we think about political actors who are guilty of (massive-scale) theft from the people, we typically go further than that. We believe that we know not only where these leaders do *not* belong – in power – but also where they *do* belong – in prison.

One might expect philosophers to be able to support such firm convictions regarding theft from the people. But the scholarly state of affairs belies this expectation. The explosion of philosophical interest in issues of distributive justice over the last fifty years has generated a significant literature on private property rights. Yet the philosophical literature offers no sustained normative account of *public* property. This is true even for influential texts devoted specifically to property. Thus for example, Tony Honore's detailed account of the different components of property, often considered the "canonical" modern treatment of ownership, does not make a single reference to public property.[6] Public property is equally conspicuous in its absence in an extensive *Nomos* volume dedicated to property.[7] Moreover, celebrated theories of distributive justice do no better. Rawls's *A Theory of Justice*, for example, features zero references to either "public property" or "state property." Dworkin, to take another illustrative example, makes only one explicit reference to public property when presenting his theory of equality of resources – and only in order to put this property outside the theory's

---

[5] Corey-Boulet, "In Burkina Faso."
[6] Tony Honoré, "Ownership," in A. G. Guest (ed.), *Oxford Essays in Jurisprudence* (Oxford: Clarendon Press, 1961): 107–147. The reference to this text as the "canonical" modern treatment of property comes from David Miller, "Property and Territory: Locke, Kant, and Steiner," *Journal of Political Philosophy* 19 (2011): 90–109, at 92.
[7] See J. R. Pennock and J. W. Chapman (eds.), *Nomos XXII: Property* (New York: New York University Press, 1980).

bounds.[8] When one turns to Rawls's and Dworkin's influential interlocutors, both liberal and socialist – for example, to Amartya Sen, G. A. Cohen, Jeremy Waldron, Richard Arneson, or John Roemer – one is similarly struck by the fact that public property plays no significant role in any of their claims, if it features at all.[9] In a "property and ownership" entry for the *Stanford Encyclopedia of Philosophy*, Waldron observes that "[m]odern philosophical discussions focus mostly on the issue of the justification of *private* property rights (as opposed to common or collective property)."[10] Waldron might very well be understating here the philosophical neglect of public property.[11]

Aiming to remedy this neglect, I search in this chapter for a persuasive normative account of public property. I proceed as follows. In 2.1, I set out some basic premises, and lay out key desiderata for a compelling account of public property. In 2.2, I employ these desiderata to criticize two views of public property. The first view derives public property from pre-political individual property. The second view is purely legalist, seeing public property as simply whatever the law declares to be publicly owned. Both of these views, I argue, are vulnerable to serious objections. In 2.3, I therefore turn to explore an alternative view, according to which the body politic is the ultimate owner of all resources found within its jurisdiction.[12] This

---

[8] Dworkin, "What Is Equality? Part II: Equality of Resources," *Philosophy and Public Affairs* 10 (1981): 283–345, at 283.

[9] Even Roemer, for instance, is keen to emphasize that his vision of "market socialism" relies on forms of ownership that are neither private nor public. See John Roemer, *A Future for Socialism* (Cambridge, MA: Harvard University Press, 1994).

[10] Jeremy Waldron, "Property and Ownership," *Stanford Encyclopedia of Philosophy*, http://plato.stanford.edu/entries/property/. Italics in the original.

[11] It is worth adding that existing treatments of collective ownership tend to focus on specific kinds of resources (especially natural resources) and on the merits of competing collective claims to these resources (chiefly the claims of separate nations versus the claims of humanity writ large). See, for example, Chris Armstrong, "Against Permanent Sovereignty over Natural Resources," *Politics, Philosophy and Economics* 14 (2015): 129–151; Mathias Risse, *On Global Justice* (Princeton: Princeton University Press, 2012]). But these debates typically have little to say regarding public ownership of other goods – of public infrastructure or income-tax revenue, for instance.

[12] This model is heterodox, for one thing, because it goes against the bulk of the territorial rights literature, which distinguishes strongly between rights of jurisdiction and rights of public ownership. (See, e.g., Miller, "Territorial Rights: Concept and Justification," *Political Studies* 60 [2012]: 252–268). Moreover, the model is heterodox in going beyond the familiar notion that

deep public ownership model, I argue, provides an appealing picture of public property, which also comports with liberal intuitions regarding the significance of private property. In 2.4, I develop another attraction of the model: its expansion of the familiar government duty to uphold the equality of all citizens. This expansion, I argue, aligns the model with the demands of liberal integrity articulated in the opening chapter. In 2.5, I take up concerns about excessive government encroachment into the private realm that the model seems to license. In 2.6, I consider how the deep public ownership model relates to several questions that have been central to the territorial rights literature. Finally, in 2.7, I briefly discuss the relationship between the model and two influential views of private property.

2.1 Setting the Stage

Let us begin with some basic assumptions, first with regard to the components of property rights. Different theorists have offered different lists of these components, with some lists including as many as eleven different "incidents" of property rights.[13] Here I shall work with a more limited list. I shall assume that an agent enjoys the full bundle of property rights over an object when four normative conditions are satisfied. First, the agent has rights to control the object's use. Second, the agent has rights to compensation in case others use the object without the agent's permission. Third, the agent has the power to decide whether to transfer its control and/or compensation rights to others. Finally, the agent is entitled to the enforcement of its rights regarding control, compensation, and transfer.[14]

> property rights require political institutions for their specification and enforcement. I share the anti-libertarian thrust of the many Kantian accounts making this point. (See, e.g., Arthur Ripstein, *Force and Freedom: Kant's Legal and Political Philosophy* [Cambridge, MA: Harvard University Press, 2009]; Stilz, *Liberal Loyalty* [Princeton, NJ: Princeton University Press, 2009]; Lea Ypi "Self-Ownership and the State: A Democratic Critique," *Ratio* 24 [2011]: 91–106). Yet I also want to explore the idea that the body politic creates (rather than merely specifies) individual property rights. The weight of this distinction should become clear later.

[13] See Honoré, "Ownership." For a different list, see Boudewijn Bouckaert and Gerrit De Geest (eds.), *Encyclopedia of Law and Economics, Vol. II. Civil Law and Economics* (Cheltenham: Edward Elgar, 2000): 332–379.

[14] For the moment, I leave open whether the entitlement to have rights enforced is an entitlement of the agent itself to enforce its own rights, an entitlement to have

I shall assume that we can treat the collectively sovereign members of a political community – taken together as "the body politic," "the public," or "the people" – as a collective agent that can also enjoy this "full bundle" of property rights. These collective rights, in turn, I shall refer to as rights of public property.

In principle, one could reflect on rights of public property by asking whether such rights should exist at all. Here, however, I opt for a different strategy. I presuppose the existence of public property, and seek a morally compelling account of such property. If a given view turns out not to align with the very existence of public property, I take that to be a fatal objection to the view.

What requirements, then, must a persuasive account of public property meet? The most basic requirement can be traced back to political tales of the kind noted above: a persuasive account of public property must be able to capture the moral complaint against de facto rulers stealing from the people. Millions around the world, not just in Burkina Faso, but also in countries as different from one another as South Africa, Russia, and South Korea, have protested in recent years about "theft from the people."[15] We have ample reason to be suspicious of an account that tells all of those millions that they are simply confused.

But capturing such popular theft allegations, while necessary, is not sufficient. A compelling account of public property should satisfy three additional desiderata. First, such an account must meet what we can term the *collectivist requirement*: it must fit with the intuition that the status of public property cannot change simply due to the uncoordinated

---

other agents enforce these rights, or both. I also want to make room for the possibility that a sufficiently nuanced conception of public property will show that even the "fullest bundle" of private property rights is never quite as full as is commonly assumed.

[15] See, e.g., Norimitsu Onishi and Selam Gebrekidan, "'They Eat Money': How Mandela's Political Heirs Grow Rich off Corruption," *New York Times*, Apr. 16, 2018, at www.nytimes.com/2018/04/16/world/africa/south-africa-corruption-jacob-zuma-african-national-congress.html; "South Korea's Presidential Crisis," *BBC News*, Apr. 6, 2018, at http://bbc.com/news/world-asia-37971085; "Sweeping Arrests amid Anti-Putin Protests across Russia," *CBS News*, May 5, 2018, at www.cbsnews.com/news/alexei-navalny-putin-foe-russian-opposition-leader-detained-protest-moscow-today-2018-05-05/; see also Hannah Beech and Austin Ramzy, "Malaysia's Ex-Leader, Najib Razak, Is Charged in Corruption Inquiry," *New York Times,* Jul. 3, 2018; Drazen Jorgic and Mubasher Bukhari, "Ousted Pakistan PM Arrested on Return, as Bomber Kills Scores," *Reuters*, Jul. 13, 2018.

2.1 Setting the Stage

activities of isolated individuals acting as private persons. Thus for example, any sensible view of public property should be able to account for the idea that the American body politic as a collective agent owns the Statue of Liberty, given by the French as "a gift to the American people." But no sensible view of public property would confer on each American citizen as a private person the unilateral power to sell any portion of the statue (however infinitesimal), simply at his or her own discretion.

Second, a cogent account of public property must also satisfy the *private property requirement*: it must show how we can make significant room for public property without forsaking private property. The relationship between public and private property is complex, and much of what I will say in this chapter bears on it. Yet at this stage we can settle for simply noting, with Allen Buchanan for example, that "any just society will have a prominent place for private property."[16] A persuasive liberal view of public ownership, at least, should align with this observation.

Third, it is important for an account of public property to illuminate political issues that extend beyond property alone. Even if, upon reflection, we think that public property deserves independent attention, we clearly also want our conception of public property to support broader moral intuitions – to serve as part of a broader moral *framework*. This framework should show how ideas regarding public property join compelling moral ideas derived from other sources, to form an appealing whole.

This last thought, even more than the requirements preceding it, makes clear the deep contrast between my approach in this chapter, and the premises of the most trenchant public property skeptics – namely, libertarians. Before I turn to the substance of my claims, it might be helpful to offer a few remarks about this contrast. Libertarians understand property rights as a single foundation for political morality, from which everything else is supposed to follow derivatively. There is no real room in libertarian accounts for any moral concerns not themselves grounded in claims of ownership. It should be clear, already at this point, that I think this libertarian approach is misguided. Yet I will not be trying to "convert" libertarians of any sort. Like many other theorists, I believe libertarianism to be both

---

[16] Allen Buchanan, "The Making and Unmaking of Boundaries: What Liberalism Has to Say," in Buchanan and Margaret Moore [eds.,] *States, Nations, and Borders* (Cambridge: Cambridge University Press, 2003): 231–261, at 233-234.

implausible as a matter of philosophical principle,[17] and (often) repugnant as a matter of political practice.[18] But because I take this belief to be widespread in the mainstream of contemporary political philosophy, my principal effort in this chapter is to advance *non*-libertarian thinking about public property. In fact, I believe that it is especially important for non-libertarians to theorize public property, because the most influential liberal model of this property is vased (as we will see shortly) on a premise that few non-libertarians accept – thus making the need for an alternative model even more pressing.

However, although I am presupposing here the rejection of libertarianism, I also think that it is important to pay close attention to the exact grounds for this rejection. This is especially the case when we consider forms of public encroachment on private affairs that everyone – not just libertarians – ought to oppose. In order to see how non-libertarians too can resist such encroachment, it is important to be precise about which libertarian claims non-libertarians must reject. Such precision will allow us to extend the scope of "the public" far beyond its libertarian borders, without licensing morally dangerous forms of public intrusion into private life. I will try to show below how my favored conception of public property can provide this nuanced extension.

2.2 The Challenges of Accounting for Public Property

How, then, should we understand public property? Arguably the most influential answer, at least within the liberal tradition, sees public

---

[17] See, e.g., Thomas Scanlon, "Nozick on Rights, Liberty, and Property," *Philosophy & Public Affairs* 6 (1976): 3–25; Thomas Nagel, "Libertarianism without Foundations" in Jeffrey Paul (ed.), *Reading Nozick* (Totowa, NJ: Rowman and Littlefield, 1981): 191–205. As will become clear below, I am especially suspicious of libertarian principles regarding natural property claims that extend beyond the body. Moreover, I am convinced by authors such as Barbara Fried that these claims fail when made by left-libertarians just as much as they fail when made by right-libertarians. See Fried's "Left-Libertarianism: A Review Essay," *Philosophy & Public Affairs* 32 (2004): 66–80 and her "Left-Libertarianism, Once More: A Rejoinder to Vallentyne, Steiner, and Otsuka," *Philosophy & Public Affairs* 33 (2005): 216–222.

[18] See, for example, Brian Barry's review of "Anarchy, State and Utopia," in *Political Theory* 3 (1975): 331–336, as well as Samuel Freeman, "Illiberal Libertarians: Why Libertarianism Is Not a Liberal View," *Philosophy & Public Affairs* 30 (2001): 105–151, passim; Thomas Pogge, *Realizing Rawls* (Ithaca, NY: Cornell University Press, 1989), passim, e.g., at 49–51.

2.2 The Challenges of Accounting for Public Property

property as parasitic upon individual property. On this view, whatever "we the people" own collectively is simply the aggregation of what each of owns individually. Tax revenue collectively owned by the people, for example, consists of nothing but the agglomeration of each individual taxpayer's private resources. And the same is true for any other object of public ownership – from government buildings to public parks. Any public property is made up of the sum of private properties.[19]

This *private aggregation model* of public property, as we might call it, clearly aligns with moral intuitions that are important to the self-conception of many liberal societies. In particular, this model represents a natural ally for the widespread intuition that individuals have (at the very least) a presumptive moral claim to *all* of their pre-tax income. The private aggregation model supports the familiar thought that individuals are entitled to this income – and that this entitlement forms a moral baseline against which any public "taking" of private earnings is to be evaluated.[20]

Insofar as it gives private property pride of place, the private aggregation model obviously satisfies the individualist requirement.[21] Yet this model also suffers from two fundamental problems. The first has to do with the collectivist requirement. I have said that a compelling account of public property must show why the status of public property cannot change as a result of uncoordinated individual actions. But it is not clear how the private aggregation model can satisfy this requirement. After all, if public property is nothing but the aggregation of individual holdings, then it is not clear why individuals cannot unilaterally withdraw from public political institutions, taking "their portion" of public property with them.[22]

---

[19] See, for example, A. John Simmons, "On the Territorial Rights of States," *Philosophical Issues* 11 (2001): 300–326, as well as Simmons, *Boundaries of Authority* (New York: Oxford University Press, 2016).

[20] This baseline is often used for satirical effect, as in the aforementioned *Yes, Prime Minister*. When Prime Minister Hacker proposes a tax cut, for example, arguing that "the money is not the Treasury's, it is the taxpayers'," he is promptly informed by Sir Humphrey that "this is not the view that the Treasury takes." And upon learning of Hacker's proposal, the Treasury's Permanent Secretary is duly appalled: "My staff are horrified. There are waves of panic running through the Treasury. Giving away one and a half billion pounds of our money is unthinkable." See Lynn and Jay, *Yes, Prime Minister*, 188, 190.

[21] And we can say this independently of whether a moral entitlement to pre-tax income is ultimately defensible – something that (along with many contemporary theorists) I will dispute shortly.

[22] Stilz raises this problem with Lockean theories in her "Why Do States Have Territorial Rights?" *International Theory* 1 (2009): 185–213.

The second crucial problem with the private aggregation model is the fact that – at least in its dominant formulations – it hinges on the notion of pre-political property. The guiding idea behind this model is that, already prior to political institutions, individuals enjoy determinate property rights in objects external to their body: public property is the aggregation of *pre-political* individual holdings. This, however, is an idea that virtually all anti-libertarians reject. This camp does not believe that individuals have determinate pre-political property rights in anything external to their body. Later on, I shall say more about why anti-libertarians consider such rights to be a "myth."[23] At this point, however, I am simply going to proceed on the assumption that there are no individual pre-political property rights over external objects. Such rights are a political artifact – they are created by the body politic.

This denial of pre-political property rights, I suspect, is so obvious to many liberal egalitarians that they do not even feel the need to dwell upon it. Yet I believe that this denial deserves more attention, if nothing else because it leads to a valuable account of public property. We can begin to see the contours of this account by examining how the idea that the body politic creates private property rights affects our understanding of the core issue of taxation. If the body politic is the creator of individual property rights, then it follows that everyday moral discourse is mistaken in assuming each taxpayer's moral entitlement to his or her pre-tax income. When there are changes to the income-tax regime, for example, this obviously affects which portion of each taxpayer's salary is "taken away." But there is no real moral sense in which the law is taking away money that "belongs" to each individual taxpayer. Rather, the tax law itself defines what "belongs" to each taxpayer.

Now, it may seem tempting to think that this point can also ground public property. After all, just as the laws might designate a certain portion of "your" income as your property, so the laws may designate the remaining portion as public property. If private property rights are a function of what the law says, then why should not the same be true for public property rights as well? Why not adopt a purely legalist

---

[23] See, e.g., John Christman, *The Myth of Property: Toward an Egalitarian Theory of Ownership* (New York: Oxford University Press, 1994); Liam Murphy and Thomas Nagel, *The Myth of Ownership: Taxes and Justice* (New York: Oxford University Press, 2002).

outlook, and say that public property is whatever the law defines as publicly owned?

The main answer is the following. If public property is whatever the laws define as publicly owned, then even de facto rulers who engage in the most blatant corruption cannot be accused of stealing public property, so long as they bother to go through the charade of giving their larceny the trappings of legality. By the way of illustration, imagine a case where, in the absence of any formal legislation pointing one way or the other, a de facto ruler routinely pockets ten percent of the state's tax revenues. This taking is public, and visible for all to see – the strongman does not even try to hide it: everyone knows that once a month his personal armored trucks stop in front of the treasury and take their fixed portion into his personal vaults elsewhere in the capital, protected by his personal bodyguards. Surely we can be confident here in saying that the strongman is systematically stealing from the people. Now compare this case to one in which everything is the same, only that here the strongman bothers to go through the façade of "legality": the strongman has now issued a formal executive order "approving" his takings (or got his puppet parliament to issue a law to this effect). It does not seem as if such formalities really undermine the charge that the strongman is stealing his people's property. However, if public property simply is what the law defines as publicly owned, and if the law defines only ninety percent of tax revenue as public property, then the strongman's taking of the other ten percent cannot count as theft from the people. This unsavory conclusion strongly suggests that a purely legalist perspective cannot provide an appealing – or even a plausible – account of the people's property. If we want to avoid such disturbing conclusions, we need an alternative.

2.3 The Deep Public Ownership Model

The alternative that I wish to propose shifts our attention away from the laws made by any de facto state authorities, and toward the sovereign people, from whom the powers of the state ultimately ought to derive. Few ideas are as fundamental to modern political thought as the notion that the state and its laws must ultimately represent rather than replace the sovereignty of the people. Notwithstanding enduring controversies regarding Rousseau's legacies, all of us moderns are Rousseauians in our rejection of the absolutist ruler's "I am the state." The sovereignty of the people means that the people – not the individuals wielding effective power – "are" the state. To the extent that we take this thought for granted, this is because modernity is the victim of its own success. We rarely consider, for example, just how pregnant with meaning is our common everyday reference to state employees not as servants of "the state" but as public servants. This locution clearly suggests that state officials ought to be nothing more than merely "officers" enacting the will of the sovereign people, rather than themselves sovereign.[24]

These ideas, I suspect, are so familiar, that their radical potential is in many ways hiding in plain sight. If we pause to reflect on them – rather than treating them as so obvious so as to make them invisible – we should be able to identify a distinctly attractive model for thinking about the people's property.[25] This model sees the people's property as antecedent to, rather than as the result of, any specific legislation.

We can return to the case of income tax in order to make the basic idea here more concrete. Suppose that your income is subject, by law, to a forty percent income tax. Following the reasoning presented above, we should be able to say that the relevant law has designated sixty percent of the income as your property. But that is not the only thing we should be able to say. Given the right sort of political institutions, at least, we should also be willing to say that the relevant law ultimately reflects the will of the sovereign people. You get to own sixty percent of 'your' income because the sovereign people decided to allocate to you rights of ownership over that portion.

---

[24] Jean Jacques Rousseau, "The Social Contract," in Victor Gourevitch (ed.), *The Social Contract and Other Later Political Writings* (Cambridge: Cambridge University Press, 1997), Book 3, Chapter 18, 1. "None of the canonical political theorists," as Bryan Garsten observes, "defended the sovereignty of the people more insistently than Rousseau did." See Garsten's "Representative Government and Popular Sovereignty," in Ian Shapiro, Susan Stokes, Elisabeth Wood, and Alexander Kirshner (eds.), *Political Representation* (New Haven: Yale University Press, 2009), at 93. Rousseau stands out in this regard, even if he was far from the only political theorist who drew a fundamental distinction between the sovereign (people) and the government. For ample illustrations, see Richard Tuck, *The Sleeping Sovereign: The Invention of Modern Democracy* (Cambridge: Cambridge University Press, 2015).

[25] There are some hints of this model in Wenar's *Blood Oil* (passim), though Wenar's legal argument focuses on natural resources. In contrast, I am in pursuit here of moral rather than legal foundations, and (as I noted above) my aims extend beyond natural resources.

2.3 The Deep Public Ownership Model

So far, you might say, so familiar. But here is the additional, more radical step. On the "deep public ownership" model that I wish to defend, the people's sovereign power is intertwined with the people's property rights: the moral power of the sovereign body politic to create private property rights over certain objects itself involves a claim to be the ultimate owner of these very objects. In claiming the authority to decide which portion of 'their' income individual citizens will get to keep, for instance, the sovereign body politic is claiming deep ownership over their entire income. And what is true with regard to income tax is true for a whole host of other objects in which property rights can be created. In claiming the moral power to create property rights in object (or set of objects) X – and specifically in claiming the moral power to create rights of control, use, and transfer over X – the body politic is itself claiming more fundamental control over X. The body politic, in other words, is claiming the moral power to decide what shall be done with X. And because this moral power, in turn, is the "central core of the notion of a property right,"[26] we can understand the body politic's more fundamental control over X as itself embodying a claim of fundamental ownership over X.[27] Thus the deep public ownership model concludes that the sovereign people is the fundamental owner of *all* of the resources encompassed within its jurisdiction.[28]

---

[26] Nozick, *Anarchy*, 171. I am assuming that one can agree with Nozick on this particular point without accepting any of Nozick's substantive views.

[27] As Philip Pettit has pointed out in conversation, the more accurate phrase might be "proprietary rights" rather than "ownership," since in some cases the body politic will be staking a claim to property that does not yet exist (just as a scientific institution, for example, may claim proprietary rights over inventions that its individual employees might develop in the future). So the "deep public ownership model" might be best construed as a "deep public proprietary rights model." I employ the shorter phrase simply for terminological ease.

[28] I am inclined to follow Dworkin in drawing "a prophylactic line" around the human body, "making body parts not part of social resources at all." See Dworkin, "Comment on Narveson: In Defence of Equality," *Social Philosophy and Policy* 1 (1983): 24–40, at 39. I believe the best defense of this "prophylactic line" pivots on the rejection of the libertarian link between bodily rights and rights over external objects. As many critiques of libertarian "labor-mixing" arguments have shown, one can grant that individuals have robust and exclusive pre-political rights of control over their body, while also denying the libertarian claim that these bodily rights extend in any way to cover external objects. This denial, in turn, means that "collectivizing" rights over external objects does not commit us to collectivizing the body in any way. For discussion, see, e.g., Wenar, "Original Acquisition of Private Property," *Mind* 107 (1998): 799–819; Robert Taylor, "Self-Ownership and the Limits of Libertarianism," *Social*

We often lose sight of this fundamental public ownership, including even its more direct manifestations. In some cases, this is because we simply take the relevant public property for granted – for instance, publicly owned street pavements.[29] In other cases, we overlook deep public ownership because its direct manifestations, though significant, are rare. The practice of eminent domain – of public authorities taking private holdings for public use – is a clear example.[30] In other cases still, we fail to notice direct manifestations of the public's proprietary claims because their impact on private property holders is minimal. A case in point is the copyright regulation associated with the Library of Congress in the United States. This regulation, known as "mandatory deposit," requires that each "owner of copyright or the exclusive right of distribution" who wishes to distribute copyrighted work in the United States will "deposit in the Copyright Office for the use of the Library of Congress two complete copies."[31] Virtually every piece of commercial music that you may hear, any movie that you may watch, and almost every book that you may read (including this one), are bound by this mandatory deposit requirement. But because the effect of this requirement on private transactions in these and other types of intellectual works is so small, it is exceedingly easy to overlook.

With these observations in mind, let us now examine how deep public ownership fares with regard to the requirements outlined in 2.1. Start with the requirement of capturing the complaint about de facto rulers stealing from the people. Plainly, the deep public ownership model satisfies this requirement. Thus, for instance, to take the scenario discussed above, the model can easily explain why the strongman who routinely appropriates ten percent of the state's tax revenues is guilty of

---

Philosophy and Policy 31 (2005): 465–482; Fried, *Left-Libertarianism*, 80, 91–92. For the claim that we should re-think our axiomatic rejection of the body as a legitimate object of redistributive efforts, see Cécile Fabre, *Whose Body Is It Anyway: Justice and the Integrity of the Person* (Oxford and New York: Clarendon Press, 2006).

[29] This example comes from G. A. Cohen's "Capitalism, Freedom and the Proletariat," in *The Idea of Freedom*, ed. Alan Ryan (Oxford: Oxford University Press, 1979): 163–182, at 174.

[30] This point is a comparative one – in some countries eminent domain is much more widely used than in others. For a comprehensive overview, see Iljoong Kim, Hojun Lee, and Ilya Somin (eds.), *Eminent Domain: A Comparative Perspective* (Cambridge, UK: Cambridge University Press, 2017).

[31] See US Copyright Office, "Mandatory Deposit" at https://copyright.gov/help/faq/mandatory_deposit.html.

2.3 The Deep Public Ownership Model

theft from the people, whether or not he has the law – however nominally – on his side. The reason is simple. On the deep public ownership model, the people own state resources not because of any specific law that a strongman may alter or cancel, but because sovereignty rests with the people rather than with the strongman.

The deep public ownership model fares equally well with regard to the collectivist requirement. "Unilateral privatization" of public property, of the kind licensed by the private aggregation model, is not an option under deep public ownership. Bizarre privatization results, such as the aforementioned "unilateral withdrawal" of portions of the Statue of Liberty, can thus be happily averted. Because the model derives private holdings from public ones, rather than the other way around, it does not provide any individual citizen with the power to alter the ownership status of any public property through isolated, solitary action.

Another appealing feature of the deep ownership model is that it sharpens our understanding of existing practices regarding public property, in a way that helps us see better the collective claims embodied in such property. The example of eminent domain is again pertinent. Whereas the private aggregation model has a fundamental problem making any sense of this practice, the deep public ownership model encounters no obstacle here. Rather than seeing eminent domain as a power of the body politic to take pre-political property for public use, the model leads us to understand eminent domain as a reflection of deep public ownership. This ownership comes to the fore when crucial public needs lead the body politic to reclaim the property that it has assigned to certain individuals.

Now, things may appear more difficult when we turn to the individual property requirement. Deep public ownership may seem to conflict with entrenched intuitions – especially among liberals – regarding the significance of private property. But this apparent conflict should seem far less problematic once the following three points are borne in mind.

First, the idea of deep public ownership is perfectly compatible with the thought that individuals ought to be able to enjoy, vis-à-vis one another, all the familiar immunities and prerogatives associated with private ownership. The point is simply that these immunities and prerogatives are not derived from any pre-political property. Rather than this Lockean picture, the view of private property that I am proposing is much more Rousseauian – it insists that while individuals certainly exercise private property rights, they do so as "trustees" of goods owned by the public.[32]

Second, to insist on this point is not to say that the public – acting through government institutions – might leave individuals with no private property.[33] To be sure, the deep public ownership model rejects appeals to pre-political property as a fundamental constraint against government taking of all privately held resources. But, *contra* libertarians, we should not hasten to conclude that no alternative liberal constraint can be found. In particular, it is crucial to note that although the deep public ownership model rejects the libertarian idea of pre-political property, nothing in the model conflicts with the concern for individual autonomy that all liberals, by definition, share. All liberals – including the most trenchant anti-libertarians – agree that protecting citizens' ability to plan and pursue their own personal projects is a core task of any morally viable government. Personal property, in turn, is a pivotal tool in this task. Without the stable expectations that personal property allows us to foster regarding the resources on which we may rely over time, we cannot form and execute any personal project that extends over time. Insofar as the deep public ownership model aligns with this simple but crucial point, it comports with the liberal conviction that personal property, as Rawls for instance puts it, "is necessary for citizens' independence and integrity."[34]

Finally, because it can accommodate the familiar liberal concern with individuals' stable expectations, the deep public ownership model also aligns with liberal concerns regarding the pace with which public authorities may change society's distribution of resources. If, for example, future American legislators decided to re-enact the much more progressive tax brackets that existed in the country during the

---

[32] See Joshua Cohen, *Rousseau* (Oxford: Oxford University Press, 2010), 140. For a detailed analysis of Rousseau's conception of property, see also Burke Hendrix, *Ownership, Authority, and Self-Determination* (University Park, PA: Pennsylvania State University Press, 2008).

[33] I am referring here to the public "acting through government institutions" since in the present context (in contrast to the context of our discussion earlier in the chapter) we can assume an institutional environment in which the public as a collective agent authorizes the actions of government officials. Here the acts of government, in other words, ultimately are the acts of the sovereign people (as argued, for example, in Pettit, *On the People's Terms* [Cambridge: Cambridge University Press, 2012]).

[34] *TJ*, XV.

1950s, they would not be doing anything intrinsically wrong, even though such reform would massively increase top earners' tax burden. What *would* be wrong is if such reform – rolling back seventy years of tax policy – would be fully implemented upon being announced, without any time for citizens to adjust their expectations. This is because the need for stable expectations around which individuals can structure their life plans requires a property system in which, as Rawls also says, "[t]axes and restrictions are all in principle foreseeable."[35]

2.4 Deep Public Ownership and Social Equality

In Section 2.1 of this chapter, I noted that a persuasive account of public property should fit within a broader, attractive framework. My preceding remarks, as to how to the deep public ownership model fits with independent concerns regarding personal autonomy and stable expectations, should provide an initial sense of how such a moral framework might look. This section aims to add further details to this broader framework by examining how the deep public ownership model can inform our thinking about relations of social equality. In particular, I want to show that the model extends a liberal government's duties with regard to racial discrimination – a phenomenon that is clearly anathema to social equality.

I should stress that the extension in which I am interested does not derive from deep public ownership alone. This is because, in my view, one must appeal to moral principles, that are not themselves grounded in any form of ownership, in order to explain why a government has a duty to combat racial discrimination to begin with. However, if we assume such a duty, then the deep public ownership model can still perform a distinctive service: it can show us just how far a government has to go in order to make good on this duty.

We can begin to make this thought more concrete by considering the ways in which private property rights are often assumed to shield private discrimination from the reach of the law. This assumption, unsurprisingly, has been explicitly invoked by lawmakers with libertarian predilections. For such lawmakers, landmark legislation such as the US Civil Rights Act, which intervenes in the decisions of private property owners, extends the government's anti-discriminatory agenda

---

[35] Rawls, *Political Liberalism* (New York: Columbia University Press, 1996), 283.

beyond its appropriate, public bounds. US Senator Rand Paul, for example, opined: "I like the Civil Rights Act in the sense that it ended discrimination in all public domains, and I'm all in favor of that ... [yet] I don't like the idea of telling private business owners – I abhor racism ... but, at the same time, I do believe in private ownership."[36]

This reasoning has quite dramatic implications. Take, by way of illustration, the US Fair Housing Act. This Act makes it illegal to refuse to sell or rent a residence to any person because of their race, color, religion, sex, familial status, or national origin. It similarly prohibits discrimination in the terms, conditions, or privileges of sale or rental of a residence due to such attributes.[37] Even if these prohibitions are driven by the right sort of moral ends, Senator Paul's position suggests that their enactment is still morally wrong, insofar as they infringe upon private property rights.

The issue looks markedly different, however, from the perspective of the deep public ownership model. Imagine for example that, buoyed by Paul's reasoning, a racist real estate developer contests a fine from the state by saying "I own this property, and so I get to decide who to allow into it." The deep public ownership model answers: "You only get to own this property under the provisions set by public authorities, and if public authorities decide that racial exclusion is unacceptable, then your exercise of your property rights has to align with this public judgment."[38]

From this perspective, it is eminently appropriate that the Fair Housing Act gives no consideration to private property claims as a constraint against government "intervention" in the decisions of private actors. And so it is also eminently appropriate that landlords who are accused of violating this act cannot simply appeal to their rights of private ownership as a defense, whatever other appeals they might make.

---

[36] Quoted in Glenn Kessler, "Rand Paul's Rewriting of His Own Remarks on the Civil Rights Act," *Washington Post*, Apr. 11, 2013.

[37] See Cornell Law School, Legal Information Institute, "42 US Code Subchapter I – Generally" at https://law.cornell.edu/uscode/text/42/chapter-45/subchapter-I.

[38] A parallel response can be made in less fraught contexts as well. Think for, example, of the familiar legal requirement that private owners of "historically valuable" homes refrain from altering these homes' historical features. See, e.g., UK Parliament, "Living Heritage: Preserving Historic Sites and Buildings" at https://web.archive.org/web/20100423162120/.

2.4 Deep Public Ownership and Social Equality

We can bring the significance of this point into sharper relief by considering a specific historical example. In the 1970s, the Trump Management Corporation was sued by the US Justice Department due to evidence of heavy bias against minorities in its New York rental policies. Trump Management was charged, among other things, with systematic misrepresentation of apartment availability to African-American apartment seekers. It was also accused of giving explicit instructions to rental agents working on its behalf, to "rent only to Jews and executives and to disregard the applications of blacks." As a result, "in a sampling of 10 Trump buildings, only 1 to 3.5 percent of the occupants were minorities, making it one of the strongest cases the Justice Department had ever seen for violations of the Fair Housing Act."[39]

The head of Trump Management, Donald Trump, vigorously contested these allegations. Trump initially labeled the charges "ridiculous." He then sued the Justice Department for $100 million in damages. Finally, Trump announced that the settlement he eventually reached with the Department did not "constitute an admission of guilt."[40] But at no point – neither before nor after Trump Management was charged with violating the terms of its settlement – did the law allow Trump to respond to the charges by appealing to private property rights. The deep public ownership model provides an immediate explanation of why it was appropriate for the law to prevent private landlords such as Trump from having this option.[41]

---

[39] See Jennifer Rubin, "Trump's Ingrained Racism," *Washington Post*, Sep. 28, 2016, at www.washingtonpost.com/blogs/right-turn/wp/2016/09/28/trumps-ingrained-racism/?utm_term=.113c3dd843fd.

[40] See Michael Kranish and Robert O'Harrow Jr., "Inside the Government's Racial Bias Case against Donald Trump's Company, and How He Fought It," *Washington Post*, Jan. 23, 2016.

[41] An anonymous reviewer asks whether the same result can be obtained by simply postulating that certain uses of one's private property are deemed impermissibly harmful of others – a view that can be supported even by proponents of pre-political property rights. One problem with this alternative is that even after we distinguish morally permissible harms from impermissible ones, we still need a further account moving us from moral to *legal* judgments. On a strict view of pre-political property, owners should have the legal prerogative of imposing many morally impermissible harms on others – and there is no obvious reason why this prerogative should not extend to the harms involved in racial discrimination. So a harm-based argument requires a more complicated defense here than one may initially think. Comparatively, at least, that should increase the attraction of the simple reasoning offered by my model.

I should stress, however, that the model does not only show why a government is morally *permitted* to sanction private landlords engaged in discrimination. Assuming that we accept a moral requirement for government to take certain actions with regard to public sector discrimination, then the model also suggests that some of these government actions are morally *required* with regard to discrimination in the private sector. Take the Fair Housing Act once again. If we assume that governments ought to avoid discrimination in publicly owned housing, then the deep public ownership model suggests that governments generally ought to avoid racial discrimination in the private housing market as well.[42] After all, both cases ultimately feature public property, even if in the private case the relevant public property can be seen, along the Rousseauian lines noted above, as managed by private trustees. Therefore, given the assumption that a liberal government ought to refrain from racial discrimination in its direct management of public property, it also ought to combat racial discrimination evident in major private actors' market decisions regarding property that they hold, but that ultimately belongs to the people.[43]

Moreover, the denial of any bright line separating private from public property has important implications for anti-discriminatory government action, even in contexts where the relevant discrimination has a more complex relationship to property. We can see this point by considering the example of racial discrimination in private education. Historically, public property was used to support such discrimination directly – for instance, through tax exemptions given to racially discriminatory private schools. The deep public ownership model can obviously show why a government that is committed to treating all of its citizens as equals must not pursue such public measures. But the model carries further, less obvious, implications for public action targeting discrimination in private education.

A specific case will again help to make these distinctive implications concrete. Bob Jones University (BJU), a private Christian school in

---

[42] I discuss a possible exception to this duty in Section 2.5.
[43] I take it to be obvious that this point remains politically relevant long after the 1970s, as various political philosophers have emphasized. See, e.g.,
Elizabeth Anderson, *The Imperative of Integration* (Princeton University Press, 2010); Christopher Lebron, *The Color of Our Shame: Race and Justice in Our Time* (New York: Oxford University Press, 2013).

2.4 Deep Public Ownership and Social Equality

South Carolina, did not admit black students until 1971. From 1971 until 1975, BJU admitted black students only if they were married; after 1975, the university admitted unmarried black applicants, but denied admission to applicants who engaged in, or even supported, interracial marriage or dating. The university also imposed a disciplinary rule that prohibited, on pain of expulsion, interracial dating or even support for interracial dating. During the 1970s, The Internal Revenue Service (IRS) tried several times to revoke BJU's tax-exempt status, claiming that the federal government's anti-discriminatory policies justified treating BJU differently from non-discriminatory private schools that receive this status. After a protracted legal process, in 1983, the Supreme Court finally upheld this IRS measure in *Bob Jones University vs. the United States*, basing its decision primarily on "government's fundamental, overriding interest in eradicating racial discrimination in education."[44]

Now, assuming a government commitment to combating racial discrimination, the model condemns the direct use of public tax revenue to facilitate discrimination of the kind practiced by BJU. Yet the model further suggests that revoking tax exemptions was only one among several financial sanctions that the federal government could have justifiably imposed in response to BJU's discriminatory practices, which endured long after its tax-exempt status was revoked.[45]

It should not be difficult to see why. BJU could not function without exercising private property rights – without such rights it would not, for example, be able to sustain its physical infrastructure or pay its employees. But, on the deep public ownership model, these private property rights have been allocated to the university through the decision of public authorities representing the people as the property's ultimate owner. And this public decision is not qualitatively different from a public decision to grant tax exemptions to the university. Therefore, there was no fundamental moral constraint forcing the government to limit its sanctions of BJU so as to cover only the university's tax exemptions. Assuming that the

---

[44] See US Supreme Court, *Bob Jones University v. United States*, 461 U.S. 574, at http://caselaw.findlaw.com/us-supreme-court/461/574.html

[45] It was only in 2000, following media uproar surrounding a campus visit by then-presidential-candidate George W. Bush, that BJU dropped its formal ban on interracial dating; it was only in 2008 that the university apologized for its racist policies. See "Bob Jones Univ. Apologizes for Racist Policies," *Associated Press*, Nov. 21, 2008, at http://nbcnews.com/id/27845030/ns/us_news-life/t/bob-jones-univ-apologizes-racist-policies/.

withdrawal of these exemptions was justifiable, then further financial penalties might also have been justifiable.

The question of the exact design of such additional penalties is obviously important.[46] However, rather than delving into this design, I want to conclude this section with two broader observations connecting the deep public ownership model to the collective integrity framework I elaborated in the Chapter 1. First, the deep public ownership model, like the integrity framework, prevents government from disavowing responsibility for certain forms of private conduct. Practices which public authorities clearly ought not pursue themselves out of respect for the demands of equality should also trigger extensive formal scrutiny, and at least in some cases be outlawed altogether, when pursued by private actors. Public authorities cannot deny their moral responsibility to address pervasive societal wrongs by simply saying that the relevant wrongs are a matter of private conduct rather than public policy; some forms of private conduct, at least, should be disturbing enough to trigger certain public policies.

The second, very much related observation, has to do with the rejection of libertarianism. As we have seen earlier, the deep public ownership model denies libertarian claims regarding the existence and significance of pre-political property. Yet the model also challenges a broader libertarian claim: that there is always a fundamental moral distinction between what the laws officially call for or support, and what the laws are simply silent about. Hardly any libertarian would defend laws that *officially* call on prominent actors in the private housing market to discriminate against people of color, for example. But libertarians have a much harder time explaining what would be wrong with the 'mere' silence of the law in the face of such discrimination. In fact, some libertarians, as we have already seen, think that the law ought *not* to intervene in such cases. However, the deep public ownership model holds otherwise. This model, like the collective integrity framework, sees the legal system as (at least potentially) blameworthy even when it merely meets private discrimination with inaction. As I noted in Chapter 1, it might very well be especially disturbing for the law to officially call for or support certain wrongs, as compared to

---

[46] Two intuitive ideas here would be to have gradual increases in the size of the fines over time, and to direct the resulting revenue to public campaigns promoting egalitarian norms.

the law being silent about the same wrongs. But we can admit that the former problem is worse than the latter, even while insisting that both problems must feature in our moral evaluation of how a political community structures its legal system.

2.5 The Scope of the Private

The deep public ownership model, I have just argued, joins the collective integrity framework in challenging the libertarian understanding of a legal system's moral responsibilities. But this challenge may seem to carry costs of this own. This is because the deep public ownership model appears to invite excessive, even draconian, government reach into private lives. This, at least, may seem like a natural result of making even distinctly private conduct a subject of active concern for public authorities wielding the power of law.

One response to this worry is the following. It is true that it would be implausible to respond to certain forms of private conduct with legal punishment. It would be odd, to say the least, to demand for example that the law punishes individuals who have made racist choices about who to invite to a dinner party at their home. But there is no reason to think that the deep public ownership model forces us to endorse such counterintuitive policies with regard to micro-level conduct. For one thing, in order to settle the question of whether government intervention in any given private affair is ultimately morally warranted, we will typically have to consider various factors, including whether government intervention through law is even feasible with regard to the case at hand, whether it is likely to be effective, and whether its benefits will outweigh its costs. It seems extremely likely that in most if not all cases of truly micro-level private conduct, the result of this overall calculus will go against the use of the law.

Some may worry, however, that such an emphasis on feasibility, effectiveness, and cost-benefit analysis is too contingent: it does not generate fundamental moral constraints against public intervention in private life. Might we not have to turn to private property after all in order to generate such constraints?

I believe that the answer is no. Just as it is mistaken to think that we need the libertarian picture of property rights in order to take private property seriously, so it is mistaken to think that we always need the idea of private property in order to take seriously fundamental constraints shielding certain forms of private conduct from the reach of the law. We can see this point by examining another private housing issue. If a homeowner who is letting out a few rooms in his own place of residence refuses to accept any person of color as a tenant, should he be subject to legal punishment? In my view, there might be a fundamental moral constraint against the law sanctioning such a racist homeowner. But this constraint has to do with rights of privacy rather than property.[47] A person should be allowed to engage in racial discrimination in his intimate space, not because he owns this space, but rather because of the intimate nature of the interactions ongoing within it.[48]

The preceding paragraphs should make clear why the deep public ownership model does not commit us to excessive government encroachment into private affairs. But while this point is crucial, a further point should also be borne in mind. There are specific cases where the deep public ownership model does indeed push public authorities to employ the law to scrutinize what is typically seen as purely private, micro-level conduct. But in those rare instances we should consider very carefully whether the relevant conduct does not have an essential public dimension. If so, then formal public scrutiny of this conduct may in fact be morally appropriate even if it goes further than existing law in making private conduct a public affair.

Consider, by way of illustration, US law concerning politicians' tax returns. American politicians currently face no legal obligation to make their tax returns public.[49] The deep public ownership model, however, suggests that politicians should be legally obligated to publicize their tax returns. This is because the public has a compelling interest in knowing whether individuals who seek public office have been reliable trustees of public property. Where they have not – where the relevant

---

[47] In saying this, I do not mean to suggest that the idea of a right to privacy (or its precise relationship to rights such as freedom of association) is straightforward. I only mean to endorse a simple thought – namely, that "everyone needs some choice about how close or how distant they want to be from different others." See Andrei Marmor, "What Is the Right to Privacy," *Philosophy & Public Affairs* 43 (2015): 3–26, at 11.

[48] See in this spirit the remarks from Senator Hubert Humphrey on exceptions to the Fair Housing Act, quoted in James Walsh, "Reaching Mrs. Murphy: A Call for Repeal of the Mrs. Murphy Exemption to the Fair Housing Act," *Harvard Civil Rights-Civil Liberties Law Review* 34 (2013): 605–634.

[49] See, e.g., Adam Levy, "California Legislature Tries to Force Trump to Release Tax Returns," *CNN*, Sept. 16, 2017, at http://cnn.com/2017/09/16/politics/california-legislature-trump-tax-returns/index.html.

individuals have sought every trick in the tax code to advance their personal position at the public's expense – the public has a moral right to know, and to be able to employ this knowledge in decisions about whether these individuals should hold public office. There is no good reason, in turn, why this moral right should not be translated into a legal right – and certainly no reason that can be traced to any immunities associated with politicians' private property.

2.6 The People's Property in the Real World

Up to this point, I have spent this chapter elaborating a particular model of the people's property. But in order to have a full view of how this model bears on actual politics, we need to identify the world's "peoples," and the territories within which they make public property claims. Consider, for instance, the statement that the Canadian people ought to be treated as the ultimate owner of all resources within Canada's territory. For this statement to be intelligible, we need to be able to identify, at least in a rough way, the individuals that ought to be considered part of "the Canadian people." And we also need to identify, at least in a rough way, the physical locations marking the borders of Canada's rightful territory. But how does such identification proceed?

Since I have expressed support for many of Rawls's claims regarding property rights up to this point, I should also confess that I share Rawls's core position with regard to territorial rights, despite the fact that this position is far less popular than many of Rawls's other ideas. According to Rawls, if we seek to identify the world's rightful territories, we should start by looking at the world's map. If we think that normative reflection "must always start from where we now are,"[50] and if we accordingly examine international questions by proceeding "from the international political world as we see it,"[51] then it makes eminent sense to "take peoples as they are"[52] – to adopt the presumption (which I made explicit already in the introduction to this book) that existing, stable international borders demarcate rightful territories, and that all of the individuals who permanently reside within each of these territories ought to comprise – at least on

---

[50] Rawls, *The Law of Peoples* (Cambridge, MA: Harvard University Press, 1999) (hereafter *LP*), 121.
[51] *LP*, 83.   [52] *LP*, 17.

first approximation – the different sovereign peoples who make collective property claims within each of these territories.

Now, one obvious concern about this presumption has to do with the territorial claims of minority groups residing within existing borders. In actual politics, various minorities, especially ethnic, religious, and linguistic minorities who consider themselves to be victims of historical wrongs, seek to secede from existing political communities and to form their own separate state institutions, over what they see as their own separate territory. Does it really make sense to simply put aside such secessionist aspirations?

Questions of this sort are important for our purposes, partly because they bring to the fore another important meeting point between the collective integrity and the collective property frameworks. When elaborating the idea of the people's integrity in Chapter 1, I emphasized the moral hope that joint civic activity will, over time, serve as a core component of collective identity, which would allow co-citizens to transcend differences of ethnicity, religion, and language, even in extremely fraught political circumstances where these differences may seem quite explosive. And this hope does generate a presumption against secession.[53]

This presumption, in turn, is strengthened whenever existing state institutions are willing and able to accommodate various forms of autonomy for distinct minorities in a way that will mitigate pressures for secession that such minorities might exert. At the very least, this is the case when state institutions are reasonably democratic, and serve the fundamental interests of all citizens. In such an institutional context, as Rawls observes, it should be "possible . . . to satisfy the reasonable cultural interests and needs of groups with diverse ethnic and national backgrounds."[54]

The same thought, it should be noted, can be strengthened even further once we bear in mind yet another function of the idea of stable expectations. If we are willing to view territorial claims as intertwined with property claims, in the manner I have been suggesting, then we should be led quite naturally to the thought that claims of historical

---

[53] Though the presumption can be outweighed, for example, when ethnic, religious, or linguistic minorities suffer systematic repression at the hands of a majority. See, e.g., Allen Buchanan, *Justice, Legitimacy, and Self-Determination: Moral Foundations for International Law* (Oxford: Oxford University Press, 2004).

[54] *LP*, 25.

2.6 The People's Property in the Real World

wrongdoing regarding territory are, at some point in time sufficiently far from the occurrence of the wrong, superseded by the stable expectations that later generations form around the territory in question.[55]

This principle, to be sure, might have qualifications. There might be instances where the wrongs perpetrated in the past are still sufficiently identifiable so as to make some form of compensation (even if not necessarily restitution) a live option. In other instances, historical wrongs have been so grave, and their effects so enduring, as to bolster the case for special forms of autonomy for the groups who have been wronged, insofar as their distinct identity itself persists into the present (aboriginal populations being a classic example).[56] Yet the principle nonetheless has clear, practical implications. It suggests that, within any polity that has existed in its current territorial borders for a substantial amount of time, citizens legitimately come to organize their lives around the assumption that these borders will remain in place, with the resources that they encompass. And this in turn means that it would be morally impermissible for various kinds of minorities to declare unilateral secession from larger political communities to which they currently belong, insofar as this necessarily involves taking away a part of the existing communities' territory. Hence Catalans who have long resided within the borders of Spain, for example, might

---

[55] The most important statement of how stable expectations supersede historical wrongs remains Jeremy Waldron's "Superseding Historic Injustice," *Ethics* 103 (1992): 4–28. For the enduring influence of this position see, for example, Stilz's review of Simmons's Boundaries of Authority, in *Notre Dame Philosophical Reviews*, at https://ndpr.nd.edu/news/boundaries-of-authority/

[56] See for example Jeff Spinner-Halev, *Enduring Injustice* (Cambridge: Cambridge University Press, 2012). Note, moreover, that one does not have to appeal to property rights in order to explain why it is wrong to displace aboriginal communities. All that is needed here is a more minimal, and distinct, notion of occupancy rights, which, unlike property, can obtain even in the absence of state institutions. For elaboration, see Stilz, "Occupancy Rights and the Wrong of Removal," *Philosophy & Public Affairs* 41 (2013): 324–356, e.g., at 327–328: "an occupancy right ... includes a liberty to reside permanently in a particular space and to make use of that area for social, cultural, and economic practices [and] a claim-right against others not to interfere with one's use of that space in ways that undermine the shared social practices in which one is engaged. [But] occupancy does not extend to full liberal ownership of a territory. It does not include rights to income from the natural resources situated there, nor does it involve the power to alienate or bequeath the territory. Occupancy may not always extend to a right to exclude outsiders from access to the territory, if their access is not disruptive to one's residence there and one's ability to participate in shared social practices."

demand the exclusive "right to decide" themselves whether to form their own state, but, in my view at least, all the citizens of Spain – all the individuals who together comprise the Spanish people – ought to be able to participate equally in the decision over whether the Catalans will have such a right.

The ideas canvassed in the preceding paragraphs should help explain how one might answer questions regarding the conflicting territorial claims of ethnic minorities and civic "peoples." Yet these ideas, especially concerning stable expectations and a civic identity evolving through time, also give us a clue as to how the model of the people's property developed here can align with a sensible conception of the one component of territorial rights that I have put aside for most of this chapter, and that has an obvious bearing on the composition of "peoples" – namely, rights of border control, especially as they concern immigration.

On the one hand, as I noted in Chapter 1, endorsing a civic rather than ethnic basis for peoplehood allows us to see all of the world's individuals as potential members of any people. At least, this is the case so long as the individuals in question are willing to immerse themselves in the people's particular political culture, revolving around its particular historical struggles to realize the equality of all citizens – and eventually to play a part in these struggles, insofar as they continue to unfold over time. But on the other hand, the emphasis on the expectations that current members of the people legitimately develop regarding the resources available to them within their territory provides a natural way to ground the intuition that a receiving political community has a moral right to insist that immigration will occur gradually, both in terms of process (so a person will not receive full citizenship immediately upon entering the people's territory), and in terms of numbers (hence the receiving community can permissibly refuse to grant simultaneous admission to a number of individuals that is too large compared to its existing population). I should hasten to concede that a complete defense of this balance would require a far more comprehensive discussion of the ethics of immigration than I can offer here.[57]

---

[57] For some of the relevant debates, see Seyla Benhabib, "The Law of Peoples, Distributive Justice, and Migrations," *Fordham Law Review* 72 (2004): 1761–1787; Christopher Heath Wellman and Phillip Cole, *Debating the Ethics of Immigration: Is There a Right to Exclude?* (New York: Oxford University Press, 2011); Joseph Carens, *The Ethics of Immigration* (New York: Oxford

2.6 The People's Property in the Real World

Yet assuming that this balance has at least prima facie plausibility, then the emphasis I have been placing on sovereign peoples' property claims might be less exclusionary than it may seem: after all, through immigration, all human beings can in principle partake in the people's ownership.[58]

Now, to be sure, even with these additions, there will be readers who will contest my willingness to begin with "peoples as they are" in the world, demarcated through stable territorial borders. This starting point, some readers might complain, simply begs a question that has been fundamental to the territorial rights literature – namely, why a particular people can claim rights over a particular territory.[59]

I believe that the best answer to this question goes through the pragmatic orientation to political philosophy that I have been emphasizing since the introduction to this book. Thinking pragmatically about the tasks of political philosophy means focusing on practical problems as they actually arise, and regarding which philosophy might realistically seek to offer guidance. This pragmatic emphasis is important here because it suggests that the familiar question of "why this particular people has a right to this particular territory" might in fact be

---

University Press, 2013); Michael Blake, "Immigration, Jurisdiction, and Exclusion," *Philosophy and Public Affairs* 41 (2013): 103–130.

[58] I should perhaps note here a few other respects in which my view is amenable to cosmopolitan sensitivities. For one thing, when considering the most ideal reaches of "ideal theory," nothing in the model of public property presented here rules out a vision in which the relevant public comprises all human beings, as members of a single world state. Furthermore, such a world state also seems like the natural home for much-debated cosmopolitan proposals, such as that of a global difference principle. Moreover, at the level of non-ideal theory, my argument here is fully compatible with the endorsement of stringent and weighty moral duties of assistance on the part of affluent nations, to sacrifice some of their property to assist in combating global poverty (duties on which I say more in Chapter 4). The one classic cosmopolitan proposal of which I am skeptical has to do with a global redistribution of natural resource wealth – a proposal that, in my view, does not have anything like the distinctive significance that various cosmopolitans have attributed to it, neither at the level of ideal theory, nor in the context of manifestly non-ideal problems. For elaboration, see my "Who's Afraid of a World State?" *Critical Review of International Social and Political Philosophy* 16 (2013): 1–23; "Liberal Global Justice and Social Science," *Review of International Studies* 42 (2016): 136–155; and "Global Poverty, Global Sacrifices, and Natural Resource Reforms," *International Theory* 11 (2019): 48–80.

[59] For a comprehensive lay of the land, see Margaret Moore, *A Political Theory of Territory* (Oxford: Oxford University Press, 2015).

misleading. At least, this question is misleading, if we take it to imply that territorial rights issues should be considered as if they arise in a world that human beings have never inhabited before – as if a theory of territorial rights has to specify what territorial rights should be "assigned" to distinct groups of individuals as they land in, say, Alpha Centauri. But if we focus on tractable practical problems as they arise within the "basic standing features of this world,"[60] then our moral analysis of territorial rights has to factor in from the outset the morally important expectations that existing political communities have developed over time with regard to the stable territories within which they have actually resided.

This pragmatic orientation, in turn, can also help explain why we should limit our aspirations when philosophizing about cases where territorial borders are extremely unstable – where disputed borders shift constantly, and often violently. It is far from clear that philosophy has any real hope of offering distinctive guidance with regard to such cases. Beyond obvious moral principles that require little philosophical analysis (such as the thought that past violence perpetrated against a group does not, in itself, justify the group's violent retaliation in the present), it seems plain (to my mind, at least) that any peaceful resolution of violent territorial conflicts, even one that ends with a result that is morally suboptimal, is preferable to enduring violence, even when some parties to this violence are pursuing a morally superior end state.[61]

[60] Pogge, "Cohen to the Rescue!" *Ratio* 21 (2008): 454–475, at 466–467.
[61] Despite disagreements on many other fronts, on this particular score I agree with Chandran Kukathas, "The Mirage of Global Justice," *Social Philosophy and Policy* 23 (2006): 1–28. Partly given Kukathas's essay (which discusses the Israeli-Palestinian conflict in some detail), and partly in response to a query from an anonymous reviewer, a few remarks on this conflict (which will feature in Chapter 5) might be appropriate here. In particular, I would like to preempt any expectation of a detailed property argument seeking to adjudicate questions such as "Who owns the West Bank" or "Who owns Jerusalem." One reason why I do not offer any such argument is that, on the Israeli side at least, the conflict has not traditionally been seen as revolving around ownership claims. For the majority of Jewish Israelis, especially among the secular, ideas such as "we own the West Bank" play little if any role. The standard hawkish, right-wing view among Jewish Israelis does not emphasize ownership claims, but rather distrust. "The problem with the Palestinians," according to this view, is not that they are claiming what belongs to the Jews by right. Rather, the (ostensible) problem is that they cannot be trusted not to threaten Jewish existence in the region. For the centrality of such distrust in Jewish Israelis' public discourse in general, and in Prime Minister Netanyahu's worldview in

2.7 Deep Public Ownership, Property as an Instrument, and Property as a Convention

If my claims here have been cogent, then the deep public ownership model, notwithstanding its pragmatic elements outlined in Section 2.6, provides an attractive way of accounting for public property. Given this attraction, it seems appropriate to end the chapter by asking why this model has not featured so far in the vast literature on property. I would like to conjecture that the reason has to do with two other positions on private property that have been prominent in the literature and that seem to provide a powerful alternative. The first position holds that all ownership arrangements are simply derivative, to be fixed by the choice of the best social institutions, as identified by independent normative criteria. Notwithstanding appearances to the contrary, the deep public ownership model actually incorporates this position. The idea of deep public ownership is situated *above* derivative property rights: it pushes us to keep our attention focused not on the criteria in light of which derivative property rights will be created, but rather on which agent will create these rights.

The second influential position parts ways with deep public ownership by associating property rights with conventions. While this view too rejects the libertarian notion of robust pre-political property rights, it does not see the body politic as creating a property regime. Instead, the thought is that property rights are "created" by a set of interpersonal understandings – conventions – which can precede the institutions of the

> particular, see Ben Caspit, *The Netanyahu Years* (New York: St. Martin's Press, 2017, trans. Ora Cummings) e.g. at 435–436. Outside the very religious right, no prominent Israeli politician has argued in recent decades that territories ought to be held because "we rightly own them." The lands occupied in 1967 (certainly outside of Jerusalem) were originally seen simply as a bargaining chip to be used in peace negotiations. What happened over the last fifty years has often been a tragic reluctance – on one or both sides – to actually make the bargain. Now, things are obviously different with regard to Israel's religious right. But if the Israeli-Palestinian conflict really were solidified as a religious conflict – a danger on which I will have much to say in the final chapter – then there would surely be no role for any philosophically respectable theory of property in adjudicating the conflict. If both sides really came to believe that "God gave us this land," it would be odd for contemporary philosophers in general – and for property theorists in particular – to wade into this kind of theological dispute. The right thing to say would be that *both* sides are making morally implausible claims, and to simply hope that the conflict will be resolved with as little violence as possible.

body politic. These institutions are needed to anticipate and adjudicate conflicts that arise from disagreements about property claims, and they accordingly define the authoritative rules of property. But the source of property claims lies with mutually recognized conventions, which can be independent of and prior to political regulation.[62]

The main problem with this position is that its key distinction, between the body politic creating property and political institutions specifying property on the basis of conventions, is too weak to bear the burden placed upon it. The reason is that conventions ultimately obtain their force – not only practically but also morally – from the decisions of the body politic. This point is evident when widely divergent conventions exist simultaneously regarding a certain property, or when there is a dominant convention but one that the body politic deems utterly unacceptable. "The people" as a plurality of individuals might have a plurality of conventions regarding ownership of land, for instance. But the people as a totality – the body politic – might ignore many of these conventions, and in principle even *all* of these conventions, when employing its higher-order power to create property rights in land.[63] Hence saying that this higher-order power is merely a power of specifying property rights on the basis of antecedent conventions gets things backward. Ultimately, whatever force conventions may have is dependent upon political decision, not the other way around.

It seems, then, that the apparent alternatives to deep public ownership are less persuasive than they may initially appear. This does not mean, of course, that other alternatives too would necessarily fall short. But it does mean that we should at least entertain the thought that deep

---

[62] This is in many respects a Humean thought. See, e.g., Samuel Freeman, "Property as an Institutional Convention in Hume's Account of Justice," *Archiv für Geschichte der Philosophie* 73 (1991): 20–49.

[63] One upshot of this point is that even if certain conventions exist regarding collective ownership below the level of the overarching political unit (for instance, conventions regarding collective tribal ownership), it is the broader political collective – the body politic – that enjoys ultimate ownership. That is why we should not treat ownership by the body politic as simply one among many types of collective ownership (in contrast to what is implied, for instance, in Stephen Munzer's *A Theory of Property* [Cambridge: Cambridge University Press, 1990] e.g., 25; see also Robert Ellickson, "Property in Land," *Yale Law Journal* 102 [1993]: 1314–1400).

public ownership is not only an attractive way to go; it may very well be the best way to go, if we are to take public property rights seriously.

Conclusion

Equipped with these observations, we can now circle back to the case of Blaise Compaoré's Burkina Faso, with which we started this chapter. Specifically, we can return to the popular protests that led to Compaoré's downfall, and to the people's "re-appropriation" of resources amassed by his family. If the deep public ownership model developed in this chapter is right, then this popular re-appropriation really did represent, as the more radical protesters believed, a reclaiming of what had belonged to the people "all along." This model, moreover, may be the best way to make sense of our firmest convictions regarding the theft that numerous de facto leaders – not just in Burkina Faso, but in so many other places around the world – have committed against their peoples.

Admittedly, the deep public ownership model is not free of challenges. This model is heterodox in its conception of private property, insofar as it suggests that individuals exercise rights of ownership as trustees of goods that are ultimately owned by the body politic. However, I have tried to show that the model is nonetheless compatible with mainstream intuitions regarding the significance of private property, and that it satisfies multiple other desiderata for an account of public property – better, at least, than the going alternatives. Moreover, I have sought to show that this model clarifies and expands our understanding of the moral duties incumbent upon a liberal democracy committed to treating all of its citizens as equals.

In Chapter 3, I utilize the deep public ownership model to investigate a related, but distinct, set of topics. I examine how this model of the people's property, together with the ideas in Chapter 1 regarding the people's integrity, can help us think about morally complex threats that de facto leaders pose to the equality of all citizens. As we will see, one part of this problem has to do with authoritarians who are more willing to fight against their people than was Compaoré at the end of his rule. But another part of the problem has to do with genuinely elected leaders, who abuse the power conferred upon them by the people.

3 The People's Integrity, the People's Property, and the Abuse of Political Power

"Our constitution works. Our great republic is a government of laws and not of men. Here, the people rule."

Gerald Ford, upon assuming the presidency, Aug. 9, 1974[1]

I have spent the opening chapters of this book developing two frameworks relating to the people as a collective agent. My aim in the remainder of the book is to show how these two frameworks, revolving around the people's integrity and property, can illuminate public policy dilemmas. In this chapter, I am interested in dilemmas associated with various forms of abuse of political power. I examine how senior politicians' abuse of their office can trigger moral complexity in real-world politics, and how ideas regarding the people's integrity and property can help us confront this complexity.

This chapter has two main parts. The first part (3.1–3.2) discusses the practice of formally shielding senior members of an elected government from the ordinary reach of the law. The main argument in favor of such formal immunity is that repeated lawsuits against senior members of government – and especially against the head of the executive branch – can disturb the functioning of government in non-trivial ways. But in 3.1, I argue that this worry is typically outweighed by considerations associated with collective property and collective integrity. These considerations show that rather than wide-ranging immunity, there is – at most – a case for special review procedures anticipating politically motivated lawsuits against the head of government.

However, while these conclusions apply in normal circumstances, it is also important to identify morally appropriate responses to drastic cases, where abuse of elected office for private gain has been a pervasive

[1] See "President Gerald R. Ford, Remarks on Taking Office," The History Place: Great Speeches Collection, http://historyplace.com/speeches/ford-sworn.htm

phenomenon.[2] In such circumstances, pursuing the full extent of the law against each and every suspect politician may involve the very real possibility of leaving virtually no one to run the country, with all of the attendant political and economic risks. In 3.2, I argue that collective property and collective integrity arguments can enhance our thinking about such manifestly non-ideal situations, by outlining distinctive recommendations as to when and how it might be appropriate to enact temporary forms of executive immunity.

The latter part of the chapter turns to pardons and amnesties. In 3.3, I discuss the practice of presidential pardons. I contend that collective integrity and collective property ideas militate strongly in favor of abolishing this practice. Using the example of the Watergate scandal and its aftermath, I show how these ideas militate especially strongly against pardoning of former democratic leaders. Finally, in 3.4, I examine in detail the granting of amnesties to former leaders of repressive regimes, as a method of facilitating democratic transitions. I show how the property and integrity frameworks yield distinctive practical proposals with regard to such complex transitional issues.

Before I start to develop these arguments, it would be helpful to say something about the sequence in which I discuss them. Each of the chapter's two parts is meant to allow us to proceed gradually, in the following sense. In each part, we start with practices (executive immunity in 3.1, pardons and amnesties in 3.3) that intuitively trigger suspicion. We buttress our confidence in the collective property and integrity frameworks by seeing how they capture, and refine, this instinctive suspicion. We then proceed to harder, manifestly non-ideal conditions (pervasive corruption in 3.2, fragile transitions to democracy in 3.4), where our intuitions are less secure. In this second step, we build on the confidence we have acquired in the collectivist

---

[2] This remains the dominant definition of corruption in the corruption literature. Susan Rose-Ackerman has been one of the most influential proponents of this definition. See, for example, her *Corruption: A Study in Political Economy* (New York: Academic Press, 1978), 6–7, as well as *Corruption and Government: Causes, Consequences, and Reform* (New York: Cambridge University Press, 1999), 9; see also Rose-Ackerman, "Corruption and Purity," *Daedalus* 147 (2018): 98–110. Definitions that focus on the norm of impartiality are sometimes proposed as an alternative. But I believe these definitions are more problematic, partly for reasons noted in Robert Sparling's "Impartiality and the Definition of Corruption," *Political Studies* 66 (2018): 376–391.

frameworks, to see where, in less well-charted territory, they may lead us.[3]

3.1 Immunity for Elected Politicians (I): General Doubts

Let us start, then, with the practice of executive immunity. The typical executive immunity regime protects the head of the executive branch from prosecution during his or her term in office.[4] The basic reason in favor of executive immunity is straightforward. Shielding the head of the executive branch from the normal reach of the law while in office is a way of preventing disturbances to effective government. The possibility of bringing the head of government to trial might very well be abused by politically motivated actors, or even simply by individuals seeking money or publicity. And the resulting specter of a president or a prime minister repeatedly having to appear before the police or the courts can hardly help the smooth functioning of government.[5]

This argument notwithstanding, the practice of executive immunity – at least in its standard form – is unjustified. This is so for four main

---

[3] Readers familiar with Rawls' philosophical method will recognize this two-step progression. See, e.g. *TJ*, 17–18.

[4] Article 67 of the French constitution, for example, states that "Throughout his term of office the President shall not be required to testify before any French Court of law or Administrative authority and shall not be the object of any civil proceedings, nor of any preferring of charges, prosecution, or investigatory measures." See *Constitution of October 4, 1958* at www.conseil-constitutionnel.fr/conseil-constitutionnel/root/bank_mm/anglais/constiution_anglais_oct2009.pdf. Note that constitutional immunity for the largely ceremonial head of state is more common than immunity for the head of the executive branch (compare "Head of State Immunity" at www.constituteproject.org/search?lang=en&key=hosimm with "Head of Government Immunity" at www.constituteproject.org/search?lang=en&key=hogimm). Note also that some constitutions avoid immunity with regard to certain offenses. Portugal's constitution, for example, decrees that "No member of the Government shall be detained, arrested, or imprisoned without the authorisation of the Assembly of the Republic, save for a serious crime punishable by imprisonment for a maximum term of more than three years ... " *Constitution of the Portuguese Republic, Seventh Revision* (2005) at www.europam.eu/data/mechanisms/FOI/FOI%20Laws/Portugal/Portugal_Constitution%20of%20the%20Portuguese%20Republic_1976%20last%20amended%202005.pdf.

[5] For a forceful statement of this argument, see Joseph Isenbergh, "Impeachment and Presidential Immunity from Judicial Process," *Yale Law & Policy Review* 18 (1999): 53–109.

reasons, neatly captured by the collective integrity and collective property frameworks.

First, the collective integrity framework alerts us to a simple fact: no people pursuing the collective project of realizing equal rights through the law can plausibly claim to be successful, if its legal system does not uphold the equality of all citizens before the law. But if we are committed to equality before the law, and to having the law of a liberal democracy "speak with one voice," we should be deeply suspicious of any arrangement that frees elected leaders from the hold of laws they demand ordinary citizens obey. We can bring this concern into especially sharp relief by considering countries where there are no constitutional limitations on how long any given head of the executive can be in office. In such circumstances, the worry that the executive branch is effectively above the law seems especially salient. And the worse are the offenses that the head of the executive branch may commit with impunity, the more we may think that he or she seems like a monarch rather than an elected leader equal to his or her fellow citizens.

Second, very much related, not only is there an integrity intuition that elected leaders ought to be bound by the law in just the same way as ordinary citizens, there is also the further intuition that elected leaders ought to be subjected to especially stringent standards when it comes to upholding the law in their own conduct. If we expect elected leaders to be at the forefront of the collective project of realizing equal rights through the law, then it makes intuitive sense to subject them to especially high standards of compliance with the law. This general observation, in turn, is reinforced by our firm intuitions about specific cases, including cases that concern public property. Thus for instance, whatever is the appropriate legal sanction for an ordinary citizen who is guilty of tax evasion, the sanctions imposed on a finance minister guilty of tax evasion clearly ought to be harsher. Along similar lines, whatever is the appropriate sanction for a junior public servant convicted of systematically soliciting bribes in exchange for abusing public property, the sanction clearly ought to be harsher when it is the prime minister who is guilty of such an offense. But these intuitions do not sit easily with the idea of shielding the most senior members of government from the normal reach of the law.

Third, while it may seem tempting to think that such legal protection for senior government members furthers the effective running of government affairs, hardly anyone would argue in favor of applying such protection beyond the time when individuals occupy the relevant political office. Yet this would be the foreseeable result if other measures, that are arguably more essential to the effective running of government affairs, are implemented.

The easiest way to see the relevant measures is to note what it really takes for the most senior member of government to do his or her job effectively. For one thing, much before immunity from legal proceedings, the prospects for effective performance of the duties of highest office are dramatically enhanced by political experience. A constitutional requirement that the head of the executive branch be above a certain age reflects formal awareness of the need for some level of experience. But one can envision additional mechanisms seeking to ensure that the holders of highest office have had at least minimally adequate preparation for their responsibilities, including, for instance, a requirement that one cannot be the head of the executive branch without first holding other government positions for a certain number of years. Moreover, concerns about effective government push not only in favor of having more experienced politicians at the helm, but also in favor of having them at the helm for longer periods. Critics of electoral systems often point out that democratic decision-making is characterized by endemic short-sightedness, with politicians inevitably prioritizing short-term electoral gain over their country's long-term interests. One way to mitigate this worry is to have longer terms in office. Electing a president, for example, to serve a five- or seven-year term rather than a two-year term is a way of advancing effective government not only by ensuring that the president will be more experienced, but also by increasing the time horizon that is relevant for his or her electoral calculations.[6]

Why does all this matter here? The answer is simple. If effective government considerations militate in favor of more experienced

---

[6] This is not to say, of course, that the rigidity often associated with longer terms in office is devoid of costs or risks, or that the wisdom of having such terms is independent of broader institutional design choices, such as that between presidential and parliamentary systems. For one classic debate on these issues in comparative politics see Juan Linz, "Presidential or Parliamentary Democracy: Does It Make a Difference?" in Juan J. Linz and Arturo Valenzuela, (eds.), *The Crisis of Presidential Democracy: The Latin American Evidence* (Baltimore: Johns Hopkins University Press, 1994); Scott Mainwaring and Matthew Shugart, "Juan Linz, Presidentialism, and Democracy: A Critical Appraisal," *Comparative Politics* 29 (1997): 449–471.

politicians, who reach highest office at a reasonably advanced stage of their careers, and who can hold that office for a significant number of years (even allowing for term limits), then it follows that by the time the relevant politicians leave that office, they will likely be far from young. Add to this the slow pace of many legal proceedings, and it becomes even more probable that by the time the legal process has been completed, politicians taken to court once they have finished their term as head of the executive branch will simply be too old to be forced to face the consequences, even if they are found guilty.

The example of Jacques Chirac is a case in point. Chirac became president of France after more than thirty years in politics, during which he served as minister of agriculture, minister of the interior, mayor of Paris, and prime minister. Having served as president for twelve years, Chirac retired from politics in 2007, at the age of seventy-four. Because of France's executive immunity regime, it was only at that point that Chirac could be prosecuted for embezzlement of public funds and abuse of public confidence that had occurred in the 1990s, during his tenure as mayor of Paris. The legal process concluded with a conviction in December 2011, a few weeks after Chirac's seventy-ninth birthday.[7] This example is important for our purposes partly because the simple passage of time made it far too predictable that Chirac would be medically incapable of appearing in court.[8] Moreover, it was far from surprising that the court, explicitly citing Chirac's health and age, avoided sending him to prison, although Chirac was convicted of charges that could have seen him spend a decade behind bars. Insofar as Chirac's trajectory is representative of the trajectory we would expect of an experienced politician who rises to highest office, it suggests that executive immunity officially extended only to a person's term in office is not at all unlikely to become, effectively, immunity for life. But this probable consequence of executive immunity defies equality before the law to an extent that hardly anyone would want to defend.

---

[7] See *Associated Press*, "Jacques Chirac Found Guilty of Corruption," Dec. 15, 2011, at https://theguardian.com/world/2011/dec/15/jacques-chirac-guilty-corruption.

[8] The specific cause was a serious stroke that Chirac had suffered some years before, and which had generated "irreversible memory problems" (*Associated Press*, "Jacques Chirac Found Guilty of Corruption").

So far I have offered three considerations against the standard practice of executive immunity, pertaining to equality before the law, to stringent expectations of elected leaders, and to concerns associated with whether the law can really reach certain leaders once they leave office. The fourth and final consideration has to do with the fear of opportunistic lawsuits that makes executive immunity seem attractive. This fear, I believe, can be addressed through procedures that are much more minimalist, and that align much better with equality before the law and with our moral expectations of elected leaders, than wholesale executive immunity. One could imagine, for instance, a supreme court being tasked with the responsibility to review any lawsuit submitted against a sitting head of the executive branch, in order to determine whether the lawsuit bears on the public interest – paradigmatically, when it bears in some way or another on public property. When this is not the case – when the lawsuit has no meaningful bearing on the executive's public duties – the court may order that the case be heard only once the executive has left office.

Considering these claims, some may worry that my position is overlooking alternative institutional procedures, which can be combined with executive immunity. Suppose, for example, that instead of standard courts ensuring that the head of the executive branch is bound by the law, the legislature would be vested with broad powers of impeachment, to be used if the executive flagrantly violated the law. What would be wrong with such an alternative? What would be the problem with having the legislature act as a tribunal, instead of allowing regular lawsuits to be brought against a sitting head of government?[9]

My main answer is that there is no obvious reason why we should trust members of the legislature to behave more fairly in their tribunal capacity than we should trust ordinary citizens who may wish to launch lawsuits against the head of government. Members of the legislature who are contemplating impeachment inevitably find themselves considering a variety of political pressures. The revenge of a head of government who survives an impeachment attempt that legislators support is one obvious pressure, as is the promise of benefits from the head of government if they vote against impeachment. Partisan calculations focused on toppling an opposing party's government are another obvious factor. None of these factors, however, would be

---

[9] This is Isenbergh's proposal. See Isenbergh, *Impeachment*, passim.

equally germane in a case where ordinary citizens (or, for that matter, public servants) are deliberating whether to take the head of government to court. And if ordinary citizens let irrelevant considerations guide their conduct on such questions, the legal system can still put obstacles in their way, in the manner I proposed above, whereas it could not do so in the case of a legislature that has voted to impeach a president or prime minister.

3.2 Immunity for Elected Politicians (II): The Problem of Endemic Corruption

"But then the situation came to a head. Long-standing corruption – commonly practiced and commonly submitted to at every level as an unwritten rule but always in force among the most widely respected – came to the surface thanks to a sudden determination of the judiciary. The high-level crooks, who at first seemed few and so inexperienced that they were caught with their hands in the till, multiplied, became the true face of the management of the republic."

Elena Ferrante, *The Story of the Lost Child*[10]

If my arguments up to this point have been convincing, then, in morally normal circumstances, we should have serious doubts about an executive immunity regime. But what about morally *ab*normal circumstances? Here, I believe, executive immunity might have more of a role to play – though this role is still conditional and temporary.

It would be good to spell out precisely what "abnormal circumstances" I have in mind. Imagine a country where the overwhelming majority of elected politicians, in the executive as well as in the legislature, have been implicated in severe corruption scandals. To make things more concrete, imagine that there is serious evidence that the lion's share of the country's top elected representatives have been systematically abusing public funds and soliciting bribes surrounding government contracts. Whether to bring all of these elected representatives to trial is a difficult moral question, since such a step is very likely to trigger deep political and economic uncertainty. With the bulk of the country's political class in prison, who would be left to govern? The instability that is bound to result from such a political vacuum

---

[10] Elena Ferrante, *The Story of the Lost Child*, trans. by Ann Goldstein (New York: Europa Editions, 2015), at 432. Ferrante is referring here to the *Mani pulite* (clean hands) investigations that shook Italian politics in the early 1990s.

might very well have grave social and economic repercussions, which every sensible moral analysis has to take into account. That is why pervasive corruption can pose genuine moral dilemmas.

These dilemmas, it is worth stressing, are not merely theoretical constructs. They can arise in any country in which corruption has long been central to the political landscape. In fact, such dilemmas currently arise in some countries. Brazil provides what is probably the most dramatic example. The roots of Brazil's dilemma lie with a federal police investigation that started in 2014 with a focus on money laundering, and has since been expanding as multiple plea bargains reveal a corruption scandal of unprecedented proportions.[11] One focal point of the scandal is Petrobras, the state-owned oil company, whose contracts with multiple construction companies were massively inflated in exchange for huge bribes transferred by these companies to scores of senior politicians. Another focal point is the construction companies themselves – most notably Odebrecht, Latin America's biggest construction firm, which has been running an entire department devoted exclusively to bribing officials in order to secure inflated government contracts for dams, bridges, roads, and power plants. After Odebrecht's senior directors signed what has been dubbed an "end-of-the-world" plea bargain, the attorney general's office used their testimonies to refer charges against more than three hundred politicians to different levels of the judiciary. In March 2017, the list already featured "almost everyone who has had any power over the past 10 to 20 years," including, for example, "five members of the cabinet, two former presidents – Luiz Inacio Lula da Silva and Dilma Rousseff – the current and former heads of both houses of Congress and at least two former opposition leaders."[12] A year later, with Lula already sent to prison, the list continues to expand as more and more plea bargains are made.[13]

---

[11] See, e.g., Andrew Jacobs and Paula Moura, "At the Birthplace of a Graft Scandal, Brazil's Crisis Is on Full Display," *New York Times*, June 10, 2016, at https://nytimes.com/2016/06/11/world/americas/brazil-corruption-dilma-rousseff-operation-car-wash.html?_r=0.

[12] Jonathan Watts, "Brazil's Corruption Inquiry List Names All the Power Players – Except the President," *The Guardian*, Mar. 16, 2017, at https://theguardian.com/world/2017/mar/15/brazil-corruption-investigation-list-politicians-michel-temer.

[13] An essential part of the Brazilian corruption drama has to do with Lula personally, not only because of his tremendous popularity as president but also because, even behind bars, Lula was the front-runner in Brazil's 2018 presidential race – until the Supreme Court prohibited him from running. The

3.2 Immunity for Elected Politicians (II)

If all high-level Brazilian politicians implicated in corruption find themselves in prison, it is not at all obvious who will be left to govern the country. And this point is especially salient given that Brazil has been going through the worst recession in its history. The recession – one of the main causes of Rousseff's 2016 impeachment – saw the economy contracting almost 4 percent in 2015, and a further 3.6 percent in 2016. Notwithstanding a modest improvement in 2017, as of January 2018 more than one in every eight working-age Brazilians was unemployed.[14] Despite some optimism about long-term trends, the country still faces stark political and economic decisions, evident, for example, in government efforts to reform the pension system and to impose formal limitations on social spending that will bind future governments.[15] All of these facts seem to amplify the need for experienced politicians at the helm. But it currently appears

---

prime beneficiary has been Jair Bolsonaro, an extreme right-wing populist, who, at the time of writing, is set to be inaugurated as Brazil's president. Bolsonaro's case is complex enough to warrant independent analysis that I cannot provide here. I will only note parenthetically that from an integrity perspective, there would have been at the very least a *pro tanto* moral case in favor of prohibiting *both* Lula and Bolsonaro from running. In Lula's case his conviction for grand corruption would have been sufficient as a moral basis for such a prohibition (contra, for example, Jorge Castañeda, "Why Lula Should Be Allowed to Run for President," *New York Times*, Aug. 21, 2018). In Bolsonaro's case, his repeated celebration of Brazil's past military dictatorship would arguably provide a compelling moral ground for barring him from running (see, e.g., Carol Pires, "Brazil Flirts with a Return to the Dark Days," *New York Times*, Aug. 24, 2018; Cateno Veloso, "Dark Times Are Coming for My Country," *New York Times*, Oct. 24, 2018). More specifically, it is not, I believe, a trivial fact that Bolsonaro publicly dedicated his congressional vote to impeach former president Rousseff – who was tortured by the dictatorship – to the head of the military torture center (see, e.g., Jonathan Watts, "Dilma Rousseff Taunt Opens Old Wounds of Dictatorship Era's Torture in Brazil," *The Guardian*, Apr. 19, 2016, at https://theguardian.com/world/2016/apr/19/dilma-rousseff-impeachment-comments-torture-era-brazil-history). Together with other elements of his open contempt for rudimentary norms of liberal democracy, this appalling public posture seems to me to suffice to call into question the plausibility of allowing Bolsonaro to seek or hold a democracy's highest elected office. But I am aware that I cannot fully defend this claim here. For an insightful discussion of how democratic institutions might deal with those openly willing to destroy them from the inside, see Alexander Kirshner, *A Theory of Militant Democracy* (New Haven, CT: Yale University Press, 2014).

[14] See Trading Economics, "Brazil's Unemployment Rate," at https://tradingeconomics.com/brazil/unemployment-rate.

[15] See, e.g., United Nations, Human Rights, Office of the High Commissioner, "Brazil's 20-Year Public Expenditure Cap Will Breach Human Rights, UN

as if virtually all the experienced politicians on offer are implicated in massive corruption. What, then, is the right response to their apparent transgressions?

There is no easy way to solve this question. But I want to suggest that the property and integrity frameworks can nonetheless provide some distinctive answers. Let me start with the property side. First, if we follow the deep public ownership model developed in Chapter 2, then, *contra* the private aggregation model, we should be willing to treat public property as more than just the sum of private holdings: it is, rather, the property of the people as a collective agent. But if this is so, then we should think that the people as an owner enjoys a morally important *collective* freedom, which parallels a moral freedom we commonly attribute to individual owners: the owner's freedom to set back its own interests.

This claim is important here, because it points to an attractive solution to the question of how to handle pervasive political abuse of public property: let the people decide. The people should be directly involved, through one or multiple referenda, in decisions as to how to respond to pervasive corruption associated with its property.

If we understand public property rights in a strongly non-paternalistic manner, then it makes eminent sense, at least in manifestly non-ideal circumstances, to let the people make direct decisions about the response to pervasive political abuse of public property. For one thing, when a given agent's property is routinely abused, and when there are unusual risks involved in prosecuting the perpetrators, it is natural to design our response – at least to a significant extent – on the basis of the direct wishes of the property's owner.[16] Moreover, if we think about public property in a non-paternalistic manner, we should also accept risks that the people, as the owner of this property, is willing to take when responding to pervasive abuse of its property. If the people vote in a referendum to immediately pursue the full extent of the law against all

Expert Warns," Dec. 9, 2016, at http://ohchr.org/EN/NewsEvents/Pages/DisplayNews.aspx?NewsID=21006.

[16] The caveat "to a significant extent" is meant partly to acknowledge the fact that, in normal circumstances, it is often thought that criminal offenses should be prosecuted independently of the wishes of their direct individual victims. But one can acknowledge this point while also holding that in morally abnormal circumstances, some exceptions might be appropriate.

3.2 Immunity for Elected Politicians (II)

of the politicians who have abused public property, then, from a non-paternalistic viewpoint, this vote has considerable moral weight even if some may believe that it is imprudent. Although such a vote would involve serious risks to political and economic stability – and indeed, to the economic value of public property itself – the people would be acting within its rights as an owner if it would decide to assume these risks.[17]

Some readers may wonder whether the private aggregation model (which, after all, is perfectly compatible with a non-paternalistic conception of private property) can also support the referendum proposal. I believe that the answer is negative: the private aggregation model is incompatible with anything like a referendum on how to deal with pervasive corruption. The reason, in fact, is simple. Since, on this model, public property is nothing but the amalgamation of individual holdings, it follows that each citizen must enjoy the power to veto collective decisions as to how to handle abuse of public property. A referendum on how to handle pervasive corruption, then, could only work if it featured unanimity – meaning that it could not work at all. The deep public ownership model, in contrast, easily avoids this kind of dead end: nothing in the model commits us to any such veto. Decisions concerning public property, on this view, have to align – both procedurally and substantively – with some plausible interpretation of the equality of each citizen. But there is no reason why unanimity procedures have to feature in this requirement. A democratic majority would clearly do.

Bearing in mind this significant link between deep public ownership and the referendum proposal, we should also note a general advantage of the proposal. By involving the people directly in a decision on how to

---

[17] Recall here Rousseau's insistence: "A people is in any case always master to change its laws, even the best of them; for if it pleases to harm itself, who has the right to prevent it from doing so." Jean Jacques Rousseau, "The Social Contract," in Victor Gourevitch (ed.), *The Social Contract and Other Later Political Writings* (Cambridge: Cambridge University Press, 1997), Book 2, Chapter 12, 2. This seems to me a key part of the normative answer to empirically based skepticism about ordinary citizens' political competence. For one particularly trenchant form of such skepticism see Christopher Achen and Larry Bartels, *Democracy for Realists: Why Elections Do Not Produce Responsive Government* (Princeton, NJ: Princeton University Press, 2016). For sustained empirical criticism of Achen and Bartels's arguments, see the symposium on their book in *Critical Review* 30 (2018), especially Susan Stokes, "Accountability for Realists," *Critical Review* 30 (2018): 130–138.

handle pervasive corruption, we can sidestep (as much as is possible) a major obstacle toward curbing pervasive abuse of public property by top politicians: the fact that it is normally top politicians themselves who have to decide whether to seek comprehensive reforms. In a thoroughly corrupt system, those who hold high office have very likely been themselves the beneficiaries of corruption in the past, or, at the very least, have present ties to other politicians implicated in corruption and hopes of future gains from such ties. Hence to ask top politicians in a thoroughly corrupt system to push for reform of this very system is effectively to ask them to combat the norms that have very likely been integral to their own power, benefits, and prominence. We should rarely expect politicians to settle this "reformer's dilemma" in the direction of change.[18] In fact, it is far more likely that politicians will do everything they can to block reforms, as has been the case in Brazil,

[18] I borrow this phrase from Dennis Thompson, *The Persistence of Corruption* (unpublished manuscript). Some empirical political scientists emphasize a similar problem when criticizing the "agent-principal theory" that has long influenced economists' study of corruption. According to this theory, "corruption arises when a benevolent principal delegates decision-making power to a non-benevolent agent" (see Toke Aidt, "Economic Analysis of Corruption: A Survey," *Economic Journal* 113 [2003]: F632–F652, at F633), and so the natural solution to corruption is for the "benevolent" principal to alter the agent's incentive structure in such a way as to steer the latter away from corruption and toward societally efficient behavior. However, as the theory's critics point out, "in most systemically corrupt systems, one should take for granted that it is the actors at 'the top' who are the presumed principals who earn most of the 'rents' from corruption." (See Bo Rothstein and Aiysha Varraich, *Making Sense of Corruption* [Cambridge: Cambridge University Press, 2017], 19). The result, as Rothstein puts it elsewhere, is "a collective action problem of the second order. Why would agents that either stand to gain from corrupt practices or who can only lose by refraining from corruption at all be interested in creating such 'efficient' institutions?" (see Rothstein, "Anti-Corruption: The Indirect 'Big Bang' Approach," *Review of International Political Economy* 18 [2011] 228–250, at 235; see also Alina Mungiu-Pippidi, *The Quest for Good Governance: How Societies Develop Control of Corruption* [Cambridge: Cambridge University Press, 2015]; for a more optimistic view on the ability of individual leaders to inspire change see Robert Rotberg, *The Corruption Cure: How Citizens & Leaders Can Combat Graft* [Princeton NJ: Princeton University Press, 2017]). Bearing this debate in mind, it is important to stress that this book endorses an "agent-principal" approach only as a normative ambition, rather than as an empirical model. In particular, when I endorse Rousseau's insistence that elected leaders can only serve as "officers" of the sovereign people, rather than as sovereign themselves (as I did in Chapter 2), I am making a normative claim as to how the relationship between the people and its leaders ought to be structured. I am *not* making any

3.2 Immunity for Elected Politicians (II)

where multiple senior politicians have been accused of appointments aimed to stem police investigations, and where members of Congress have been openly discussing an amnesty law that will protect them from prosecution.[19] If reform is going to happen, it is much more likely to come from the people than from those who exercise direct control over reform decisions.

However, even if the referendum proposal has intuitive appeal, it requires further refinement in order to be compelling. The integrity framework, I believe, can provide the necessary refinement. We can start to see this contribution by noting the following point. In Chapter 1, I argued that one benefit of the integrity framework is that it organizes important intuitions concerning the relationship between the people in a liberal democracy and the promise of equality that is essential to a liberal legal system. By casting the legal realization of equal rights as an identity-grounding project for a liberal people, the integrity framework captures the conviction that a legal system that truly realizes equality is not something a people can enjoy simply as "manna from heaven." A legal system that fulfills the promise of equality, I said, requires continuous civic engagement.

This emphasis on civic engagement explains why the integrity framework aligns with the people deciding directly how to deal with pervasive corruption. After all, the collective egalitarian project at the heart of this framework ultimately points to the people: at bottom, this is the people's project, rather than the project of those who normally wield de facto political power. That is partly why, even in the best of circumstances, when elected leaders actually do their job of leading this collective effort, ordinary citizens ought not to treat active participation in this collective project as redundant. But this civic duty receives added weight once we step away from the "best of circumstances." In manifestly non-ideal circumstances, such as those of pervasive corruption, elected leaders do not advance the collective project of realizing equal rights through the law. Rather, elected leaders themselves pose a threat to this project. And when this is the case, it would be especially wrong of the people to simply leave elected representatives to sort things out. Such conditions amplify the people's duty to step in, and

---

empirical claim about how this relationship is actually structured in many real cases.

[19] Watts, "Brazil's Corruption Inquiry."

to actively shoulder some of the burden involved in the collective project of realizing equality.[20] Hence the collective integrity framework supports the thought that the people should decide directly, through a referendum, how exactly to respond to problems such as pervasive political corruption.

However, while the integrity framework supports the referendum proposal, it also helps us to refine this proposal in a way that incorporates two important intuitions. First, as a general matter, we would not want the people to replace an actual judge or jury in deciding the legal fate of politicians charged with abusing public office for private gain. It would be disturbing if the people literally set the verdict (or the sentence) of politicians accused of corruption. Second, more specifically, there is also the intuition that it would be disturbing for the people to simply let elected leaders "off the hook" – to have the legal system entirely overlook these leaders' transgressions.

In turn, what is underlying both of these intuitions is the same familiar principle emphasized above – equality before the law. The integrity framework, moreover, not only casts this principle as pivotal to a liberal democracy's collective project. The demands of integrity also mean that even in extreme circumstances, where some deviation from this principle might be warranted, it is morally imperative to keep this deviation as minimal as possible. In particular, the idea of steadfastness that I have been associating with the integrity framework – the willingness to incur costs for the sake of our principles – helps us see why it would be wrong for the people to simply decide to erase all charges against a senior elected politician, or – to consider again the other extreme – to try suspect politicians directly. A society cannot be genuinely committed to the rule of law, and to equality before the law, if it is willing to simply abandon these commitments whenever living up to them is inconvenient. But precisely such abandonment is what

---

[20] One recent case in point is the massive anti-corruption demonstrations in South Korea (2016–2017), which were essential in the impeachment of President Park Geun-hye. See, e.g., Anna Fifield, "South Koreans Gather en Masse to Protest against President," *Washington Post*, Nov. 12, 2016, at https://washingtonpost.com/world/south-koreans-gather-en-masse-for-protest-against-president/2016/11/12/602cf658-a85c-11e6-ba46-53db57f0e351_story.html?utm_term=.57e300c3d6d1; Choe Sang-Hun, "South Korea Removes President Park Geun-hye," *New York Times*, Mar. 10, 2017, at https://nytimes.com/2017/03/09/world/asia/park-geun-hye-impeached-south-korea.html?mtrref=www.google.com.

3.2 Immunity for Elected Politicians (II)

happens when a society is willing to have (often extremely unpopular) politicians be tried directly by the people, or when it is willing to remove all criminal charges against politicians that it deems "too important" or "too popular" to face trial. In both of these cases, insisting on fidelity to the principles of the rule of law and equality before the law may very well be costly, and even painful. But such insistence, to repeat, is a key part of what acting with integrity means.

Given all this, we can draw a fairly direct line from the integrity framework to the two intuitions I just noted. We can use the integrity framework to buttress our conviction that elected leaders facing legal charges should undergo the same procedure as ordinary citizens: just as we would want ordinary citizens facing legal charges to be tried in a court of law rather than by the people, we should aim for elected leaders to be tried in the same fashion. And we can similarly use the integrity framework to support the thought that it would be wrong for the people to have the law ignoring grave, systematic transgressions committed by elected leaders, insofar as such transgressions would never be ignored if committed by ordinary citizens.

How can we structure a referendum proposal that incorporates these integrity concerns associated with equality before the law? In order to see the answer, note first that virtually any feasible referendum proposal on a topic of political significance features a limited set of options for the citizenry to vote on. A workable referendum cannot accommodate an endless array of policy choices: there always has to be a fairly fixed menu for the public to choose from. Moreover, since the matter at hand ultimately involves legal proceedings, it seems natural to task a part of the legal system with setting the parameters of a referendum on how to deal with pervasive political corruption. For illustrative purposes, let us suppose that the attorney general's office, in some special capacity, would be responsible for this task. In line with the points made above, the Attorney General should not provide citizens the option of "clearing" the record of any politician from corruption charges. Yet the attorney general's office can and should give citizens the ability to defer the commencement of legal proceedings against elected representatives. This means that a referendum would feature, in the simplest case, two options. Citizens would choose whether legal authorities immediately bring all relevant politicians to trial, or whether legal proceedings pertaining to each politician are to be postponed until this politician leaves office. Alternatively, we could envision specific additional options: for instance, alongside these two alternatives, citizens may be presented with a third option, under which legal authorities would bring to immediate trial only those politicians whose alleged crimes occurred within a certain time frame (say, the previous ten years).

Of course, further variants are also conceivable. But my aim here is not to give a complete specification of the referendum proposal. The finer details may be impossible to settle in abstraction from the precise features of the particular corruption problem to which the relevant referendum is meant to respond. Nonetheless, I hope that even this broader outline of the proposal suffices to give a sense of how it might work, and of how it could incorporate the property and the integrity intuitions highlighted above.[21]

Before moving to the next stage of our inquiry, it may be useful to note one more comparative advantage of the referendum proposal. The best way to see this advantage is to return to the case of Brazil yet again. As the country's enormous corruption scandal has unfolded, Brazilian media has been debating the degree to which legal authorities are being selective with regard to which politicians they are charging with corruption, with regard to the timing of pressing charges, and with regard to their determination to impose immediate sanctions.[22] Debates of this kind are important to bear in mind, because they alert us to the

---

[21] One natural way to add further details to the proposal would be to examine debates surrounding the policy issues regarding which referenda are typically held – especially the creation of new states and constitutions, and the transfer of core government powers to either subnational or supranational institutions. (For a comprehensive survey, see Stephen Tierney, *Constitutional Referendums: The Theory and Practice of Republican Deliberation* [Oxford: Oxford University Press, 2012]). Here I will only point out that it seems clear that once a referendum is held, it is seriously wrong of politicians to simply ignore its results – no matter how much the substantive verdict reached by the referendum may be morally misguided. This point constrains politicians' options in cases as different from one another as the Brexit vote in the UK, and the FARC peace agreement vote in Colombia. In future work, I hope to say more about the many moral complexities of such cases. For some of the relevant issues, see Christine Bell, "Lex Pacificatoria Colombiana: Colombia's Peace Accord in Comparative Perspective," *American Journal of International Law* 110 (2016): 165–171; Ron Levy, "Shotgun Referendums: Popular Deliberation and Constitutional Settlement in Conflict Societies," *Melbourne University Law Review* 41, No. 3 (2018) available at https://papers.ssrn.com/sol3/papers.cfm?abstract_id=3182298.

[22] Thus for example, in late 2016, Renan Calheiros, the former head of the Brazilian Senate, refused to obey an order from a Supreme Court justice to step down while he was being investigated. The full Court, however, chose not to punish Calheiros; instead, the Court only announced that Calheiros, despite

3.3 Pardons

simple fact that in the delicate circumstances of pervasive corruption, *someone* has to decide whether and how fears regarding political and economic stability should lead us to deviate from applying the normal workings of the law to suspect politicians. Yet it is surely morally better for the people to decide in a transparent process whether such deviation is warranted than it is for legal officials to informally arrogate to themselves the right to make this momentous decision in an opaque manner and without any kind of formal mandate from the people.

3.3 Pardons

"The right of pardoning or exempting the guilty from a penalty imposed by the law and pronounced by the judge belongs only to the authority which is superior to both judge and law, i.e., the Sovereign; each its right in this matter is far from clear, and the cases for exercising it are extremely rare. In a well-governed State, there are few punishments, not because there are many pardons, but because criminals are rare; it is when a State is in decay that the multitude of crimes is a guarantee of impunity . . . Frequent pardons mean that crime will soon need them no longer . . . But I feel my heart protesting and restraining my pen; let us leave these questions to the just man who has never offended, and would himself stand in no need of pardon."

Rousseau, *The Social Contract*, Book 2, Chapter 5, para. 7

Having examined how the collective integrity and property frameworks might bear on circumstances of pervasive corruption, let me now turn to the practice of government pardons. Pardons bear on the

---

being head of the Senate, had to give up his place in the succession line to the presidency (see Associated Press, *"Brazil's Top Court Overturns Ban on Senate Head Renan Calheiros,"* Dec. 8, 2016, https://theguardian.com/world/2016/d ec/08/brazils-top-court-overturns-ban-on-senate-head-renan-calheiros). This lenient approach may well have stemmed from Calheiros's central role in pushing for economic changes to combat the ballooning government deficit. On the other end, in some cases legal officials have also been accused of excessive determination to convict senior politicians, even if this means deviating from due process. See, e.g., Alex Cudaros, "The Rot at the Heart of Brazil's Anti-Corruption Crusade," *The Atlantic*, Feb. 2, 2018, at https://theatlantic.com/in ternational/archive/2018/02/brazil-lula-carwash-corruption-temer-due-pro cess-dilma/552056/. It should be clear at this point that collective integrity rules out such deviations, even in cases where they could very well lead to considerable deterrence gains.

abuse of political power when considering those who issue them, and when considering those who benefit from them. Pardons may be issued in response to past abuses of power by those who previously held power. But, equally importantly, the pardoning power itself may be abused by those who wield it.

Considering both of these phenomena, I advance three claims with regard to the practice of pardons. First, there are weighty reasons against the very existence of government pardons, which mean that, at the very least, their scope should be extremely limited (3.3.1). Second, there are especially weighty reasons against vesting any single person with an unaccountable power to pardon, particularly when this person is the head of the executive branch (3.3.2). This means, for example, that the unaccountable power of the president of the United States to issue pardons is morally dangerous. Finally, building on these arguments, I turn to discuss pardons given to former elected leaders (3.3.3). Taking the pardon given to Richard Nixon following Watergate as my key example, I argue that such pardons undermine, rather than protect, the dignity of highest office.

3.3.1 General Objections to the Practice of Pardons

Let me start with some general doubts about the very practice of pardoning. A pardon constitutes an external, irregular intervention in the workings of the legal system. To reduce or remove a sentence that has been imposed upon someone who was convicted following due legal process, is to disturb the integrity of that process in a way that is at least prima facie suspicious, especially since pardons typically cannot be appealed once given. How, then, can the practice of pardons be justified?

The most familiar argument for the practice is reflected in Rousseau's invocation of "the heart": pardons provide an easy way – even if one to be taken only rarely – to extend mercy to those convicted of a crime. "The criminal code of every country," as Hamilton put it in the *Federalist Papers*, ". . . partakes so much of necessary severity that without an easy access to exceptions in favor of unfortunate guilt, justice would wear a countenance too sanguinary and cruel."[23]

---

[23] Alexander Hamilton, *The Federalist Papers: No. 74*, Mar. 25, 1788 at http://avalon.law.yale.edu/18th_century/fed74.asp.

3.3 Pardons

This may seem like an intuitive argument. But it encounters at least two obvious problems. First, there are multiple stages preceding the granting of a pardon, in which lenience can be introduced into the legal process itself. Thus, for instance, the prosecution may avoid pressing the most severe charges against a defendant, or avoid asking for the most severe penalties against a defendant who has been convicted. A judge, in turn, also may show lenience when sentencing. Similarly, the appeal procedure internal to the standard workings of the judicial process can be used to seek more lenience from the law. These points suggest that, at minimum, there should be a very strong presumption in favor of forbidding pardon requests prior to the exhaustion of standard legal procedures. Second, if, despite these procedures, the legal system frequently metes out sentences that are deemed overly harsh, the main way to address this issue is not through the institution of a pardon, but through reform of the legal system.[24]

Consider, then, another argument in favor of the practice of pardons. Some activities that trigger criminal prosecution and conviction at a given point in time may come, at a much later point in time, to be seen as far from criminal due to changes in both societal values and the legal code. The practice of pardons allows a swift and easy resolution to such cases: by pardoning someone convicted of a past unjust law, we are able to restore some of the moral balance, even if the damage that was done can never be fully repaired.

The main difficulty with this argument is that when the relevant laws are clearly profoundly unjust, it makes more sense to declare these laws, and the convictions associated with them, to be void, than it does to pardon the convicted. After all, to accept a pardon means to admit guilt, but if the relevant laws are profoundly unjust, then it seems mistaken to expect that those convicted of violating these laws will admit any guilt; if anything, we should expect the government to admit the mistakes of past laws through some form of apology. Thus for instance, when the British government announced at the end of 2016 that thousands of gay and bisexual men would be pardoned for violating homophobic laws decades earlier, some of the pardon's intended

---

[24] This is perhaps most obvious in the context of capital punishment. Rather than having pardons as a "safety valve" preventing executions, it makes much more sense to prohibit capital punishment altogether.

beneficiaries reasonably insisted that what they sought was an apology rather than a pardon.[25]

Let us consider one more argument in favor of pardons. A convict's attempts to appeal a verdict or a sentence can often be complicated, lengthy, and costly. This fact is especially significant when a convict's economic resources are limited, and when the costs of the relevant legal process are considerable. Hence it makes sense to have pardon requests as a tool that is at least sometimes available to the less well-off, who do not have the resources to utilize the full range of options internal to the legal system. Rather than undermining the legal system, the practice of pardons may advance its core values by helping to achieve greater de facto equality before the law – balancing out the inevitable advantages that the better-off enjoy with regard to access to legal services.

One response to this argument is that here as well, the main focus should be on changes that are internal to the standard workings of the legal system, rather than on pardons functioning as a "deus ex machina." Most importantly, convicts seeking to appeal a verdict or a sentence should be able to rely on a robust public defender system: if they cannot afford the costs of the appeal process, there should nonetheless be adequate legal services, funded by the public, available to them.

Another response is that a pardoning mechanism may turn out to deepen, rather than mitigate, inequality before the law. Even if such a mechanism provides to the less well-off some legal possibilities that may normally be available only to the affluent, it also provides the affluent with further avenues through which they may translate their resources into protection from the law. Most obviously, the affluent may try to effectively purchase pardons by contributing to the finances of those politicians with the power to issue them.[26] The complexity of

---

[25] Thus one of the intended beneficiaries noted: "To accept a pardon means you accept that you were guilty. I was not guilty of anything. I was only guilty of being in the wrong place at the wrong time." Quoted in "'Alan Turing Law': Thousands of Gay Men to Be Pardoned," *BBC News*, Oct. 20, 2016, at http://bbc.com/news/uk-37711518.

[26] President Bill Clinton famously had to face accusations of this nature surrounding his pardon of businessman Marc Rich in the final hours of his second term. See, e.g., Jessica Taylor, "More Surprises: FBI Releases Files on Bill Clinton's Pardon of Marc Rich," *NPR*, Nov. 1, 2016 at www.npr.org/2016/11/01/500297580/more-surprises-fbi-releases-files-on-bill-clintons-pardon-of-marc-rich.

3.3 Pardons

detecting, proving, and punishing such deals should, at the very least, cause us to be skeptical about the egalitarian benefits of the institution of pardons.

3.3.2 Pardons as a Presidential Prerogative?

The concerns about due process and equality before the law, which I have associated with the idea of collective integrity, underlie the arguments I have just offered against the very existence of pardons. But I now want to use other aspects of the collective integrity framework – as well as the collective property framework – to discuss another issue surrounding pardons. Almost one hundred and thirty active constitutional schemes around the world currently feature pardoning mechanisms.[27] Realistically, one should expect at least some such mechanisms to endure into the future. We should therefore ask not only whether the practice of pardons makes moral sense. We should also ask how the practice should be structured, assuming, realistically, that (in some way or another) it is here to stay.

The collective property and collective integrity frameworks yield some powerful answers. In particular, both frameworks alert us to the need to keep pardoning privileges away from the hands of individuals who hold highest office. A historical perspective will help us see the rationale for this conclusion.

Historically, pardoning powers rested exclusively with the individual who stood above the legal system – the monarch. The power to pardon was the monarch's prerogative, to be exercised at his (or, less commonly, her) discretion without any need for justification. As Kathleen Moore puts it,

> The pardoning power of the great monarchs of seventeenth and eighteenth century Europe was analogous in theory and practice to divine grace. Like grace, the freely given, unearned gift of divine favor, a royal pardon was thought of as a personal gift. Therefore, it required no justification and was not subject to criticism. As personal favors, acts of beneficence, and benevolence, pardons were beyond the reach of both positive and moral law. Thus, pardons could be granted for any reason whatsoever or for no reason at all.[28]

---

[27] See Constitute Project, "Pardon" at https://constituteproject.org/search?lang=en&q=pardon.

[28] Kathleen Moore, "Pardon for Good and Sufficient Reasons," *University of Richmond Law Review* 27 (1993): 281–288, at 282. See also Moore's *Pardons: Justice, Mercy, and the Public Interest* (Oxford: Oxford University Press, 1989).

The monarchs repeatedly made strategic use of their "divine grace," so as to serve their political and economic needs. Thus Moore continues:

> The monarchs used "gifts of grace" to reward their friends and undermine their enemies, to populate their colonies, to man their navies, to raise money, and to quell rebellions. Unusual only in the price he charged, James II sold pardons for 16,000 pounds sterling, of which he received "one half and the other half was divided among the two ladies then most in favour."[29]

These conventions regarding the monarch's pardoning powers stemmed, both directly and indirectly, from the monarch's *sovereign* status. For one thing, the monarch could override the legal system's decisions because, as sovereign, this system was subordinate to his or her will. Furthermore, the monarch's "prerogative of mercy" would naturally apply to crimes committed against the state, because as sovereign, the monarch, to paraphrase Louis the Fourteenth, *was* the state. This equivalence between the state and the person of the monarch explains why, since the middle ages, a crime against the state was known as "high crime," "in respect of the royall majesty against whom it was committed."[30] And this equivalence also explains why it was so common for monarchs to sell pardons, especially when the pardons concerned crimes related to state property. Since, as sovereign, the monarch was the owner of state property (theft of such property long being recognized as one of the "high crimes"), the monarch could issue pardons "forgiving" violations of "his" property rights, for the right price.

Unsurprisingly, the ideas that I have been emphasizing regarding the people's integrity and the people's property point in a very different direction. After all, if we follow the collective integrity framework, we should see the legal system as the creation of – and as subordinate to – the sovereign *people* rather than any monarch. Similarly, if we follow the public property framework, then we should insist that state property belongs to no 'elevated' individual, but to the people as a whole. These ideas in turn mean that pardoning, including pardoning for abuses of state property, should not be a prerogative available to a

---

[29] Moore, *Pardon for Good and Sufficient Reasons*, 282.
[30] Edward Coke, *Institutes of the Laws of England; Concerning High Treason and Other Pleas of the Crown* (London, W. Clarke & Sons, 1817), quoted in Isenbergh, IMPEACHMENT, 68.

3.3 Pardons

single individual who is supposedly interchangeable with the state, but rather should be collectivized as much as possible.

There is a sense in which this collectivist sentiment should be obvious. It is hard to reconcile basic democratic impulses with the idea of a single person being able to override the legal process and release suspects or convicts from the full reach of the law, irrevocably, simply at his or her own discretion. And it is especially hard to see how a democratic ethos can be reconciled with the most powerful person in the land enjoying such discretion.

It is striking, then, that this is precisely the situation that the American constitution creates with regard to the president's pardoning powers. According to the constitution, the president may grant "reprieves and pardons for offenses against the United States, except in cases of impeachment."[31] The constitution sets no further limits on the president's pardoning powers, nor does it subject pardoning decisions to any kind of formal oversight by any other branch. Even more strikingly, up until the 1920s, the US Supreme Court treated the president's pardoning power as "akin to the divine or royal prerogative,"[32] understanding presidential pardons as a personal "act of grace."[33]

Of course, unlike a monarch, a president who clearly abused the pardoning privilege would risk his or her own impeachment. Yet this fact should not be too much of a comfort. For one thing, as several jurists have noted, this risk is much less salient when a president is just about to leave office – the time when a disproportional share of presidential pardons are issued.[34] Moreover, it seems plausible to think

---

[31] US Constitution, Article II, Section 2.
[32] Moore, *Pardon for Good and Sufficient Reasons*, 283.
[33] Compare *Biddle v. Perovich*, 274 US 480 (1927) to *United States v. Wilson*, 32 US (1 Pet.) 150, 160 (1833). See also Carolyn Strange, *Discretionary Justice: Pardon and Parole in New York from the Revolution to the Depression* (New York: New York University Press, 2016). In the court's defense, this "royalist" understanding of the president's pardoning powers was consonant with an important strand of American constitutional thought that stretched all the way back to the revolutionary era. See Eric Nelson, *The Royalist Revolution: Monarchy and the American Founding* (Cambridge, MA: Harvard University Press, 2014).
[34] See, for example, the symposium on "Suspending the Pardon Power during the Twilight of a Presidential Term," in *Missouri Law Review* 67 (2002). The awarding of presidential pardons just before leaving office has in fact become so widespread that the media often treats a president's final days in office as the natural time to call for pardons. See, e.g., "Editorial: Mr. Obama, Pick Up Your

that there are cases where a pardon is seriously troubling, yet is nonetheless unlikely to lead to impeachment of a sitting president.

Furthermore, in thinking about the implications of the president's pardoning power, it is also important to extend our gaze beyond the president himself or herself. One result of giving the president the power to single-handedly issue pardons is that members of the president's administration might very well expect to be pardoned if they run into legal troubles in the course of advancing the administration's agenda. As a result, such members may be more willing to act in contravention of the authority of other branches of government, to abuse their office, and, in various cases, to direct public resources to serve the administration's plans against the explicit instructions of other branches of government acting within their authority. One example of such dangers is the Iran-Contra scandal of the late 1980s, which saw several senior members of the Reagan administration engineering – against Congress's explicit instructions – illegal arms trade with the Iranian regime and illegal use of public funds to advance the administration's anti-communist agenda in Nicaragua. All of these senior officials – including Reagan's defense secretary – were pardoned by Reagan's vice president during the scandal, and later President George H. W. Bush, weeks before Bush left office. This pardon was predictable, not least because it made it "impossible to pursue already-developed plans to investigate Bush himself in greater detail."[35]

Another example is the efforts of several senior members of Richard Nixon's administration – including Nixon's chief of staff, his chief domestic advisor, and the White House counsel – to convince Nixon to issue pardons or formal immunities from prosecution, which would protect them from legal repercussions of their involvement in attempts to cover up the Watergate scandal.[36] Here as well, the presidential pardoning power encouraged those working on the president's behest

---

Pardon Pen," *New York Times*, Jan. 16, 2017, at https://nytimes.com/2017/01/16/opinion/mr-obama-pick-up-your-pardon-pen.html.

[35] Malcolm Byrne, "The Iran-Contra Affair 30 Years Later: A Milestone in Post-Truth Politics," *National Security Archive*, Nov. 25, 2016, at http://nsarchive.gwu.edu/NSAEBB/NSAEBB567-Iran-Contra-Reagan-Oliver-North-and-Post-Truth-30-years-later/.

[36] "The Administration: The Fallout from Ford's Rush to Pardon," *Time*, Sep. 23, 1974, at http://content.time.com/time/magazine/article/0,9171,908732-8,00.html.

to "go above the written law,"[37] to abuse public resources and their public office.

What, then, is the solution? The answer should be clear, at least if we follow the collective integrity and collective property frameworks. Ultimate pardoning decisions, if they are to remain available at all, should be made, not by a single individual who sits at the head of the executive branch, but by a collective body that is as far removed as possible from executive power. A distinct government agency with the sole power to grant, deny, and revoke pardons (as is the case in Canada, for example), is preferable to vesting the pardoning power in the Office of the President. This conclusion is supported both by concrete practical reasons, and by more symbolic considerations. At the practical level, a distinct agency featuring a collective body overseeing pardons significantly reduces the potential for abuse of the pardoning mechanism. This is because the likelihood of a quid pro quo between the pardoning authority and its beneficiaries diminishes considerably when that authority is not a single person. At the symbolic level, vesting pardoning powers in a collective body removed from executive control means stepping as far away as possible from the disturbing image of a single powerful person who may decide the fates of others on a personal whim, in the manner of an emperor.

3.3.3 Pardoning Former Elected Leaders

Let me now turn to one last question surrounding pardons: how should we think about pardons given to former heads of government? In considering this question, it is worth distinguishing between different contexts in which it may arise.

One context in which a pardon to former heads of government may seem like an attractive idea is in circumstances featuring a profound transformation of the entire political system – for instance, when a military dictatorship is replaced with a democratic system. I take up this complex issue in 3.4. But prior to doing so, I want to use the

---

[37] The phrase comes from the congressional testimony of a participant in the Iran-Contra cover-up efforts. See Dan Morgan and Walter Pincus, "Hall Testifies of Necessity 'To Go above Written Law,'" *Washington Post*, Jun. 10, 1987, at www.washingtonpost.com/wp-srv/local/longterm/tours/scandal/fawnhall.htm.

collective property and integrity frameworks to examine other contexts where pardoning former senior officials – and especially a former head of government – may seem appropriate.

To get a sense of the contexts I have in mind, consider the reasoning underlying one of the most dramatic pardoning decisions of the twentieth century: the "full, free and absolute pardon" that President Ford gave his predecessor, Richard Nixon, in September 1974, in the immediate aftermath of the Watergate scandal.[38] Over time, prominent journalists and politicians have come to think that this pardon was justified. "I concluded," Bob Woodward, for example, said, "that the pardon was the right thing for Ford to do – the sensible thing to do – and the courageous thing to do."[39] In May 2001 Ford was honored with a Profile in Courage Award at the John F. Kennedy Library in Boston. In the event, Senator Edward Kennedy noted that he had originally opposed the pardon, "but time has a way of clarifying things, and now we see that President Ford was right. His courage and dedication to our country made it possible for us to begin the process of healing and put the tragedy of Watergate behind us."[40] As a *New York*

---

[38] Presidential Proclamation 4311 of Sept. 8, 1974 (President Gerald R. Ford granting a pardon to Richard M. Nixon), Record Group 11: General Records of the United States Government, 1778–1992; NARA, Washington, DC. (ARC #194597); "Text of President Ford's Pardon Proclamation" available at http://watergate.info/1974/09/08/text-of-ford-pardon-proclamation.html.

[39] See Woodward's remarks in Tian Lee, "Woodward: President Ford Knew What Needed to Be Done," Gerald R. Ford Library and Museum 25th Anniversary, *The University Record Online*, University of Michigan, Apr. 10, 2006, at http://ur.umich.edu/0506/Apr10_06/05.shtml.

[40] Quoting these remarks, Tom De Frank wrote in 2014: "It took a generation of hindsight, in fact, for the country to embrace the notion that the pardon was the right thing to do for the good of the country, even though it cost Ford dearly." See Tom De Frank, "Gerald Ford's Pardon of Nixon Doomed His Political Future. But It Cemented His Legacy," *National Journal*, Sept. 7, 2014, at https://nationaljournal.com/s/620111/gerald-fords-pardon-nixon-doomed-his-political-future-cemented-his-legacy. Stephen Carter reflected a similar sentiment when arguing that "although it was politically wrenching at the time, President Ford, in retrospect, probably made the right decision in 1974 . . . although our national anger seemed to demand punishment for Nixon's crimes, Ford believed that in the long run, the national interest would be better served by enabling the ex-President to avoid prosecution, leaving him untouched by legal proceedings that would otherwise have kept alive our national obsession with Watergate, which, in retrospect, it was plainly time to put aside" (Stephen Carter, *Integrity* [New York: Harper, 1996], 50). Below I will dispute this claim using the notion of steadfastness that I borrowed from Carter himself in Chapter 1.

3.3 Pardons

Times obituary noted upon Ford's death in 2006, "the pardon, intensely unpopular at the time, came to be generally viewed as correct."[41] A 2014 article in the *Wall Street Journal* went so far as to argue that "now there's almost universal agreement that Ford was right."[42]

In my view, however, there was no justification for this shift in the pardon's perception: Nixon ought not to have been pardoned. Ford offered three main justifications for his pardoning of Nixon. Yet I believe that, with the help of the collective integrity and collective property frameworks, we can dispute all three. Let me consider each in turn, in ascending order of significance.

First, Ford argued that "Richard Nixon and his loved ones have suffered enough," disputing "the propriety of exposing to further punishment and degradation a man who has already paid the unprecedented penalty of relinquishing the highest elective office of the United States."[43] The collective integrity framework, however, shows precisely why such "further punishment" was appropriate: this framework, as I emphasized above, leads us to be more, not less strict in our requirements of those who hold highest office. And there is nothing in Nixon's story that justified deviation from this principle. The simple fact that he had to relinquish the presidency did not, by itself, provide such a justification. Imagine, by way of comparison, a person who had to resign from the chairmanship of a prestigious major firm due to revelations of severe crimes in which he participated as head of the firm. Suppose that his victims sought to bring the former chairman to trial. Would we really say that his forced resignation was an adequate substitute for a trial? Would we really say that the former chairman's having to relinquish the power, privileges and status of his position was "punishment enough?" The answer is surely not. But if

---

[41] James Naughton and Adam Clymer, "Gerald Ford, 38th President, Dies at 93," *New York Times*, Dec. 27, 2006, at http://nytimes.com/2006/12/27/washington/27webford.html.

[42] Ken Gormley and David Shribman, "The Nixon Pardon at 40: Ford Looks Better Than Ever," *The Wall Street Journal,* Sep. 5, 2014, at https://wsj.com/articles/ken-gormley-and-david-shribman-the-nixon-pardon-at-40-ford-looks-better-than-ever-1409955912. Gormley and Shribman also cite shifts in public opinion polls regarding the pardon, as proof that "it is now clear that Richard Nixon is not the only president to have been pardoned. In a gesture that is one part generosity and one part perspective, Americans seem to have pardoned Gerald Ford as well."

[43] See Ford's speech, announcing his pardoning of Nixon, "President Gerald R. Ford Pardoning Richard Nixon," Sep. 8, 1974, The History Place: Great Speeches Collection at http://historyplace.com/speeches/ford.htm.

we will not say this to the victims of a private person's crimes, why should we speak differently when the relevant crimes are committed by the holder of highest office in his public capacity?[44]

Moreover, we can use the public property framework to further support the same conclusion. This framework draws our attention to an aspect of the Watergate scandal that is often overlooked: the fact that it involved a manifest and sustained abuse of public resources. This is perhaps clearest in the case of the significant hours that administration officials, paid by the public, devoted over an extended period of time not to the public interest, but rather to breaking the law to advance Nixon's "imperial presidency," with the president's knowledge and (apparently) active support. Now imagine that these abused, publicly funded hours could have been calculated, and that a court could have obliged the former president to pay to the US treasury even a portion of the costs of these hours. If this could be done – if Nixon could have been held legally accountable for systematic abuse of significant public resources to serve his illegal ends – it would seem even less plausible to argue that the circumstances of his resignation provided sufficient punishment. And while there may have been a whole slew of obstacles toward actually holding Nixon accountable for this particular wrong, it does strengthen the moral case against the pardon that protected Nixon from the reach of the law.

Let us move, then, to Ford's second argument. Ford claimed that pardoning Nixon would spare American society and the American political system a divisive and distracting trial. Defending the pardon decision before the House of Representatives in October 1974, Ford said:

The purpose I had for granting the pardon when I did . . . was to change our national focus. I wanted to do all I could to shift our attentions from the

---

[44] Ford also presented another kind of individual desert argument: "A former President of the United States," he claimed, "instead of enjoying equal treatment with any other citizen accused of violating the law, would be cruelly and excessively penalized either in preserving the presumption of his innocence or in obtaining a speedy determination of his guilt in order to repay a legal debt to society" ("President Gerald R. Ford Pardoning Richard Nixon," at www.historyplace.com/speeches/ford.htm). Yet this is an even weaker argument. There is simply no plausible connection between equality before the law and the idea of pardoning someone for his criminal abuses of the most powerful public office in the land. Nor is it plausible to suggest that a former president of the United States is bound to be discriminated against in criminal proceedings because he is a former president.

3.3 Pardons

pursuit of a fallen president to the pursuit of the urgent needs of a rising nation. Our nation is under the severest of challenges now to employ its full energies and efforts in the pursuit of a sound and growing economy at home and a stable and peaceful world around us. We would needlessly be diverted from meeting those challenges if we as a people were to remain sharply divided over whether to indict, bring to trial, and punish a former president.[45]

This rationale too suffers from multiple problems. One problem is that it is not obvious how precisely a Nixon trial would have "diverted" political energies from ongoing public policy tasks. In what way exactly would have a Nixon trial prevented Congress or the White House from pursuing sound economic or foreign policies? In what ways would have such a trial detracted from the "energies" of these branches of government? The task of handling a Nixon trial would have surely rested first and foremost – if not exclusively – with the judicial branch. Why would such a trial necessarily have a serious effect on the "energies" of the other branches of government?

Another problem has to do with the aforementioned demand – central to the integrity framework – that a society's legal system speak with one voice. Insofar as a presidential pardon constitutes a direct intervention in the workings of the legal system, the president's pardoning decisions, just like the system itself, ought to speak with one voice. But this intuitive principle, in turn, undermines Ford's claim that intense political disagreement justified pardoning Nixon. Ford, after all, refused to pardon Vietnam draft dodgers, a topic on which the general public was divided to a much greater extent. Similarly, if Ford thought that the general public was divided about Watergate to a degree that warranted presidential pardons to the culprits, then why did he refuse to pardon the multiple members of Nixon's staff involved in the scandal?[46]

---

[45] See "Gerald R. Ford's Statement before Subcommittee on Criminal Justice" (Washington, DC: Office of the White House Press Secretary Oct. 17, 1974) available at https://gilderlehrman.org/sites/default/files/inline-pdfs/t-02109.pdf.

[46] Ford's press secretary, who resigned in protest following the pardon, wrote to him accordingly: "As your spokesman, I do not know how I could credibly defend that action in the absence of a like decision to grant absolute pardon to the young men who evaded Vietnam military service as a matter of conscience and the absence of pardons for former aides and associates of Mr. Nixon who have been charged with crimes – and imprisoned – stemming from the same Watergate situation." Quoted in Bruce Weber, "J. F. terHorst, Ford Press

The most likely answer, I believe, takes us directly to Ford's third justification for pardoning Nixon: an end to a national trauma. Ford's famous statement upon accepting the presidency – "our long national nightmare is over"[47] – clearly reflected this understanding of Watergate, as did his speech, several weeks later, announcing his decision to pardon Nixon: "I cannot prolong the bad dreams that continue to reopen a chapter that is closed."[48] At the heart of the national nightmare, as Ford saw it, was the profound damage that Watergate caused to the dignity of the office of the president. Thus the fact that Nixon was "already ... condemned to suffer long and deeply" for Watergate was not really a salient consideration in favor of pardoning him. Rather, it was the fact that Nixon was condemned to suffer in this way, as Ford put it, "in the shame and disgrace *brought upon the office he held.*"[49]

This appeal to the dignity of the presidency was, I believe, the most significant argument that could have been offered to justify pardoning Nixon. It explains what was supposed to set Nixon apart from either his subordinates or from the Vietnam draft dodgers: the simple fact that he held the nation's highest elected office, and the one of the greatest symbolic significance. Hence the thought – shared even by key members of the Watergate prosecution team – that bringing the former president to trial for his abuse of office would have been a traumatic event for the nation as a whole. As one such member put it when reflecting on the pardon in 2006: "The specter of a former president in the criminal dock as our country moved into its bicentennial year was profoundly disturbing."[50]

We ought to ask, however, whether this disturbance was truly sufficient to justify pardoning. We can answer this question by once again turning to the notion of steadfastness that I have been associating with the integrity framework. As I stressed earlier, a steadfast commitment

---

Secretary, Dies at 87," *New York Times*, Apr. 1, 2010, at www.nytimes.com/2010/04/02/us/02terhorst.html.

[47] See *"President Gerald R. Ford Remarks on Taking Office"* at http://historyplace.com/speeches/ford-sworn.htm.

[48] Ford's pardoning speech, "President Gerald R. Ford Pardoning Richard Nixon" at http://historyplace.com/speeches/ford.htm. All italics are mine unless noted otherwise.

[49] "Ford's Statement before Subcommittee on Criminal Justice."

[50] Richard Ben-Veniste, "The Pardon in History's Hindsight," *Washington Post*, Dec. 29, 2006, at http://washingtonpost.com/wp-dyn/content/article/2006/12/28/AR2006122801054.html.

3.3 Pardons

to the principles of equality before the law means that the implications of this equality have to be carried through, even when the results are distressing – even when they yield the extremely discomforting sight of a former head of government, who is supposed to be the people's prime representative, facing severe criminal charges.

Integrity's hostility toward self-deception, emphasized in Chapter 1, further supports the same conclusion. It is mistaken, and arguably even dangerous, to think that the dignity of any public office – let alone that of the presidency – can be retained in the face of an enormous scandal simply by canceling, through a pardon, the scandal's legal implications for a former president. Such a move does not genuinely protect the dignity of the presidency. Rather, it is a way of deceiving ourselves – burying our heads in the legal sand – while the dignity of the presidency is gravely undermined. A genuine commitment to the dignity of this office required an honest, public confrontation with the lows to which events such as Watergate had brought it. And such confrontation, in turn, required a full legal process against a former president who, through criminal activities, brought upon this office "shame and disgrace." This process would have been the best way to restore – rather than undermine – the dignity of the office.

This reasoning, in turn, leads to a policy proposal that may have initially seemed surprising, but which I hope would appear natural at this point in our inquiry. Rather than allowing the former head of the executive branch to be pardoned while his subordinates face criminal prosecution, there is a significant case to be made for the *opposite* policy – for ensuring that even if subordinates may be pardoned, it will not be possible to pardon the head of the executive branch for manifest abuses of his or her office. Or, short of this more radical change, it should (at minimum) not be possible for the head of the executive branch to pardon his or her predecessor (especially when this is an immediate predecessor).[51] Therefore, if not simply a categorical prohibition on pardoning former presidents for offenses associated

---

[51] This should not be possible, at the very least, in order to prevent public suspicions of a quid pro quo between a pardoning president and his or her predecessor. Ford, for instance, repeatedly had to combat accusations that he and Nixon had arranged in advance a pardon in exchange for Nixon's resignation and Ford's consequent elevation to the presidency. But even if these accusations were mistaken in Ford's particular case (as most commentators seem to agree), the rules that make such accusations possible to begin with should be reformed.

with their former office, there should be a special procedure for the granting of such pardons – for instance, a supermajority in both houses of Congress.

3.4 Abuse of Power, Amnesty, and Democratic Transitions

Bearing in mind these critiques of the pardon given to Nixon, I now wish to turn to a set of related problems where the stakes are even higher – ones concerning fragile transitions to democracy. More specifically, these problems concern a core element of what the transitional justice literature often calls the "peace versus justice" dilemma.[52] Facing a repressive regime that is rapidly losing popular support, democratic forces on the ascent have an important choice to make.[53] Democratic forces may insist on bringing the heads of the regime to justice for major crimes committed under their rule. Alternatively, democratic forces may accept a compromise with the regime, and guarantee amnesties to its leaders, in order to precipitate the regime's actual demise. After all, if faced with certain prosecution, the regime's leaders may very well "dig in their heels," extending their repression and endangering more lives. By making concessions to the regime, democratic forces may shift these leaders' incentive structure in a less destructive direction. How, then, should democratic forces deal with such a morally fraught situation?[54]

---

[52] The relevant literature is vast. For an early influential emphasis on this dilemma (and a call for its pragmatic resolution in the direction of peace) see Samuel Huntington, *The Third Wave: Democratization in the Late Twentieth Century* (Norman, OK: University of Oklahoma Press, 1991), e.g., at 228. For more recent examples see the essays in Jon Elster, Rosemary Nagy, and Melissa Williams (eds.,), *Nomos: Transitional Justice* (New York: New York University Press, 2012), especially Elster's chapter 2.

[53] Throughout this section, I will use the term "democratic forces" to encompass formal democratic opposition to a repressive regime (for example, the African National Congress in South Africa), as well as more fluid forms of democratic opposition, such as labor unions that become politically prominent (along the lines of Poland's Solidarity movement).

[54] There are, of course, other important moral issues discussed in the transitional justice literature, including, for instance, reparations, apologies, and lustration policies (see, e.g., Ruti Teitel, *Transitional Justice* [Oxford: Oxford University Press, 2000]). But trying to offer a comprehensive account of all transitional justice policies would clearly take me too far afield, not least due to the sheer

3.4 Abuse of Power, Amnesty, and Democratic Transitions 135

In approaching this question, it is essential to avoid a key mistake to which one might be drawn by some of the empirical literature on the topic. Some empirical political scientists who discuss the question of pragmatic amnesties during democratic transitions argue that the only responsible course of action in such dire circumstances is for democratic forces to step away from "emotions" and to grant amnesties, even to murderous dictators, on the basis of a "logic of consequences."[55] But it is important to note that, appearances to the contrary notwithstanding, there is actually no clear line leading from *consequentialism* as a moral doctrine to the granting of amnesties during democratic transitions. A thoroughly consequentialist position sees only and all results of our actions as genuine moral factors.[56] Such a position would weigh the local gains that follow from amnesty deals with military dictatorships, for example, against broader losses, accruing not just across time but also across space. The short-term gains in reduction of authoritarian violence and repression would have to be balanced against the long-term loss of deterrence that follows from amnesties, not only for the relevant society, but also for other societies – for instance, for neighboring countries that also have politically ambitious militaries. Refusing to grant amnesty for crimes associated with a repressive military regime is likely to deter future military officers in other countries, who can be expected to take to heart key lessons associated with the careers of their older foreign colleagues.[57] Admittedly, some scholars believe

---

variety of transitional contexts, emphasized, for example, in Jon Elster, *Closing the Books: Transitional Justice in Historical Perspective* (Cambridge: Cambridge University Press, 2004).

[55] Jack Snyder and Leslie Vinjamuri, "Trials and Errors: Principle and Pragmatism in Strategies of International Justice," *International Security* 28 (2003): 5–44.

[56] For the consequentialist "it is not only the immediate, or short term, results that matter: long term results, side effects, indirect consequences – all these matter as well and they count just as much as short term or immediate consequences." See Shelly Kagan, *Normative Ethics* (Boulder: Westview Press, 1998), 64. For a particularly firm criticism of this view (focusing on Kagan's arguments), see James Lenman, "Consequentialism and Cluelessness," *Philosophy & Public Affairs* 29 (2000): 342–370.

[57] As one of the leading scholars in the field observes: "in the longer term, future human rights violations can be prevented through the impact of prosecutions on the new generations of military and police officers, and on civilian political leaders. Young officers who were not involved in the last round of repression may look at past leaders and draw conclusions about their future choices. They observe former leaders, perhaps imprisoned as a result of domestic prosecutions,

that the deterrence associated with post-dictatorship trials is overstated.[58] Yet it seems extremely hard to deny that some non-trivial level of deterrence can be associated with such trials.[59] Once this fairly modest claim is granted, then there should be no obvious reason why a consequentialist outlook should unequivocally favor amnesties as a way of dealing with dictatorships that are on the verge of losing power.

What I said in the last two paragraphs is not meant to deny the firm intuition that amnesties might indeed be a "necessary evil" in certain transitional circumstances.[60] My suggestion is only that this intuition actually points in a *non*-consequentialist direction. Unlike consequentialists, a non-consequentialist position can hold that "the good of the world" as a whole does not provide an appropriate basis for deciding whether to

---

or with tattered international and domestic reputations. Future military officers may decide that prosecutions have made repression and coups too costly." See Kathryn Sikkink, *The Justice Cascade: How Human Rights Prosecutions are Changing World Politics* (New York: Norton, 2011), 259. At the same time, Sikkink also argues (e.g., on p. 260) that the cross-border deterrence effect of prosecutions depends upon certain perceived affinities between perpetrators who have been facing trial and the potential recipients of the deterrent message: "Prosecutions for individual criminal accountability publicize the new norms. But not all prosecutions publicize equally ... [I]n order for the publicity effect to be 'received,' the potential recipient of the message must see himself as somehow similar to the individual being prosecuted. That is why the trial of General Pinochet had a greater impact on other military officers in Latin America than it did on US officials in Washington, DC. Geographic, cultural, and linguistic proximity can all contribute to the perception that actors are similar to those being tried."

[58] See again, Snyder and Vinjamuri, *Trials and Errors*, passim.

[59] To my mind, part of the problem in reaching confident empirical conclusions here has to do with broader, structural difficulties of social science. These difficulties are arguably present in any macro-level context, as I emphasized already in the introduction. But the limitations of social science are especially evident in the context of global inquiries. I develop this point at length in my "Liberal Global Justice and Social Science," *Review of International Studies* 42 (2016): 136–155.

[60] See, e.g., Mark Freeman, *Necessary Evils: Amnesties and the Search for Justice* (Cambridge: Cambridge University Press, 2009). Some scholars have been inclined to view such a position as suspiciously amoral (see, e.g., Amy Gutmann and Dennis Thompson, "The Moral Foundations of Truth Commissions," in Robert Rotberg and Thompson [eds.], *Truth v. Justice: The Morality of Truth Commissions* [Princeton, NJ: Princeton University Press, 2000], 22–44). But it is unclear why this is so: why cannot the likelihood of prolonged violence in the absence of amnesties count as a moral factor – even if one to be weighed alongside others?

3.4 Abuse of Power, Amnesty, and Democratic Transitions

offer amnesties to members of repressive regimes. More specifically, a non-consequentialist perspective can hold that the decision on such amnesties has to be justified to the members of the particular society in which amnesties will be enacted, and that the relevant justification cannot be put in terms of the universal impartiality that the consequentialist favors. It will not do to say to such a society: "You may suffer greatly because of a decision to withhold amnesty from members of the dictatorship, since such a decision would prolong the dictatorship. But you should see your suffering as offset by the significant benefits that this decision will yield for many other societies, where its deterrence gains will do a great deal of good." Each transitioning society can reasonably reject such a consequentialist demand, even if the predictions underlying this demand are accurate – even if it is indeed the case that a refusal to compromise with dictatorship in one society will have considerable deterrence benefits in many other societies. Even then, we might say – to put the point in integrity terms – that a transitioning society has the moral prerogative, if not the moral obligation, to *refuse* to see its collective project of establishing a liberal democracy as simply dispensable for the sake of "the good of the world" writ large.[61]

If these claims are cogent, then there are strong reasons to view the "peace versus justice" dilemma – insofar as we think it is a real dilemma – through a non-consequentialist lens. But this point does not yet tell us how to actually confront this dilemma. I now turn to develop several practical recommendations, grounded in the collective property and – especially – the collective integrity framework.

3.4.1 Amnesties and Democratic Transitions: A First Look

It is sensible to start with the main practical recommendations. At the end of Chapter 1, I emphasized the difference between integrity and

---

[61] This is true, moreover, even if "the good of the world" refers here to maximizing the number of liberal democracies in the world. The integrity framework thus aligns with a conviction that is central is to non-consequentialist moral thought more generally: that, at least in some important domains, it is a mistake to think of morality as necessarily concerned with "maximizing" anything. For different versions of this claim, see, e.g., T. M. Scanlon, *What We Owe to Each Other* (Cambridge, MA: Harvard University Press, 1998); Frances Kamm, *Intricate Ethics* (New York: Oxford University Press, 2006); Christine Korsgaard, "The Reasons We Can Share: An Attack on the Distinction between Agent-Relative and Agent-Neutral Values," *Social Philosophy & Policy* 10 (1993): 24–51.

fanaticism. Collective integrity, I argued, is not fanatic, insofar as it recognizes that we need to *live*, not only to *live up to* our principles. Collective integrity does not require of a society to behave in suicidal fashion – neither for the sake of its principles, nor for the sake of other societies.[62] It would follow, then, that collective integrity allows the granting of amnesties to members of repressive regimes, if and when such amnesties are really the only alternative to massive-scale violence.

However, collective integrity also requires that democratic forces be steadfast in their efforts to realize, to the greatest extent possible, the ideals of rule of law and equality before the law that are so essential to the identity-grounding institutions of liberal democracy. In particular, democratic forces must be trenchant – and creative – in trying to ensure that the leaders of the repressive regime they replace face significant legal sanctions, notwithstanding the pragmatic use of amnesties.

A key example of the trenchant creativity I have in mind concerns the use of conflicting interests separating different members of the repressive regime that democratic forces are working to overcome. Political scientists who support the use of amnesties to facilitate democratic transitions tend (however implicitly) to portray "the regime" as a monolithic actor that is determined to "spoil" a democratic transition in the absence of satisfactory guarantees of "its" interests. But in many cases, "the regime" is not, in fact, a monolith, and the different individuals of which it is composed will often have conflicting views and interests. These conflicts, in turn, can and should be exploited whenever they can be discerned, even when the pragmatic need for some sort of amnesty for certain crimes associated with the regime is clear. Thus for instance, even if amnesty has to be granted to many military officers if a military dictatorship is to give way without violence, it may still be the case that calculated

---

[62] As Sikkink points out (*The Justice Cascade*, 130), it is telling that during the 1980s and 1990s, the label "suicidal" recurred when political scientists, policy makers, and even human rights activists discussed trials for the members of repressive regimes during fragile transitions to democracy. However, even the most prominent trial skeptics admitted that "if civilian politicians use courage and skill, it may not necessarily be suicidal for a nascent democracy to confront the most reprehensible facts of its recent past" (see Guillermo O'Donnell and Phillipe C. Schmitter, *Transitions from Authoritarian Rule: Tentative Conclusions about Uncertain Democracies* [Baltimore, MD: Johns Hopkins University Press, 1986], 32). One way to think about the proposals I make here is to see them as tentative recommendations for civilian politicians of this kind.

3.4 Abuse of Power, Amnesty, and Democratic Transitions 139

offers of amnesty to a distinct subset of officers can go a long way toward bringing down the regime, without in any way committing democratic forces to grant any kind of amnesty to *other* members of the regime – including its most senior leaders.[63]

We can further develop this thought by considering one of the most famous social science models tying the collapse of numerous dictatorships to a certain kind of collective action problem. This model comes from Timur Kuran, who, in 1991, sought to explain why academics, policy makers, journalists and other experts were all "united in amazement"[64] at the (utterly unexpected and extraordinarily fast) collapse of the Soviet Union and its satellite regimes in Eastern Europe. Kuran's key claim was that fear of regime repression leads to *preference falsification*: the danger of repression pushes even individuals who resent the regime to hide their views. Preference falsification, in turn, renders the true political sentiments of the general public opaque; but it also renders opaque the preferences of different members of the regime, especially at the lower ranks. In this environment, the marginal status of dissent is self-sustaining: as long as only few accept the risks inherent in publicly opposing the regime, most critics of the regime – whether external or internal – assume that they are alone in their (private) opposition to the dictatorship, and thus avoid public action. That is why preference falsification is "the wellspring of stability"[65] for a great number of

---

[63] Argentina's fragile transition to democracy in the 1980s – a case of long-standing interest to transitional justice scholars – is a pertinent example, though it featured a different sequence of events. The military regime, badly demoralized following the debacle of the Falklands defeat, was unable to unify in order to challenge the effort, by Raul Alfonsin's democratic government, to try the nine most senior leaders of the military Junta. Alfonsin intended to stop with those trials, which concluded in 1985. But after these trials ended, many individual victims of the dictatorship initiated criminal proceedings on their own (relying on Argentina's criminal law, which does not vest the power to bring criminal charges solely in state prosecutors). Because of this array of private legal initiatives, hundreds of junior officers also faced criminal prosecution. And it was only in the face of this much more extensive threat that, in 1987, the military officers were able to unify sufficiently to meaningfully threaten the democratic government, forcing Alfonsin to block future prosecution through a new "due obedience" law (for this history, see Sikkink, *The Justice Cascade,* 70–83). Had this broader threat against so many of them not arisen, the junior officers may well have refrained from challenging the civilian government.

[64] Timur Kuran, "Now Out of Never: The Element of Surprise in the East European Revolution of 1989," *World Politics* 44 (1991): 7–48, at 7.

[65] Kuran, "Now out of Never," passim.

dictatorships. And that is also why, in terms of the actual individual preferences of each one of its members, a society can be on the brink of revolution without anyone realizing it. Change comes when some trigger (such as a deepening economic crisis, or geopolitical changes) takes some individuals beyond their "revolutionary threshold": that is, when some individuals who did not do so before now have sufficient incentives to express their dissent publicly and stop falsifying their preferences. Such action has the potential to very quickly snowball into all-out revolution, because the more individuals express public dissent, the more other individuals, so far concealing their opposition to the regime, have an incentive to "go public."[66]

All of this matters for our purposes because, if Kuran is right, then a well-crafted amnesty proposal made by democratic forces can have a disproportional effect on a dictatorship's survival, even if it applies only to a fairly limited segment of the regime. By way of illustration, imagine a situation where a military dictatorship that has long depended on the support of a foreign superpower can no longer rely on such support – much as was the case with Eastern European dictatorships in the late 1980s and early 1990s. Emboldened by this important shift, the leaders of the democratic opposition not only call on the regime to cede power to the people. They go further, and, faced with a governing elite that is reluctant to concede power, publicly guarantee an amnesty to a fixed number of junior officers, on the condition that these officers commit to truthfully testify as part of future court proceedings concerning political crimes perpetrated by key members of the ruling elite. If we follow Kuran's reasoning, then such a targeted use of the amnesty tool may very well suffice to generate the necessary cascade that will bring the dictatorship down with minimal bloodshed. At the very least, if democratic forces can offer credible evidence that their conditional amnesty proposals were indeed taken up by the number of officers they sought, and if preference falsification is indeed the wellspring of authoritarian stability, then the result may very well extend far beyond those particular officers. A snowball effect may very well emerge, giving pro-democracy forces the initiative and precipitating the actual achievement of democracy.

[66] Kuran's bandwagoning model thus provides a way to explain precisely why it is so often the case that revolution (as Michael Walzer famously put it) "comes unexpectedly." See Michael Walzer, "The Moral Standing of States: A Response to Four Critics," *Philosophy & Public Affairs* 9 (1980): 209–229, at 222.

3.4 Abuse of Power, Amnesty, and Democratic Transitions 141

Here is another example of trenchant creativity in the pursuit of significant legal sanctions against leaders of repressive regimes. If we follow the venerable tradition in political thought that warns of the corrupting effects of political power, then we can expect the leaders of repressive regimes – especially ones who have held on to power for many years during which they have been unconstrained by mechanisms of democratic accountability – to be corrupt in the narrow, literal sense emphasized by the collective property framework: the sense of stealing from the people. Yet in many cases, leaders of this kind are stealing to enrich not only themselves, but also their families.[67] Evocative examples are not hard to find around the globe, from the Philippines (think of Imelda Marcos's extravagance[68]), through Iran (consider the shocking opulence of the Shah's family[69]), to present-day Equatorial Guinea and Russia.[70] This point generates another sort of vulnerability for these leaders when it comes to their legal prosecution. Just as democratic forces can essentially offer plea bargains to a dictatorship's junior servants willing to testify against its leaders, so can democratic forces offer plea bargains to the leaders directly – striking a deal in which these leaders stand trial for severe crimes in exchange for their families being spared trial.[71] Both of these forms of plea bargains have been deployed

---

[67] Conversely, one may see democratically elected leaders emphasizing that they do not have children as a way of assuring voters that they have less incentive to steal from the public. India's Narendra Modi is a case in point. See, e.g., "India's 'Bachelor' Modi Admits He Is Married," *Al-Jazeera*, Apr. 10, 2014, at https://aljazeera.com/news/2014/04/india-bachelor-modi-admits-he-married-20144114 2718280976.html.

[68] See, for example, Shirley Escalante, "Imelda Marcos Shoe Museum: The Excess of a Regime That Still Haunts the Philippines," *ABC News*, Oct. 1, 2016, at http://abc.net.au/news/2016-10-02/imelda-marcos-shoe-museum:-the-excess-of-a-regime/7877098.

[69] See, e.g., Ann Crittenden, "Little Pain in Exile Expected for Shah," *The Spokesman-Review*, Jan. 14, 1979 at news.google.com/newspapers?nid=1314&dat=19790114&id=ezxOAAAAIBAJ&sjid=9e0DAAAAIBAJ&pg=6704,6136788.

[70] See, e.g., Faith Kairi and Mateo Diop, "Bugattis, Ferraris and Yachts, Oh My! African Vice President on Trial in Paris," *CNN*, Jun. 23, 2017, at edition.cnn.com/2017/06/23/africa/france-trial-teodoro-nguema-obiang-mangue/index.html; Stephen Grey, Andrey Kuzmin and Elizabeth Piper, "Putin's Daughter, a Young Billionaire and the President's Friends," *Reuters*, Nov. 10, 2015, at https://reuters.com/investigates/special-report/russia-capitalism-daughters/.

[71] The parallel between "normal" plea bargains and such transitional tactics is explicit, for example, in Eric Posner and Adrian Vermeule's "Transitional Justice as Ordinary Justice," *Harvard Law Review* 117 (2003): 762–825. I am

by many legal systems to deal with grand corruption. And it seems sensible to think that these techniques might also be put into good use when the aim is partly to create a new legal system – to replace the system imposed by the dictatorship.

I am aware that some readers may find these examples to be overly concrete. Normative political theory, such readers might worry, necessarily operates at a certain level of abstraction: it is problematic to try to deploy it to guide the choice of such specific political tactics. I think that this worry is intuitive, and important. In many cases, normative political theory, including the normative frameworks I have been developing here, should not try to offer a precise manual for political decision-making "on the ground." But the examples I just outlined, though quite specific, are not meant to be part of any such manual. Rather, these examples are meant to highlight a more general theoretical point: the way in which integrity's requirement of steadfastness pushes against the temptation to frame policy options in artificially narrow ways. Collective integrity, as I emphasized already in Chapter 1, pre-empts the self-seeking rationalizations often associated with a narrow framing of actual policy choices. It is often tempting to claim that "political realities" simply leave no way to live up to collective moral commitments. But while such limitations may obtain in some cases, the claims of integrity remind us that these limitations can be exaggerated – even in a manifestly non-ideal realm such as that of democratic transitions. Concrete examples of possible tactics, of the sort I just offered and will go on to offer, put this morally crucial fact center stage.

3.4.2 Democratic Transitions and Authoritarian Abuses of Public Property

With this clarification in hand, let me now turn to another important aspect of the "peace versus justice" dilemma. In some important cases of democratic transitions, peace may be at risk not only because the dictatorship that holds power is extremely recalcitrant. Peace may be at risk also because the dictatorship still enjoys the support of non-trivial

> inclined to agree with Posner and Vermeule that we should not be too quick to view transitional justice questions as sui generis (contra, for example, Colleen Murphy, *The Conceptual Foundations of Transitional Justice* [Cambridge: Cambridge University Press, 2017)]. But I believe that the positions I defend here are largely, if not entirely, independent of this debate.

3.4 Abuse of Power, Amnesty, and Democratic Transitions 143

portions of the population. This fact clearly complicates attempts to hold the dictatorship's leaders accountable for political crimes committed under the regime. Chile's democratic transition, for example, exhibited this structure. In the Chilean case, democratic forces had to contend not only with the fact that the military they were facing still held brute power but also with the fact that its economic policies were viewed favorably by key segments of the citizenry, including the middle class. These segments were accordingly suspicious of any (ostensibly) "ideologically tainted" insistence, by democratic forces, on criminalizing the regime's repression of political opposition.[72]

Now, insofar as the collective property and collective integrity frameworks presuppose liberal-democratic commitments, these frameworks obviously condemn such lenient attitudes toward authoritarianism: citizens who hold such attitudes are plainly wrong to do so. But these frameworks also yield important suggestions as to how democratic forces that make up the majority in a transitioning society should proceed when a sizable minority espouses such authoritarian sympathies.

One key suggestion concerns another form of trenchant creativity in subjecting the leaders of repressive regimes to significant legal sanctions. Even if lenient attitudes toward authoritarianism are too widespread to allow significant legal sanctions with regard to political crimes, it may still be possible to impose such sanctions for other serious offenses around which a divided society can unify. The example of the Pinochet regime in Chile is again pertinent. Pinochet's popularity among conservative Chileans – which endured even after he left power – played a key role in preserving his immunity from prosecution as a "senator for life." But even Pinochet's most ardent conservative supporters were dismayed once revelations emerged of the scope of personal corruption and illicit self-enrichment in which he had engaged.[73] It is therefore sensible to

---

[72] For a detailed discussion, see Cath Collins, *Post-Transitional Justice: Human Rights Trials in Chile and El Salvador* (University Park, PA: Pennsylvania State University Press, 2010).

[73] Thus in December 2006, upon Pinochet's death, the *Washington Post* noted: "Throughout his later years, Pinochet retained loyal supporters, who credited his government with instituting a fiscal discipline that helped make Chile's economy the region's strongest. But he lost many of those backers after multiple probes in recent years revealed financial corruption, including the discovery of millions of dollars in state funds held in numerous secret overseas accounts, among them several at the former Riggs Bank in Washington. As recently as October, Chilean investigators announced the discovery of 10 tons of gold,

think that a trial for corruption, which would have happened had Pinochet lived long enough, would have had a real chance of uniting rather than dividing Chilean society. Notwithstanding their profound ideological differences, those on the Chilean right who have long been apologists for Pinochet's regime could agree with their fierce opponents on the left in firmly rejecting Pinochet's abuse of public property.[74]

This reasoning is likely to attract various objections. Two objections in particular are worth highlighting. The first objection is that there is something disturbing – in general, and from integrity's perspective in particular – about a legal system that seems to be looking for excuses to sanction particular individuals. "Make dictators pay, no matter how" may be a potent political slogan, but is hardly a morally compelling strategy. My response to this worry is that nothing in my remarks here should be taken to endorse any distortion of the legal system so as to convict particular individuals of "something, no matter what." It is indeed essential that any charges brought against members of repressive regimes – including the most senior members – be handled in a manner that fully accords with the standard requirements of due process. So nothing in my view is meant to rule out any of the familiar legal protections of defendants' rights to a fair trial. The only point I do want to stress is that *if* clear evidence emerges of large-scale personal corruption by the former leaders of repressive regimes, and *if* prosecuting

---

worth an estimated $160 million, in Pinochet's name in a Hong Kong bank." See Monte Reel and J. Y. Smith, "A Chilean Dictator's Dark Legacy," *Washington Post*, Dec. 11, 2006, at https://washingtonpost.com/archive/politics/2006/12/11/a-chilean-dictators-dark-legacy/596e14a3-d86c-496f-8568-05f81c199a81/?noredirect=on&utm_term=.54e508587bee; see also Jeffrey Simser, "Asset Recovery and Kleptocracy," *Journal of Financial Crime* 17 (2010): 321–332.

[74] Another way to think about the appeal of this unifying strategy is to situate it within the empirical debate on the degree to which ordinary citizens prioritize punishment of corrupt politicians. In the context of electoral competitions in which all candidates are perceived as corrupt, voters often seem uninterested in holding particular corrupt leaders accountable, even through the ballot (see for example Jan Teorell, "Corruption as an Institution: Rethinking the Nature and Origins of the Grabbing Hand," Working paper, [Gothenburg: The Quality of Government Institute, University of Gothenburg,2007], 5). But things are different in a context where the entire political system is being transformed – as is the case with transitions from authoritarianism to democracy. Here the notion that "there is simply no alternative" is clearly far less persuasive, and indeed a firm stance against corruption can be a key part of the effort to make a sharp break with the past – to forge a new legal system, and a new set of governance norms. I say more about this sharp break below.

these leaders on corruption grounds is far less likely to undermine a precarious democratic transition as compared to legal charges focusing on these leaders' political crimes, then prosecution for corruption is an attractive strategy.

The second objection views this strategy as deficient for a different reason. According to this objection, focusing a trial of former leaders of repressive regimes on those offenses around which the polity can unify ignores important moral claims of the particular victims of the worst crimes that these leaders have committed. From the perspective of the victims of political torture, for example, the mere fact that a former dictator is languishing in prison may bring little solace. For these victims (and their families) it often matters more that the dictator (and his henchmen) languish in prison *for torturing*.

In response to this objection, I only wish to point out that my collectivist account consciously differs from the objection's focus on individual victims. On my view, the primary reason why it is so morally essential to be steadfast in pursuing severe legal sanctions against former leaders of repressive regimes has to do with the constant need to uphold, to the greatest extent possible, the core collective ideals of the rule of law and equality before the law. These collective ideals may bring only limited comfort to individual victims. But that is not the main issue here. Indeed, even if there were no individual victims left – and even if their descendants too had died or left the country – there would still be considerable value in significant legal sanctions against former leaders, which make clear that all citizens, regardless of their level of past or present political power, are equally subject to the law. This message, in turn, is surely conveyed clearly enough when a former dictator finds himself behind bars for the rest of his life, even if not necessarily for the most severe crime of which he is guilty.

3.4.3 Truth Commissions

So far in this section, I have discussed various ways in which democratic forces may seek to impose significant legal penalties on leaders of repressive regimes, even in the extremely delicate circumstances of a democratic transition. But what ought democratic forces to do when such sanctions are genuinely not feasible? When none of the creative strategies suggested above – nor any other creative methods – can really help to subject those most responsible for political crimes to legal punishment, and when trying to do so will really result only in more violence and deeper societal conflict, what is the right way to proceed?

It might be best to start with what, in my view, is certainly the *wrong* way to proceed. Collective integrity, at least, firmly suggests that even a society that cannot afford to bring those responsible for repression to trial ought not to engage in collective forgetting – it ought not pretend that repression had never happened. If the decision to pardon Nixon can be conceived as a form of "burying heads in the sand," as I argued earlier in this chapter, then this is clearly true, a fortiori, in the case of a collective decision to behave as if decades of dictatorship never took place. Thus societies such as Spain – where an almost official "pact of forgetting" has effectively forbidden any kind of discussion of the Franco dictatorship – have committed a serious collective wrong.[75] Such societies have engaged in a form of collective self-deception that is flatly incompatible with collective integrity.[76]

Now, in saying all this, it may seem that I am calling for the complete opposite of the Spanish approach. To some extent, this is indeed the case. I do think that, where standard legal proceedings are impossible, collective integrity is much better served by a model such as South Africa's, where amnesty for past political crimes was conditional upon a full public confession of these crimes.[77]

---

[75] See, e.g., Giles Tremlett, *Ghosts of Spain: Travels through Spain and Its Silent Past* (New York: Walker & Company, 2006); Omar Encarnación, "Reconciliation after Democratization: Coping with the Past in Spain," *Political Science Quarterly* 123 (2008): 435–459. See also Elster's remarks on Spain's self-conscious "disremembering" in *Closing the Books*, 62.

[76] Note that this integrity argument for the intrinsic significance of a collective confrontation with the past is not dependent upon causal claims about the instrumental benefits of truth commissions. For critiques of these alleged benefits see, e.g., David Mendeloff, "Truth-Seeking, Truth-Telling, and Postconflict Peacebuilding: Curb the Enthusiasm," *International Studies Review* 6 (2004): 355–380; Eric Brahm, "Uncovering the Truth: Examining Truth Commission Success and Impact," *International Studies Perspectives* 8 (2007): 16–35.

[77] There may be reasons to hold truth commissions alongside trials when this is feasible, though there are complex questions about the best sequence for combining these two forms of transitional justice. For discussion, see

Two further remarks are important here, however. First, there are multiple policy options that lie on the spectrum between the South African and the Spanish model. Therefore, even in circumstances where an extremely ambitious undertaking such as that of the South African truth and reconciliation commission is not feasible, smaller-scale initiatives may still be available to ensure that important historical truths are duly recognized rather than "swept under the rug." Thus, for instance, public museums, national days of remembrance, and the inclusion of painful histories in core school curricula are all important forms of collective reckoning with the past, which can and should be pursued as early as possible, even when the immediate pursuit of a comprehensive truth and reconciliation commission would endanger a peaceful transition to democracy.

Second, we should be cognizant of the fact that, at least in some cases of especially fragile transitions, where the threat from "spoilers" is especially acute, even attempts to force an immediate public reckoning with the wrongs caused by the regime may trigger a violent backlash.[78] When this is the case, the challenge is to take adequate note of this danger without resorting to "collective forgetting." Here, once again, trenchant creativity is crucial. Even if democratic forces have no real choice but to guarantee an amnesty to the leaders of the repressive regime they seek to replace, and even when democratic forces are not even in a position to force these leaders (or their associates) to publicly confess the wrongs they have committed, democratic forces can still pursue creative strategies for committing their opponents to provide morally important testimonies.

Consider the following example. When "spoilers" resist public honesty mechanisms such as truth commissions, they typically do so because they fear that such mechanisms threaten their present standing

---

Alexander Dukalskis, "Interactions in Transition: How Truth Commissions and Trials Complement or Constrain Each Other," *International Studies Review* 13 (2011): 432–451.

[78] Examples such as Guatemala are a case in point: the director of the country's 1999 truth commission was murdered two days after the commission published its report (despite the director being a bishop and despite the fact that the report did not name perpetrators). See Priscilla Hayner, *Unspeakable Truths: Confronting State Terror and Atrocity* (New York: Routledge, 2001), 244.

– whether by shaming them and thus reducing their clout, by providing evidence that may later be used against them in legal proceedings, or even by incentivizing victims and their families to pursue vigilante justice. But these fears on the part of spoilers can be accommodated – in those circumstances where there is really no choice but to accommodate them – by committing them to provide testimonies whose secrecy will be guaranteed for a certain period.

Here is one way such an arrangement might work. A third party agreed upon by democratic forces and members of the regime – be it a prominent NGO, a foreign government that has already served as a mediator between the two sides, or even an organization such as the Catholic Church – would be entrusted with formal, written confessions of political crimes committed under the regime. These confessions would be accessible to this third party, but would otherwise be kept secret until a certain amount of time has elapsed (say, twenty years), or until the authors of these confessions pass away – whichever comes first.[79] Such an arrangement is not, of course, anything like a perfect substitute for a normal trial, or even for a truth commission that imposes a heavier social cost on perpetrators. But it is nonetheless worth keeping in mind as an alternative in the most non-ideal transitional situations where there is no other feasible mechanism for holding perpetrators socially accountable. Moreover, this kind of alternative is also worth keeping in mind as a way of resisting, yet again, the overly convenient rationalization of collective amnesia as the "only" means of negotiating a transition to democracy. Instead of such rationalizations, creative institutional mechanisms, such as sealed confessions whose publication is delayed, serve to commit a society to – eventually – confronting fundamental truths about its recent past, however distressing and uncomfortable these truths might be.

3.4.4 Revoking Amnesties?

Equipped with these arguments against collective forgetting, I want to close this section – and the chapter – with one last contribution that the

---

[79] One can obviously imagine further fine-tuning. Thus, for instance, in a case where many confessions overlap – and where the confessions of one culprit may accordingly incriminate another – these confessions may be unsealed only when all relevant culprits have passed away.

collective integrity framework makes to our thinking about democratic transitions. This framework, I believe, provides a powerful unifying rationale explaining how a democratic society ought to deal with amnesties of different origins that have already been granted to the leaders of past repressive regimes.

Two different scenarios are worth mentioning here.[80] First, suppose that just before he relinquishes power, a dictator announces the passage of a general amnesty shielding himself and all of his associates from any subsequent legal charges. Following a transition to democracy, a new, reformed supreme court declares the dictator's amnesty bill null and void, and he is consequently brought to trial for various crimes. Few of us, I assume, would see such post-dictatorship developments as problematic in any way. In fact, we would have the moral expectation that the democratic government, as well as civil society, publicly support the nullification of the dictator's amnesty bill.[81]

Our intuitions seem quite different, however, in a second scenario, where the relevant amnesty bill has clear democratic provenance. Suppose that a democratic opposition offers an amnesty to the leaders of a military dictatorship in exchange for the latter's permanent retirement from politics. These leaders accept the deal, and keep their side of it. When the opposition comes to power, the amnesty is enshrined in law. Yet after democracy is consolidated and the military is weakened, the amnesty is revoked, with the firm backing (or maybe even at the initiative) of the same democratic forces that offered it. There is, I take it, something much more disquieting about this case. Yet how can we account for this intuition?

Part of what makes this intuition difficult to explain is that it strains credulity to ground it by appealing to the claims of amnesty recipients who have kept their side of the amnesty deal. It would be odd to say

---

[80] I do not mean to suggest that this pair of scenarios is in any way exhaustive of real-world possibilities – only that these particular scenarios deserve our moral attention.

[81] For an extensive empirical discussion indicating the centrality of judicial leadership, as well as an "engaged executive," in combating immunity laws, see Francesca Lessa, Tricia Olsen, Leigh Payne, and Gabriel Pereira, "Persistent or Eroding Impunity; The Divergent Effects of Legal Challenges to Amnesty Laws for Past Human Rights Violations," *Israel Law Review* 47 (2014): 105–131.

that these recipients have a moral right that the amnesty they have enjoyed will endure. The severity of these recipients' crimes, and the fact that their amnesty was only granted because of their own threats of continued violence, surely undermine any purported right on their part to continued immunity from prosecution.

A consequentialist explanation will not do better. It is true that, if it becomes clear that democratic forces have no real intention of upholding the amnesty they offer to dictators and their associates once the latter concede power, then power will simply not be conceded: amnesty deals will not get made, and the amnesty mechanism will lose its pragmatic benefits. But we have already seen that these benefits might very well be outweighed, in any thoroughly consequentialist account, by deterrence considerations that extend further in space and time. These considerations mean that there is no obvious reason why a consequentialist outlook would favor amnesties as a way of dealing with dictatorships that are on the verge of losing power. Therefore, there is also no obvious reason why a consequentialist position would oppose the ex post withdrawal of such amnesties – even if, and perhaps partly because – such withdrawal will likely prevent amnesty deals from arising in the first place.

If these claims are cogent, then some alternative argument is needed in order to ground the forceful intuition that it would be wrong for democratic forces to negotiate an amnesty with an authoritarian regime only to renege on the amnesty at the earliest opportunity. The collective integrity framework, I wish to suggest, provides the needed argument. Moreover, in doing so, the integrity framework unifies our intuitions about the significance of withdrawing amnesties that dictators have given to themselves with our intuitions about the significance of upholding amnesties with firmly democratic roots.

Let me elaborate. In Chapter 1, I argued that a people as a collective agent, just like an individual, can have an identity-grounding commitment to break with its own past, and indeed to define its core present identity as a contradiction of its "former self." And this sort of collective break with the past is clearly germane to our moral intuitions with regard to transitions away from dictatorship. It is morally essential that the democratic institutions arising in the aftermath of dictatorship are as far removed as possible from the institutions that preceded them. Moreover, this is especially true for the polity's identity-grounding

3.4 Abuse of Power, Amnesty, and Democratic Transitions 151

legal institutions. Given that the integrity of liberal democracy pivots on the realization of equal rights through the law, from an integrity perspective, it is especially important that a new democracy's legal system break with the shadows of dictatorship rather than re-create them. The need for such a sharp break, in turn, explains both why it is so important that a new democracy rescinds, at the earliest possible opportunity, an amnesty that a dictator has provided for himself, and why it is important that a democracy does *not* rescind an amnesty that was guaranteed by democratic forces. The core thought is the same in both of those cases: we do not want a liberal democracy's legal system to mimic some of the most reprehensible aspects of the dictatorship that preceded it.

We can render the fear of such mimicking more concrete by considering our instinctive alarm at transitions to democracy that are marked by kangaroo trials, even of deposed dictators. A new democracy's legal system ought to be vastly better than the dictatorship it replaces, and this difference ought to start with how the new regime treats the legal prosecution of those who previously held supreme political power. To spare such rulers of any legal process, simply because of an amnesty they have given to themselves while in power, is to betray a liberal democracy's identity-grounding commitment to equality before the law. But the opposite extreme – treating such rulers much as they had treated their opponents – betrays the collective project of a liberal democracy in a way that is arguably just as acute.

Something like this betrayal, I would suggest, was present, for example, in the Romanian revolution of 1989 that ended Nicolae Ceaușescu's communist dictatorship. Consider, for instance, Kathryn Sikkink's description of Ceaușescu's "trial":

After the fall of the communist regime . . . the leader and his wife and political partner Elena were put on trial for their crimes. The trial was about human rights violations, and the individuals were being held criminally accountable, but . . . the accused were not given even a minimally fair trial. On the morning of December 25th, 1989, the Ceaușescus appeared before an ad hoc military tribunal. Before the trial began, the panel of judges knew that it was a foregone conclusion that the Ceaușescus would be executed that afternoon. After a two-hour trial in which little hard evidence was presented and the defendants were not allowed a strong defense – as even their defense lawyer accused them of crimes – they were given a death sentence and executed "commando style" in the same room where the "trial" occurred.[82]

In my view, infamous tales such as this are worth bearing in mind when discussing a decision to renege on an amnesty that democratic forces had given to former dictators. To be sure, such a decision is not equal in its moral severity to a summary execution of a former dictator without proper legal procedure. Nonetheless, from an integrity perspective, these two wrongs belong on the same spectrum, even if they occupy different points on this spectrum. An amnesty deal that democratic forces adopt dishonestly, without any intention of keeping, may facilitate the birth of a new regime by helping to remove from power extremely unsavory rulers who would otherwise cling on to power. But such a deal also poses very real question marks as to the incoming regime's actual novelty: is this regime steadfast in its commitment to a legal system that speaks with one voice? Or does the new regime abandon this basic commitment when it requires non-trivial sacrifices? And if the latter is the case, is it so far-fetched to say that the new regime, rather than representing a genuine collective transformation, ultimately stoops to a level not too far from those it replaces?

Questions of this sort, it is worth stressing, are not merely philosophical constructs. These questions were very much alive for those charged with key aspects of certain democratic transitions. In Portugal, for instance, the new government that had replaced the dictatorship following the Carnation Revolution of 1974 had kept more than a thousand members of Salazar's secret police (PIDE) in prison for more than a year, in the absence of legal charges or a trial, and in some cases subjecting the imprisoned to abuses going all the way to simulated executions. Upon discovering this state of affairs, the newly appointed superintendent of the Commission for the Extinction of PIDE lamented "the great moral problem of the revolution. We had started to treat our enemies in the same manner that the authoritarian regime had treated its enemies."[83]

---

[82] Sikkink, *The Justice Cascade*, 13.
[83] Quoted in Sikkink, *The Justice Cascade*, 54.

Conclusion

The collective property and collective integrity frameworks that I presented in the first two chapters emphasize the unity of the people as a collective agent. In the introduction to this book, I suggested that this unity might explain why ideas regarding the people as a collective agent remain under-studied in political theory, focused as it is not on unity but on division. In this chapter I accordingly examined how the two collectivist frameworks can be used in circumstances dominated by a significant divide, between a people and its leaders. This divide is especially manifest when leaders become a liability rather than an asset for the people's collective project. I tried to show how ideas associated with the people's property and the people's integrity can help us think about the normative dimensions of various policies pertaining to such conditions.

My aim in the next two chapters is to examine how ideas regarding the people's property and integrity might inform our thinking about two other divides that have long been of interest to political theory and central to political realities. In Chapter 5, I shall examine in further detail internal ideological divisions generating acute societal conflict. Although such divisions bear on morally fraught transitions to democracy, as we have seen, their political import – and moral complexity – can be just as great in circumstances featuring transitions away from liberal democracy. Taking up the case of Israel, I shall try to show how the collective property and collective integrity frameworks can advance our thinking about such backsliding.

Prior to this effort, however, Chapter 4 explores another politically salient divide, which is more intimately related to the concerns explored here. In this chapter, I delved into domestic policy choices concerning different forms of corruption and abuse of political power. But in the twenty-first century, at least, the problem of how to deal with corruption, and with leaders who abuse their power, is rarely a purely domestic issue. This problem often implicates foreign actors as well – from foreign governments to foreign corporations. Such circumstances bring to the fore the divide between outsiders and insiders – between ordinary members of the people and external actors interacting with the people's (alleged) representatives. I now turn to examine how the property and integrity frameworks can illuminate this divide as well. I do so by focusing on foreign actors' choices regarding sovereign debt accumulated by massively corrupt autocrats.

4 | *Their Property, Our Integrity: The Democratic Response to the Problem of Odious Debt*

In Chapter 3, I deployed ideas concerning the people's property and the people's integrity to discuss domestic political decisions. This domestic focus meant that the integrity framework and the property framework applied to the same sovereign people. Yet once we turn from the domestic to the international realm, we may encounter problems with a different normative structure. In particular, we may find cases where the relevant collective integrity relates to the people of a liberal democracy, but where the relevant property belongs to a foreign people living under a manifestly undemocratic regime. In this Chapter I explore one such case, revolving around international sovereign debt practices.

With very few exceptions, every de facto government can borrow funds internationally, adding to the country's sovereign debt, and every de facto government inherits the sovereign debt incurred by previous de facto governments. This is generally the case regardless of the process through which a government comes to power, regardless of the process by which it makes public policy, and regardless of the substance of its policies.

My main aim in this chapter is to show that we can use ideas associated with the people's property and the people's integrity to construct a compelling alternative to these de facto-ist practices. These ideas, I will argue, yield a forceful condemnation of the status quo, grounding – and refining – some of the best existing proposals for reform. Moreover, the collective property and collective integrity frameworks also unify further moral intuitions concerning sovereign debt issues, in a way that yields novel policy proposals. Finally, these frameworks can help us think systematically about some hard sovereign debt problems rooted in current practices.

I develop these contributions in two main stages, which parallel the sequence pursued in Chapter 3. In the first stage (4.2 through 4.4), I highlight issues concerning de facto-ist sovereign debt practices that trigger strong moral intuitions. I argue that the property and integrity frameworks provide a coherent basis for these intuitions, generating compelling policy implications. In the chapter's second stage (4.5

through 4.8), I turn to sovereign debt issues where our moral intuitions are less secure, and examine how the property and integrity frameworks can guide our approach to these issues. Here I also anticipate challenges to my proposed alternative to customary practices.

Before I turn to these claims, however, some framing remarks will help to clarify the chapter's scope and goals.

4.1 Setting the Stage

The best way to introduce the themes of this chapter is to begin with a concrete example. Consider, then, the case of Nicaragua's sovereign debt in the aftermath of the Somoza regime. The Somoza family held Nicaragua's presidency for more than forty years, and then continued to rule the country by controlling its military (the National Guard). The last of the Somozas in particular – Anastasio Somoza Debayle – engaged in extensive repression that ended only in 1979, when his regime was defeated by the Sandinista guerrillas and the Somozas had to flee Nicaragua. By that point, "thanks" to the Somoza family, Nicaragua had "empty public coffers,"[1] while its public and publicly guaranteed external debt exceeded a billion dollars.[2] *The Wall Street Journal* described the Somozas' final days in power as follows:

> Before they left, the Somozas followed a virtual "scorched earth" policy. Besides sacking opponents' businesses, they borrowed heavily from outside using the convenient apparatus of a government that was synonymous with the family financial empire, looted the treasury and left behind a staggering short-term foreign debt... What the Somozas leave behind is a bankrupted society, its infant-mortality rate higher than that of India.[3]

The Somozas provide an extreme example of sovereign borrowing by regimes whose claim to represent the sovereign people is, to put it mildly, suspect. This is the kind of sovereign borrowing that I wish to scrutinize here.[4]

---

[1] Ann Helwege, "Three Socialist Experiences in Latin America: Surviving US Economic Pressure," *Bulletin of Latin American Research* 8 (1989): 211–234, at 222.
[2] Odette Lienau, *Rethinking Sovereign Debt: Politics, Reputation, and Legitimacy in Modern Finance* (Cambridge, MA: Harvard University Press, 2014), 175. I will rely on Lienau's extensive historical study at multiple points.
[3] Quoted in Lienau, *Rethinking Sovereign Debt*, 176.
[4] Although I will be assuming that this borrowing warrants independent attention, I do not mean to suggest that it is the only causal mechanism relevant to how

Although this inquiry covers a broad range of regimes – including ones clearly less disturbing than the Somoza government – I intend my analysis to have modest ambitions, in four ways. First, I do not intervene in debates among legal scholars, as to whether existing international law identifies debts incurred by certain repressive regimes as "odious," and therefore as non-binding on later governments.[5] Much of what I will say here will align with this odious debt doctrine. Yet whenever I will use the term "odious debt," I will be expressing a moral stance rather than a legal claim: my interest here is in what the law ought to be, rather than in what existing (international) law does or does not hold.

Second, in focusing my attention on de facto governments that can plausibly be seen as alien to their people, I will be bracketing here questions regarding sovereign debt that arise in the context of very different governments. In particular, much public attention has been given in recent years to countries where representative governments have been facing unsustainable levels of external debt (think of the Greek case, for instance). But although the normative analysis of such economic crises is clearly an important undertaking, I put it aside here.[6]

Third, I am going to assume in this chapter that given the appropriate institutional conditions, future governments may inherit debt obligations incurred by past governments even when they preside over very different generations. This is not to say that the question of how

---

extremely objectionable regimes exercise their power, or even the only mechanism in which affluent democracies are implicated. Thus, for example, the benefits that such regimes often derive from natural resource trade with affluent democracies (discussed in Chapter 1) might in some cases be at least as important for explaining their grip on power. For remarks along those lines, see, for instance, Christina Ochoa, "From Odious Debt to Odious Finance: Avoiding the Externalities of a Functional Odious Debt Doctrine," *Harvard International Law Journal* 49 (2008): 109–159.

[5] See, for example, Jeff King, *The Doctrine of Odious Debt in International Law: A Restatement* (Cambridge: Cambridge University Press, 2016); Robert Howse, "The Concept of Odious Debt in Public International Law," UNCTAD Discussion Paper No. 185 (July 2007). See also W. Mark, C. Weidemaier, and Mitu Gulati, "The Relevance of Law to Sovereign Debt," *Annual Review of Law and Social Science* 11 (2015): 395–408. For an argument focusing on domestic law see Lee C. Buchheit, Mitu Gulati, and Robert Thompson, "The Dilemma of Odious Debts," *Duke Law Journal* 56 (2007): 1201–1262.

[6] For such analysis see, e.g., Gabriel Wollner, "Morally Bankrupt: International Financial Governance and the Ethics of Sovereign Default" *The Journal of Political Philosophy* 26 (2018): 344–367.

sovereign debt obligations get transferred across generations is unimportant or devoid of moral complexity. But this question would apply even to the most morally commendable governments. Since I wish to keep my attention here on the specific case of governments that are clearly far from commendable, and to isolate what sets their moral circumstances apart, I am going to approach this case on the assumption that we can solve the broader inter-generational puzzle, of how any government can create obligations for future generations.[7]

Finally, the aims of this chapter are modest insofar as I do not wish to establish that every practical recommendation I make here can only be derived from the integrity and property frameworks developed earlier in this book. Rather, I proceed on the assumption that the reader has already been convinced that these frameworks can advance our moral thinking on certain fronts. Therefore, part of what I want to show here is that these advances are not achieved at the cost of setbacks on other fronts. Since the collective integrity and collective property frameworks centrally bear on corruption, as we have already seen, it is natural to ask what practical verdicts these frameworks yield with regard to issues such as odious debt. If I can show that none of these practical verdicts are morally implausible, this will be important in and of itself. This reassuring result does not require showing that each such verdict is uniquely traceable to ideas about collective integrity and collective property.[8]

4.2 Odious Debt and the People's Property

With these framing remarks in hand, let me return to the case of Nicaragua and the Somoza family. There is clearly something disturbing, to say the least, about rulers like the Somozas being able to borrow massive sums abroad in order to enrich themselves and fuel their repression, and then leave the resulting debt to be paid by their victims and their victims' descendants. But although the Sandinista government established

---

[7] See, e.g., Sanjay Reddy, "International Debt: The Constructive Implications of Some Moral Mathematics," *Ethics & International Affairs* 21 (2007): 33–48; Christian Dimitriu, "Are States Entitled to Default on the Sovereign Debts Incurred by Governments in the Past?" *Ethical Perspectives* 22 (2015): 369–393.

[8] That said, I do hope to show that the two frameworks allow us to capture some intuitively attractive judgments especially quickly. This too is an important finding, at least to the extent that we often worry about normative theories that require too many steps to reach plausible results.

after the Somozas' departure was able to restructure Nicaragua's sovereign debt on terms that were more favorable than usual, any attempt on its part to even hint at a principled repudiation of Somoza-era debt was met with staunch resistance by foreign creditors. Creditor banks would concede no relevant difference between the Somozas' debt and the debts accumulated by any other government, repeatedly claiming that they are not "dealing with politics," but instead with "the continuing institution of the Nicaraguan government."[9]

However, notwithstanding the banks' protests, morally speaking it seems safe to say that they got things backward. For one thing, Somoza-era debt, rather than being Nicaragua's debt serviced by successor governments, ought to have been designated as the Somozas' personal debt.[10] Moreover, given that the creditors were clearly aware of the ways in which the Somoza family wielded its power and (ab)used the funds it borrowed against the people of Nicaragua,[11] it is not obvious why there should have been any presumption at all in favor of later

---

[9] Quoted in Lienau, *Rethinking Sovereign Debt*, 177.

[10] This was indeed the view of some central figures in the Sandinista government (see Lienau, *Rethinking Sovereign Debt*, 176). This was also the view of the original proponent of the "odious debt" doctrine in international law, the Russian lawyer Alexander Sack, who wrote in 1927: "If a despotic power contracts debt, not for the needs and interest of the State, but to strengthen its despotic regime, to oppress the population that combats it, that debt ... need not be recognised by the Nation: it is a debt of the regime, a personal debt of the power that contracted it and consequently falls along with the power that contracted it." Quoted in Eric Toussaint, "The Doctrine of Odious Debt: From Alexander Sack to the CADTM," CADTM, Nov. 24, 2016, at http://cadtm.org/The-Doctrine-of-Odious-Debt-from#nb2-1.

[11] As political theorists reflecting on events at the time had stressed, toward the end of the Somozas' rule there could be little doubt – even for outsiders not immersed in the intricacies of Nicaraguan politics – that the Somoza regime was alien to the people. This was evident, for instance, in "a press statement strongly reminiscent of Woody Allen's *Bananas*," in which "Somoza stated that his was the cause of Nicaraguan freedom, since he enjoyed the support of virtually the entire National Guard." Citing this statement, David Luban added in 1980: "I do not pretend to possess a detailed understanding of Nicaraguan politics. However, it does not take a detailed understanding to realize that when the populace of a capital city cheers the guerrillas who have taken their own parliament hostage, when labor unions and business associations are able to unite in a general strike, and when a large city's residents must ask for third-party intervention to prevent their own government from bombing them to rubble, the government in question enjoys neither consent nor legitimacy." David Luban, "Just War and Human Rights," *Philosophy and Public Affairs* 9 (1980): 160–181, at 170.

4.2 Odious Debt and the People's Property

Nicaraguan governments paying the creditors. In fact, we can go even further and say that insofar as the creditors were benefiting from the repressive rule of the Somoza family,[12] the creditors ought to have paid compensation to the Nicaraguan people for their dealings with the family. Finally, very much related, the burden of justifying a different policy ought to have rested with the creditors. It should have been the creditors' duty to show, with regard to any given loan they extended to the Somoza family, why they had any kind of claim to be paid by the current government, and why they should not in fact offer compensation.[13]

The most immediate way to ground these powerful moral intuitions, I believe, is to appeal to the people's ownership of public property. From a normative perspective, "sovereign debt" can ultimately be accrued only by the sovereign people as an owner, rather than by any supposedly "sovereign" regime. A de facto regime can at most act only as a principal for the sovereign people. But a regime that is completely alien to the people – that incurs debt without anything like the authorization of the people and that routinely uses borrowed funds for purposes that have little to do with the people – cannot bind the people to sacrifice its property to pay for this debt.

These ideas regarding the people's property suggest the following general rule. Two conditions should be jointly sufficient to yield a very strong presumption against burdening a people with a debt incurred by a regime. At least in cases where (1) it is clear beyond reasonable doubt that a regime cannot plausibly claim authorization from the people to

[12] Thus, for instance, Richard Weinert explains the "flocking" of international banks to Nicaragua partly through the "uncommonly large loan commissions or fees which formed a small part of the graft and corruption which permeated Nicaragua's public sector." See Weinert's "Nicaragua's Debt Renegotiation," *Cambridge Journal of Economics* 5 (1981): 187–194, at 188.

[13] Christian Barry, for example, writes: "It seems quite implausible that oppressive elites should be entitled to incur debts in the names of those whom they impoverish (or worse) and bind present and future citizens of their country (along with others subject to their tax authority) to repay it. And it seems equally problematic that a creditor should be permitted to provide a government with resources that there are strong reasons to believe will be used to impose significant social costs on the present and future people of that government's country. Indeed, it seems quite wrong that such creditors could *escape* responsibility for compensating for the harms ... that they have thus enabled and in many cases benefited significantly from." Christian Barry, "Sovereign Debt, Human Rights, and Policy Conditionality," *Journal of Political Philosophy* 19 (2011): 282–305, at 289. Italics in the original.

borrow funds on its behalf, and (2) it is clear beyond reasonable doubt that the regime has been systematically abusing loans for manifestly illegitimate ends, there ought to be a very strong presumption against saddling the people with the resulting debt. The norm should be that the people, insofar as they are able to act through later representative governments, may repudiate such debt, and in fact demand compensation from creditors for the harms associated with the relevant loans.[14]

This rule would obviously apply to many other cases apart from Nicaragua. When the representative government that replaced Ferdinand Marcos's kleptocracy in the Philippines, for instance, considered (in 1987) repudiating even parts of the $27 billion debt that Marcos left behind, private creditors rejected such attempts outright as "departing from conventional practice," with some creditors even threatening the Philippines explicitly with "immense suffering" in case of debt repudiation.[15] Had ideas about the people's property received their due, such claims would have not been possible: it would have the creditors' burden to explain why there is any reason at all for representative governments of the Philippines to pay anything to Marcos's creditors, rather than demand compensation from the creditors.

Along the same lines, consider the constraints that Iraq's transitional government faced when negotiating sovereign debt with foreign creditors in the aftermath of Saddam Hussein's dictatorship. This government had to give up from the outset on any "odious debt" claims, partly because it became clear that insisting on these claims would make it more difficult to negotiate restructuring of legitimate debt, and partly because the government faced the burden of showing which parts of the country's debt were illegitimate.[16] In contrast, had ideas about the people's property been central, there would not have been any trade-off between restructuring legitimate debt and repudiating odious debt, because such repudiation would have been the obvious baseline. And for that reason it would also have been the creditors' task

---

[14] This point also suggests that it can often be misleading to characterize creditors as engaging in debt "forgiveness" when they avoid the pursuit of payment for certain loans. Morally speaking, creditors are not in a position to "forgive" payment to which they had no moral entitlement to begin with (as is also pointed out in Christian Barry and Lydia Tomitova, "Fairness in Sovereign Debt," *Ethics & International Affairs* 21 [2007]: 41–79, at 47).

[15] Quoted in Lienau, *Rethinking Sovereign Debt*, 187.

[16] Lienau, *Rethinking Sovereign Debt*, 212.

4.3 The Integrity Angle   161

to explain which parts of the country's debt should be considered legitimate and why.

A final, ongoing example is also worth mentioning. At the time of writing, the United States continues to insist that Cambodia ought to pay back, with interest, loans that were incurred by the massively corrupt regime of Lon Nal in the 1970s, and which Cambodia has sought to repudiate. This American stance persists despite the fact that Nal came to power through a coup; despite the fact that the relevant loans were made to purchase American rice, wheat, oil and cotton; and despite the fact that the main reason why these loans were needed to begin with is that the United States itself engaged in a massive carpet-bombing campaign in Cambodia, forcing Cambodian rice farmers to flee away from their fields.[17] The US State Department currently chooses to ignore all of these points, insisting simply that "the international financial system will fall apart if governments cannot be held responsible for their predecessors' debts."[18] But from a normative point of view, this position again paints a highly misleading picture of who ought to face the burden of justification with regard to odious debt payments.

4.3 The Integrity Angle

Having discussed how the collective property framework can capture some key intuitions with regard to odious debt, I now wish to suggest that the collective integrity framework can do the same.

One important contribution of the integrity framework is to guide democratic governments as creditors who face the burden of justification I just emphasized. The collective property framework yields the thought that it is creditors who face the burden of explaining why they should be paid anything by the people in the context of debts incurred by severely oppressive regimes. But it does not follow from this that democratic governments as public creditors, at least, should necessarily try to meet this burden.[19] The integrity framework identifies

---

[17] See Julia Wallace, "Cambodia Appeals to Trump to Forgive War-Era Debt," *New York Times,* Apr. 2, 2017, at https://nytimes.com/2017/04/02/world/asia/cambodia-trump-debt.html?_r=0.
[18] Wallace, *Cambodia Appeals to Trump to Forgive War-Era Debt.*
[19] For the moment I will put aside the moral responsibilities of private creditors, which will be discussed later in this chapter.

circumstances in which democratic governments as creditors should actually refrain from trying to do this.

Suppose, for example, that in the past a democratic government repeatedly extended loans to multiple brutal dictatorships. In many of these cases, the loans coincided both with a major purchase of arms that the relevant dictatorship used for repression, and with some investment in public infrastructure. Should these loans be 'identified' with the latter, legitimate public expense, or with the former, illegitimate expense? Note that a question of this kind can be extremely difficult to settle on empirical grounds, not least because borrowed funds are fungible: even if it could be shown that the direct effect of any given loan was to support some public infrastructure investments, this support may have made it possible to shift other funds toward arms purchases. So some significant uncertainty is likely to remain about the causal impact of any given loan on the regime's conduct. Now, imagine that the democratic government pressed this uncertainty as justification for why the relevant people should now pay back each loan, with interest. Would this be morally appropriate?

The integrity framework suggests that the answer is no. To see why, we can go back to the idea of steadfastness that I have been associating with this framework. An agent acting with integrity, I have argued, is steadfast in its commitment to moral principles – is genuinely willing to incur non-trivial costs for the sake of these principles. An agent who professes a fundamental commitment to certain moral principles but who repeatedly clings to "escape clauses" from the hold of these principles cannot be said to really adhere to these commitments. Such an agent – whether individual or collective – lacks integrity.

It follows from all this that integrity constrains a democratic government's ability to invoke uncertainty about the consequences of its actions as an exemption from moral requirements. This means, among other things, that integrity constrains a democratic government's ability to invoke uncertainty surrounding the consequences of past loans it has made to severely oppressive regimes. It would be a failure of collective integrity for such a government to repeatedly cite such uncertainty as justification for why it should be paid back by the relevant foreign peoples. At most – and even this might very well be questionable – a government can cite such uncertainty as exempting it from a duty to compensate foreign peoples who have suffered under the relevant dictatorships. But it is hard to square the integrity of liberal

4.3 The Integrity Angle

democracy with a democratic government insisting in such circumstances that foreign peoples pay the entire principal on each one of these loans – let alone that foreign peoples make such loans profitable by paying the interest that the government has negotiated with the relevant past dictatorships.[20]

These integrity considerations, in turn, are amplified in all-too-common circumstances, where the democracy that lent the funds is far more affluent than the society that suffered under the relevant dictatorship. Here again the claims of Chapter 1 are helpful. In that chapter, I linked the idea of integrity to the idea of decency, and argued that one thing that a decent person does is concede ground in (potential or actual) disputes with vulnerable others, where the costs to him are trivial and the costs to the vulnerable are tremendous. This point is pertinent here, because it obtains for an affluent democracy as a collective agent just as much as it obtains for an individual person. It is indecent of an affluent democracy to insist that an impoverished foreign people pay it back for a loan extended to a past dictatorship, even when there is considerable uncertainty about the repercussions that this loan had for the people, even when the sums involved are trivial from the affluent's point of view, and even when they are dramatic from the poor's point of view.[21] In contrast, an affluent democracy does the decent thing when it willingly accepts rather than deflects responsibility for loans that may have been deleterious for the poor.

The example of Norway is a case in point. Norway did the decent thing when it unilaterally cancelled, in the mid-2000s, the debts associated with loans it made decades before to Ecuador, Egypt, Jamaica, Peru, and Sierra Leone. The official reason for this step was that the

---

[20] This is especially true when the relevant democratic government may have already benefited from these loans through illegitimate transactions they may have facilitated. Thus, for instance, if the arms that the dictatorship bought for repressive purposes came from the same democratic government that extended the loan to the dictatorship in the first place, then it would be especially disturbing for this government to insist on being paid interest for this loan.

[21] For a special emphasis on the stringent responsibilities of the world's affluent in the face of uncertainty about their causal contributions to global poverty, see Christian Barry and Gerhard Overland, *Responding to Global Poverty* (Cambridge: Cambridge University Press, 2016), Chapter 10. For extensive empirical evidence on how uncertainty pervades policy decisions regarding loans to poor countries, see Stephen Nelson, *The Currency of Confidence: How Economic Beliefs Shape the IMF's Relationship with Its Borrowers* (Ithaca, NY: Cornell University Press, 2017).

development policy rationale underlying these particular loans was now deemed to be flawed.[22] But arguably, the deeper reason was at least partly that even if the exact consequences of these loans were uncertain, and even if there was (therefore) uncertainty about Norway's exact causal role in the economic plight of these societies, for Norway to assume the greater share of responsibility for these loans was the decent thing to do, given its affluence and these societies' poverty. In recognizing this point and acting on it, Norway acted with integrity.

4.4 Collective Integrity and the Debts of Vulnerable Agents

The collective integrity framework, I argued in the last section, captures some important intuitions as to how a liberal democracy should respond to the burden of justification it faces with regard to past loans it has extended to repressive regimes. But this is not the only kind of response that a liberal democracy has to make in the context of such loans. Liberal democracies also have to respond to morally fraught actions that other agents take with regard to these loans. Using two examples, I want to show that the integrity framework can provide useful guidance here as well.

4.4.1 Reputational Calculations and Odious Debt Payments

The first example has to do with governments that insist on paying debts incurred by their predecessors, despite their clear odiousness, in order to minimize reputational risks that might affect their own ability to borrow funds in the future. Perhaps the most striking case of such insistence was the decision of South Africa's post-apartheid government to accept debt continuity with regard to the apartheid regime. As Odette Lienau describes:

By the end of apartheid, the fundamental illegitimacy of the regime was near-universally acknowledged. Most of the foreign banks that previously provided the regime with capital had withdrawn, under pressure from a successful international civil society movement through the 1980s and early 1990s . . . the new South African regime would likely have had more goodwill than any other for a principled debt repudiation . . . Under these

---

[22] See Lienau, *Rethinking Sovereign Debt*, 200.

4.4 Collective Integrity and the Debts of Vulnerable Agents 165

favorable circumstances, the conceptual claim that the new South Africa was a distinct and discontinuous sovereign . . . should not have been overly complex for potential investors, credit rating agencies, and other international actors to register. But, by this time, the norm of sovereign debt continuity was deeply embedded and had become central to the definition of a responsible member of the international community, which South Africa wished to be.[23]

Now, the fact that the new South African government decided to assume apartheid-era debt for these pragmatic reasons is clearly understandable. But it is nonetheless intuitive to think that it would have been morally appropriate for the creditors who held (and benefited from) apartheid-era debt to insist to the new South African government that they do *not* wish it to pay this debt. And this is an intuition that the integrity framework can neatly capture.

One way in which the framework can do this goes back to another aspect of decent treatment of the vulnerable presented in the opening chapter. A decent person who acts with integrity, I argued in Chapter 1, has strong reasons against accepting what are clearly disturbing sacrifices from vulnerable others, even if the vulnerable might have the prerogative of offering these sacrifices. Yet insofar as a reluctance to accept disturbing sacrifices by vulnerable others is an important mark of integrity, we should expect it not only in individual but also in collective agents. Hence an affluent democracy as a collective agent should similarly be reluctant to accept disturbing sacrifices from vulnerable others – including other vulnerable collective agents, such as post-apartheid South Africa. We can therefore say that it would have been an act of integrity for affluent democracies in the wake of apartheid's demise, to insist to the new South African government that they do not wish it to pay apartheid-era debt.

Moreover, we can use other aspects of the integrity framework to go even further. Throughout the previous chapters, I stressed the ways in which this framework captures important intuitions as to how a liberal democracy's particular history should affect its policies. Among other things, I argued – using the key example of US ties with South Africa – that a liberal democracy whose own history has been marked by an identity-grounding struggle against racism has especially stringent and weighty reasons of collective integrity to dissociate from foreign racist

[23] Lienau, *Rethinking Sovereign Debt*, 191–192.

regimes. This point suggests that while every liberal democracy had reasons of integrity to insist that it would not want the new South Africa to pay apartheid-era debt, these reasons were especially strong for a liberal democracy with a deeply racially charged history, such as the United States.

4.4.2 The Problem of Vulture Funds

Liberal democracies have to devise policy responses toward governments that may wish to pay odious debt accrued by previous regimes, due to reputational calculations of the kind just noted. But liberal democracies also need to respond to the behavior of private actors who may try, in systematic fashion, to benefit from the vulnerability of such governments.

The actors known as "vulture funds" are a key case in point. Vulture funds are private investor firms that purchase heavily devalued debt of vulnerable governments that are on the brink of default, solely with an eye toward benefiting from these governments' dire straits. The classic vulture fund strategy is to purchase highly de-valued sovereign debt from a public creditor, and then refuse to participate in any debt restructuring, instead taking the borrowing government to court in pursuit of the loan's full original principal, plus interest. Thus for example, in 1999, following protracted negotiations over a $15 million sovereign debt owed by Zambia to Romania, the Romanian government sold its rights to collect the debt to a vulture fund called Donegal International. Although Donegal paid less than $4 million for these rights, it eventually sued Zambia in a UK court for $55 million, representing the original principal of the loan plus interest.[24] Another vulture fund, FG Capital Management, also turned to UK courts to sue the Democratic Republic of the Congo for $100 million after acquiring government debts for $2.6 million, and was only blocked by England's Privy Council in 2012.[25] US-based NML Capital, one of the most notorious vulture funds, spent four years in courts to cash "distressed" Peruvian bank loans it had bought for $11.8 million, forcing the

---

[24] The affair ended with a $15 million settlement payment. See Thomas Laryea, "Donegal vs. Zambia and the Persistent Debt Problems of Low-Income Countries," *Law and Contemporary Problems* 73 (2010):193–200.

[25] See Daniel Huang, "What Happens When the Vulture Funds Start Circling," *Wall Street Journal*, Jun. 25, 2014, at https://blogs.wsj.com/moneybeat/2014/06/25/what-happens-when-the-the-vulture-funds-start-circling/.

4.4 Collective Integrity and the Debts of Vulnerable Agents 167

Peruvian government to settle in 2000 for almost $56 million.[26] Later on, the same NML Capital sued Congo-Brazzaville for $400 million for a debt it acquired for $10 million, ultimately securing $127 million.[27]

At least in some of these cases – and many others – it could well be argued that the original debt was itself odious, given the fact that the repressive regimes incurring it clearly lacked proper authorization to borrow in their people's name and systematically abused public funds. But the vulture funds' actions added further insult to the injury of such odious debts. In a 2012 op-ed, Hector Timerman, then-minister of foreign affairs for Argentina (another of NML Capital's victims), summarized the repercussions of this injury: "This is money that should be going to build roads, schools, and other poverty reduction programs. Worst, these nations are often on the receiving end of debt alleviation and international funding – which then goes to line the pockets of ... vulture funds."[28]

The integrity framework can readily explain why affluent democracies ought to combat this phenomenon. To see this, we can go back to another claim I made in the opening chapter. A decent person acting with integrity, I argued in Chapter 1, avoids blatant exploitation of vulnerable others: such a person does not act in a way that, beyond any reasonable doubt, unfairly takes advantage of others' duress for his own benefit. And what is true for an individual person is once again true for a liberal democracy as a collective agent. In particular, we can employ the integrity framework's focus on liberal law to say that a liberal democracy should not allow actors operating under its jurisdiction to use its own law to engage in blatant exploitation of vulnerable others.

It is worth noting that something very much like this integrity rationale has already received concrete expression in actual public policy. For example, this rationale motivated the UK's Debt Relief Act, passed in 2010 and made permanent in 2011. The Act aimed "to make sure that Vulture Funds will never again be able to exploit the poorest countries in the world within the UK's courts."[29] The same rationale

---

[26] See, e.g., Barry and Tomitova, *Fairness in Sovereign Debt*, 54.
[27] Hector Timerman, "Africa and Latin America Still Fight Vulture Funds," *Huffington Post*, Nov. 14, 2012, at http://huffingtonpost.com/hector-timerman/africa-latin-america-vulture-funds_b_2100827.html.
[28] Timerman, *Africa and Latin America Still Fight Vulture Funds*.
[29] "Government Acts to Halt Profiteering on Third World Debt within the UK," HM Treasury, May 16, 2011, at https://gov.uk/government/news/government-acts-to-halt-profiteering-on-third-world-debt-within-the-uk.

drove Belgium to enact parallel legislation in 2015.[30] The major creditor countries organized through the "Paris Club" have also followed suit, agreeing not to sell their loans to vulture funds, as did other EU countries.[31] From the perspective of collective integrity, these are all steps in the right direction.

4.5 Is Cancelling Odious Debt Always Appropriate?

So far in this chapter, I have sought to show how we can use the collective property and collective integrity frameworks to capture a variety of powerful intuitions as to how affluent democracies ought to respond to problems of odious debt accumulated by past repressive regimes. But up to this point I have been assuming that such regimes have been replaced by governments that are far more representative of their people. And unfortunately, there are many cases where this is not true. To take a key example, consider the thirty-nine nations designated by the IMF and the World Bank as Highly Indebted Poor Countries.[32] Many members of this group were not only ruled in the past by repressive regimes that are alien to the population, but are still being ruled by such regimes. Therefore, unconditional cancellation of these countries' debts may have the unintended consequence of strengthening the position of current repressive rulers, at their population's expense. Christian Barry captures this concern as follows:

---

[30] Unsurprisingly, vulture funds have been trying to contest this legislation. See, e.g., Antonio Gambini, "Vulture Fund Takes the Belgian Government to Court – and Belgian NGOs Join the Defence Team," Eurodad, Mar. 5, 2018, at www.eurodad.org/vulture-funds-belgium.

[31] See, e.g., Ben Hall, "Paris Club Steps Up Vulture Fund Action," *Financial Times*, Jun. 12, 2008. See also UNCTAD, "Sovereign Debt Restructurings: Lessons Learned from Legislative Steps Taken by Certain Countries and Other Appropriate Action to Reduce the Vulnerability of Sovereigns to Holdout Creditors," Oct. 2016, at http://un.org/en/ga/second/71/se2610bn.pdf.

[32] See, e.g., International Monetary Fund, "Factsheet: Debt Relief under the Heavily Indebted Poor Countries (HIPC) Initiative," Sep. 20, 2016, at http://imf.org/external/np/exr/facts/hipc.htm. The thirty-nine countries are Afghanistan, Benin, Bolivia, Burkina Faso, Burundi, Cameroon, Central African Republic, Chad, Comoros, Republic of Congo, Democratic Republic of Congo, Côte d'Ivoire, Eritrea, Ethiopia, The Gambia, Ghana, Guinea, Guinea-Bissau, Guyana, Haiti, Honduras, Liberia, Madagascar, Malawi, Mali, Mauritania, Mozambique, Nicaragua, Niger, Rwanda, São Tomé & Príncipe, Senegal, Sierra Leone, Somalia, Sudan, Tanzania, Togo, Uganda, and Zambia.

4.5 Is Cancelling Odious Debt Always Appropriate? 169

The granting of debt relief ... may not only fail to promote the fulfilment of human rights within the debtor country, but be counterproductive to this aim ... Reducing the debt burden of a country will do little to promote the fulfilment of the human rights of its population if its government uses the revenues freed up by debt relief on military equipment that does not enhance the security of its people, or to buy the latest-edition Mercedes to transport its ministers, or if its expenditures benefit only a few relatively well-off segments of the population.[33]

How, then, should we address this concern? One way to do so (recommended by Barry) is to re-think our conception of conditionality agreements promoted by institutions such as the IMF and the World Bank. Contrary to the familiar NGO tendency to view such agreements with automatic suspicion, we can be cognizant of the potential benefits of making debt cancellation, for example, conditional on a government credibly committing to use the freed-up revenues toward public ends rather than simply to cement its hold on power. There is nothing inappropriate about making debt cancellation vis-à-vis a repressive regime conditional on the regime credibly committing to direct the freed-up funds toward goals such as decreasing infant and maternal mortality rates, or increased access to improved sanitation and water sources.[34]

Now, there might very well be cases where such credible commitment cannot be had. The logistical obstacles toward this kind of commitment may be too great – whether because of the substitutability problem mentioned earlier, or even because of a basic lack of infrastructure to effectively monitor public expenses. Moreover, the repressive regime may be unwilling to commit to transparency about its use of public funds, or, even if officially willing, the regime's track record may be too disturbing to take its official proclamations seriously. When

---

[33] Barry, *Sovereign Debt, Human Rights, and Policy Conditionality*, 290–291.
[34] While NGOs often complain that IMF conditionality agreements represent an undue imposition of certain political and economic goals on foreign societies that may not share them, few NGOs would deny the universal applicability of these Millennium Development Goals, measured by the IMF and World Bank as part of debt cancellation initiatives. See, e.g., International Monetary Fund, "Heavily Indebted Poor Countries (HIPC) Initiative and Multilateral Debt Relief Initiative (MDRI) – Statistical Update," March 2016, at http://imf.org/e xternal/np/pp/eng/2016/031516.pdf. For an empirical perspective on some of the relevant debates see Stephen Nelson and Geoffrey Wallace, "Are IMF Lending Programs Good or Bad for Democracy?" (forthcoming, *Review of International Organizations*).

such circumstances obtain, there might be at least a *pro tanto* case for affluent democracies insisting on the regime paying back even odious debt. But it is essential – in line with the notion of steadfastness emphasized above – that affluent democracies do not take such circumstances as an excuse for simply keeping the relevant funds, as if the loans that generated them were entirely unproblematic. Rather, affluent democracies should publicly commit themselves to pursuing whatever means they can to ensure that these funds actually help the relevant country's most vulnerable population rather than its ruling elites.

The best way to pursue this goal will obviously depend on each relevant country's specific political and economic dynamics. In some cases, direct cash or goods transfers to needy families might be an important way of bypassing grasping regimes.[35] In other cases, it might be wiser to simply place the relevant funds in a trust, which will be transferred to the control of the relevant country once it has at least a minimally accountable government (an idea on which I will say more later in this chapter).[36] In other cases still, it might be that the most a given affluent democracy can do for a foreign people suffering under a severely repressive regime is to open its doors to potential or actual refugees fleeing the regime.[37] The property and integrity frameworks cannot tell us which of these policies is optimal "in general"– arguably no normative account can do this detached from specific empirical contingencies. But the property and integrity framework can tell us that these policies are not merely supererogatory – something that affluent democracies may initiate out of "kindness." At least in cases where democratic governments themselves extended key odious loans to begin with, they have a moral duty to

---

[35] See, for example, Christopher Blattman and Paul Niehaus, "Show Them the Money: Why Giving Cash Helps Alleviate Poverty," *Foreign Affairs* 93 (2014): 117–126.

[36] This is a parallel to Leif Wenar's proposal regarding natural resource trade with kleptocrats. See, e.g., Wenar, "Fighting the Resource Curse," *Global Policy* 4 (2013): 298–304. I think the idea of such a trust is actually easier to implement in the case of odious debt, but I will not try to show this here. I will note, though, that such trusts already feature in affluent democracies' response to corruption in countries such as Equatorial Guinea (one of Wenar's prime cases) and Kazakhstan. See, e.g., Kieron Monks, "Nigerian Group Requests $500 Million from Trump Administration," *CNN*, Jan. 3, 2018, at https://cnn.com/2017/02/15/africa/nigeria-lost-assets-trump/index.html.

[37] For remarks along similar lines see David Wiens,"Natural Resources and Government Responsiveness," *Politics, Philosophy & Economics* 14 (2015): 84–105.

4.6 The Challenge of Future Loans

4.6.1 The Basic Approach

Let me now turn from backward-looking questions regarding odious debt to forward-looking issues. Undermining de facto-ism regarding odious debt accumulated in the past is obviously important. But we must also consider future-oriented criteria for morally fraught loans, since without such criteria, the problems of the past will only recreate themselves.

My suggestion is that we adopt future-oriented criteria that parallel our backward-looking considerations. In other words, the presumption ought to be that liberal democracies refrain – and make sure private creditors they regulate refrain – from lending funds to a regime that they have good reason to believe is guilty of two infractions: (1) lacking popular authorization to borrow funds in the people's name; (2) systematically abusing public funds. Creditors need to have special reasons for deviating from this presumption, and should face the burden of defending such exceptions on a case-by-case basis.

Collective property considerations clearly support this view. Stepping away from customary practices regarding sovereign borrowing – not just with regard to past debts but also with regard to future loans – is justified partly as a way of respecting foreign peoples' ownership over state property. This ownership does not align with massively corrupt and manifestly unaccountable rulers having the capacity to borrow funds in the people's name. If we take public property seriously, we cannot allow such rulers to commit their peoples to relinquish portions of public property in the future in order to pay for what is essentially the rulers' private borrowing.

Collective integrity considerations push in the same direction. The most immediate way to see this point is to go back to what I called in Chapter 1 the "global integrity test." This test requires each liberal democracy to assess whether foreign practices facilitated by its own law could be incorporated into its domestic institutions in a way that would still keep its identity-grounding institutions intact. It should be clear that this is not the case here. A reality in which de facto leaders are able to borrow massive funds in their people's name, without anything like the people's authorization and while systematically abusing these funds for their private ends, would distort liberal democracies' identity-grounding institutions beyond recognition. This means that there are strong reasons of integrity for each liberal democracy not to have its law facilitate such practices beyond its borders.

In turn, both of these sets of considerations have a decidedly non-consequentialist character. From a property perspective, reform of customary practices is meant to ensure that the rules governing sovereign borrowing do not wrong foreign peoples by violating their property rights, independently of whether these rules have good consequences for these peoples. The integrity claim – the thought that its own integrity should push each liberal democracy to disentangle from "odious borrowing" by certain foreign rulers – has a similarly non-consequentialist character. This claim is not dependent on whether disentanglement would produce good consequences for the peoples living under the relevant rulers.

However, while the property and integrity factors give us non-consequentialist foundations for reform of sovereign borrowing, the consequences of reform are clearly a morally important factor as well. In particular, it would be implausible – and morally irresponsible – to simply ignore the consequences that reforms driven by property and integrity concerns might yield for some of the world's most vulnerable people. I will accordingly spend much of the remainder of this chapter discussing how my future-oriented proposal, despite its non-consequentialist roots, can make coherent room for these consequentialist concerns.

4.6.2 *Private Creditors' Incentives*

One way to approach some of the relevant consequentialist challenges is to spell out further the two criteria of popular authorization and systematic regime abuse of public funds. In line with several other proposals for reforming de facto-ist practices surrounding sovereign borrowing, I am going to assume that popular authorization to borrow funds in the people's name requires democratic procedures. Hence regimes that manifestly violate the requirements of free and fair elections – typically, in the twenty-first century, not by avoiding elections but rather by engaging in large-scale electoral

4.6 The Challenge of Future Loans

fraud[38] – can be said to lack popular authorization to borrow in their people's name.[39]

Non-democratic regimes, of course, may not necessarily engage in systematic abuse of public funds, and even when they do engage in such abuse, its severity will likely vary from case to case. These facts may give rise to a particular kind of consequentialist worry – that a reform of customary practices regarding sovereign borrowing will generate too many "false negatives." If we are not careful, there will be many cases where loans that should be permissible are instead prohibited, resulting in potentially significant setbacks to the interests of vulnerable populations in developing countries that could very well reap significant fruits from these loans.[40]

The best way to address this worry, I believe, is to design an alternative to the status quo that is sufficiently flexible. Thus, for example, creditors who wish to defeat the presumption against lending to a given authoritarian regime could do so, at least to some extent, by proving that the regime has made significant improvement over the last several years in using borrowed funds for public rather than private ends. Similarly, if creditors can show that the funds they will lend will be

---

[38] See, e.g., Susan Hyde, *The Pseudo-Democrat's Dilemma* (Ithaca, NY: Cornell University Press, 2011), as well as Ashlea Rundlett and Milan Svolik, "Deliver the Vote! Micromotives and Macrobehavior in Electoral Fraud," *American Political Science Review* 110 (2016): 180–197.

[39] Notice, in particular, that the mere absence of popular protests cannot signify anything like valid authorization for a regime to control public funds or specifically borrow on the people's behalf. One reason, highlighted by various commentators, is that absence of popular protests may simply be the result of effective coercion by the regime. Another reason follows directly from the collective property framework: if we take seriously the people's ownership over public property, then we cannot infer from the people's silence that it authorizes the regime's use of public resources, just as we cannot infer from an individual owner's silence that she authorizes another agent's use of her property. The presumption, at the collective as at the individual level, is that if the owner is silent then manipulation of the owner's property by others is prohibited.

[40] Concerns of this sort animate, for example, Scott Wisor's "Conditional Coercion versus Rights Diagnostics: Two Approaches to Human Rights Protection," *Politics, Philosophy & Economics* 15 (2016): 405–423. Wisor apparently views the withdrawing of customary borrowing privileges as posing similar risks to the welfare of the vulnerable in developing countries, as compared to other international commercial sanctions. For some doubts on this score see Seema Jayachandran and Michael Kremer, "Odious Debt," *American Economic Review* 96 (2006): 82–92.

spent in sectors where there the relevant regime has had little or no record of corruption, this should help in mitigating the presumption against allowing loans to the regime.

Given the aforementioned logistical obstacles toward verifying the causal effects of any given loan, some may think that even this kind of flexibility is insufficient. In particular, some may argue that even if creditors could in principle justify certain prospective loans, the costs and complications involved would be too steep for the effort to be financially viable. The result would be private creditors avoiding such complications by shifting their portfolios away from many developing countries ruled by authoritarians, again depriving poor populations of much-needed funds.[41]

This is an important objection. Yet we should not overestimate its force. This is partly because of the particular features of the status quo. For one thing, as previously emphasized, there are very strong grounds for thinking that many ongoing loans to dictatorships ruling some of the world's poorest people are a curse rather than a blessing for these people. So even if there is a real danger of "false negatives," effectively preventing private creditors from extending loans that will help the world's poorest, there is also a very real danger of "false positives" – of allowing loans that will harm the world's poorest.[42] Additionally, for many extremely poor countries, there is no current pool of private loans that will be taken away in case we depart from the status quo, since their macroeconomic situation already deters private creditors from lending.[43]

Moreover, it is sensible to think that setting up different ground rules for sovereign borrowing can positively affect private creditors' attitude on an issue that is at least as crucial for poor countries as is the volume of private lending: the issue of precedent. Over the last several decades, virtually every government from a developing country that has sought debt restructuring has found that the mere mention of "odious debt" would alarm private creditors concerned with setting up "dangerous" precedents. The result was that even when the value of the relevant debt

---

[41] Another possible result, which might very well seem equally problematic, is that private creditors will charge risk premiums on such loans that would be too high for poor countries to afford.

[42] Indeed, for some at least the latter danger will be a key part of the motivation for disputing customary practices regarding sovereign borrowing.

[43] See International Monetary Fund, "Factsheet: Debt Relief under the Heavily Indebted Poor Countries (HIPC) Initiative."

was minuscule from the creditors' perspective, they would refuse to erase the debt out of fear that many other debtor countries would seek similar "exceptions."[44] But if the ground rules regulating sovereign borrowing were altered in the direction proposed here, then cancelling odious debt would no longer be an "exception," but rather the norm. It is true that this shift may deter private creditors from making some loans that could be morally beneficial. But because it will also render moot the creditors' worry about "setting up dangerous examples," this shift will allow creditors, at least in some cases, to bargain far less harshly on debt restructuring. And that is an issue of profound importance for a very large number of poor countries.

To these specific points regarding the implications of the status quo for the world's poorest, we may add three more general observations concerning the complex regulations that creditors will have to face in case of reform. First, there are many areas of business activity where we intuitively accept the need for often-complex government regulations, even while recognizing that these regulations may derail generally valuable economic exchange. This is the case for anything from mortgage and stock market regulations inhibiting banks' activities to environmental regulations limiting the operations of coal and oil corporations. In these and many other contexts, we simply recognize that the potential benefits of unregulated economic activity are outweighed by countervailing moral considerations. The same is arguably true here.

Second, very much related, insofar as such complex regulations place obstacles in the way of private firms, this is primarily because the additional costs they pose yield lower profit margins. But there are many contexts – from child labor to safety regulations regarding certain products – where firms clearly ought to accept these margins as

---

[44] This point was clear in how commercial banks treated negotiations over Nicaragua's sovereign debt after the Somozas' downfall. As Weinert (*Nicaragua's Debt Renegotiation*, 189) puts it, "The banks' obsession was with precedent. They entered the negotiations knowing they would have to reschedule and that the circumstances both demanded and justified somewhat more lenient terms than usual. But at stake was more than the sums involved, which, while substantial in the aggregate, were generally less than a month's earnings for any of the individual banks involved. However, the concurrent negotiations with Jamaica, Sudan, Zaire, and Turkey and untold future negotiations were a constant undercurrent at the negotiating table."

normal, or at least accept the relevant regulations as a given. The same is again true in the case of morally risky loans to authoritarians.

Finally, where there are compelling moral grounds, all things considered, for extending certain loans to a particular authoritarian regime, despite its systematic abuse of public resources, the issue of low profit margins may be addressed partly through more significant involvement by public creditors. By stepping in where private creditors are reluctant to enter for commercial reasons, public creditors may provide loans that are ultimately beneficial to vulnerable populations (as is currently the case concerning the Highly Indebted Poor Countries). Additionally, public creditors may also be able to assuage private creditors' fears about certain lending strategies, despite new costs that these strategies will involve for creditors. By implementing these strategies where private creditors will be reluctant to try them, public creditors will shoulder the initial risks to show to private creditors that the relevant loans can be commercially viable.

4.7 Institutional Design and the Problem of Collective Action

The previous section focused on criteria for evaluating future loans to de facto governments that differ from customary practices. But I have not said much about the institutional mechanisms that should support this proposed alternative. To fill this gap, it might be helpful to consider two existing proposals with which my position aligns to a significant extent.

One proposal comes from Thomas Pogge, who envisions constitutional amendments in fragile democracies, announcing *ex ante* that if a dictatorship comes to power, debts it incurs will be repudiated by future legitimate governments. Pogge notes that such an amendment may incentivize future dictatorial regimes to refuse to pay the external debts of democratic governments (since these regimes will not be able to borrow abroad anyway), and this in turn will push creditors to refrain from lending even to fragile democratic governments, out of fear that in case of authoritarian regress they will not see their debts respected. Anticipating this problem, Pogge proposes that affluent democracies contribute to a "democracy fund" that will service debts incurred by fledging democratic governments, in case a dictatorship repudiates them. Pogge further suggests the establishment of a "Democracy Panel," comprised of neutral foreign experts, who will

4.7 Institutional Design and the Problem of Collective Action

define whether the government that incurred a given debt was democratic.[45]

Another proposal comes from Jonathan Shafter, who envisions an existing or new international organization determining whether a given regime is "odious debt prone" – that is, whether it is "either unwilling or unable to provide for a reasonable modicum of public consent to its policies and where the likelihood that levels of sovereign borrowing material to the nation's economy will be used for illegitimate purposes crosses an unacceptable threshold."[46] Once a regime is designated as odious debt prone, potential creditors have to present a plan specifying both the legitimate ends for which their funds are intended and the exact ways in which they will monitor the actual use of these funds. A loan would be "invalidated" – that is, the debtor country will not have an obligation to pay back the loan – only if "the funds were diverted toward illegitimate ends and the lender failed to make a good faith effort to comply with its own pre-approved due diligence plan."[47]

The approach I presented above obviously has a great deal in common with these two proposals. In fact, one conceivable way of implementing my approach would be to adopt something like the institutional mechanisms that Pogge and Shafter outline. Yet the collective property and collective integrity frameworks can nonetheless refine our thinking about these mechanisms in at least three ways, which we may mention in ascending order of significance.

First, considering the details of Shafter's proposal, the approach I favor can be seen as more stringent in an important respect. On Shafter's model, a private creditor that sought to extend loans to "odious debt prone" regimes even without a "due diligence" plan would be allowed to do so, but would not be defended if the relevant debtor country later sought to repudiate the debt. In contrast, the arguments presented here suggest that in such cases creditors should not be allowed to make the loan to begin with.

Second, considering the details of Pogge's specific proposal, the approach I have been defending can be seen as more comprehensive,

---

[45] Thomas Pogge, "Achieving Democracy," *Ethics and International Affairs* 15 (2001): 3–23.
[46] Jonathan Shafter, "The Due Diligence Model: A New Approach to the Problem of Odious Debts," *Ethics & International Affairs* (2007): 49–67, at 59.
[47] Shafter, "The Due Diligence Model," 51.

at least insofar as it is not limited to countries that have some history of democratic government. In contrast to Pogge, on the view I am proposing, the presumption that each liberal democracy ought to implement against lending to certain kinds of regimes is not dependent upon democratic governments preceding these regimes and passing any constitutional amendment. This point is important partly because many of the world's poorest countries – and indeed the vast majority of the world's Highly Indebted Poor Countries – have never had reasonably democratic governments.

Third, insofar as both Pogge and Shafter emphasize the role of international institutions in reforming customary practices, their proposals are vulnerable to the collective action problems that often haunt attempts at international cooperation, of the sort highlighted in the opening chapter. Thus for instance, one can imagine various democracies excusing themselves from contributing resources to the "democracy fund" by citing the lack of credible commitment from other countries, and insisting that this lack of commitment makes the moral gains from such a fund too limited and uncertain to justify their own sacrifices. One can also imagine such "ineffective sacrifice" excuses arising more generally, as each democracy points out that whatever business opportunities it will avoid with odious regimes will simply be taken up by less scrupulous countries and creditors. In contrast, the ideas of collective property and collective integrity allow us to preempt such collective action excuses by alerting us to the ways in which each specific democracy acting independently can and ought to initiate reform. After all, if each democracy has at least a *pro tanto* duty to disentangle itself from lending to odious regimes, partly as a matter of its own integrity and partly as a matter of respecting the property rights of the people living under such regimes, then no democracy can "pass the buck" to others. At least to some extent, each democracy would have to reform its own conduct, and the conduct of private companies based in its own jurisdiction, independently of other democracies' policy choices. Each democratic government, for example, ought to review and potentially rule out creditors' "due diligence" plans concerning loans to odious regimes, independently of any international collective action regarding loans to such regimes.[48]

---

[48] This is not to deny the importance of such collective action in the long run. Moreover, insofar as the property and integrity frameworks bolster the demand

4.8 The Exile Proposal

> He was one more incognito in the city of illustrious incognitos ... he had returned to Geneva after two world wars ... the years of glory and power had been left behind forever, and now only the years of his death remained ... The President stood up and, instead of buying a daisy from the flower vendor, he picked one from the public plantings and put it in his buttonhole. She caught him in the act. "Those flowers don't belong to God, Monsieur," she said in vexation. "They're city property."
>
> Gabriel Garcia Marquez, Bon Voyage, Mr. President [49]

I am aware that, notwithstanding the various claims I have already made in the course of this chapter, some readers are likely to remain concerned about sad realities that my arguments here may seem to ignore. For one thing, there is the sad reality of odious debt cases where conditions on the ground mean that there is truly no way to circumvent grasping dictators who are effectively holding their population hostage. In these cases, customary loans – for all of their shortcomings – really do seem like the least worst of possible worlds. Furthermore, although unilateral action has the virtue of circumventing the collective action problems I just emphasized, it is also inherently limited in its structural potential. Short of extreme measures such as unilateral military action, of which we have ample reason to be deeply suspicious, unilateral action – even by powerful affluent democracies – will typically do little to promote structural change in developing countries suffering under extremely corrupt strongmen.

One response to these worries goes back to a point that was already stressed in Chapter 1. Even in circumstances where all the policy choices available to liberal democracies leave a great deal to be desired, the collectivist ideas that I have been developing – and especially the notion of collective integrity – can be helpful in capturing the tragic nature of the relevant policy dilemmas.

There is also, however, a more constructive response that we might make to the pessimist here. Taken together, the two collectivist frameworks support at least one distinctive proposal for breaking out of the deadlock of unlikely collective action and ineffective solitary action.

---

for each democracy to lead by example, these frameworks might make such future collective action more likely.

[49] In Marquez, *Strange Pilgrims*, trans. Edith Grossman (New York: Alfred Knopf, 1993), 3–6.

The proposal that I have in mind concerns a particular kind of exile deal. Here is how such a deal might work. Consider once again a Nicaragua-style case, where there is little doubt that the regime is systematically abusing loans extended by foreign creditors. Suppose further that simply boycotting the regime – completely halting the supply of loans – could have serious deleterious consequences for the people living under the dictatorship. But suppose that instead of accepting this dire state of affairs as immune to change, even one affluent democracy tackles it in a new way. This democracy does not boycott the dictatorship. But it also refuses to simply ignore the striking abuse of the loans extended to the dictatorship. Instead, the relevant democracy offers the dictator and his family a safe but conditional exile within its own borders.[50] This exile is conditional not only upon the dictator's permanent retirement from politics, but also upon his revealing, and forfeiting, all of the family's secret bank accounts within the relevant democracy's jurisdiction.[51] The relevant democracy, in turn, will go on to hold all of the funds in these accounts in trust for the people who have been living under the dictatorship.

Such a deal should be more tempting to the dictator the more he has domestic threats to fear, and the more these threats are likely to be lethal. A strongman who steals billions from his people, and is widely

---

[50] I am assuming here that the relevant dictator, while massively corrupt, is not guilty of atrocities such as mass killings or mass torture, which would trigger involvement by the international criminal court (ICC). These more extreme cases obviously present different – moral and practical – complexities. For a recent empirical discussion, distinguishing more moderate, "merely corrupt" dictators who seek exile from human rights violators, see Daniel Krcmaric, "Should I Stay or Should I Go? Leaders, Exile, and the Dilemmas of International Justice," *American Journal of Political Science* 62 (2018): 486–498.

[51] In some cases, such a deal will also help affluent democracies themselves, whose regulatory agencies cannot (even in the best-case scenario) conceivably monitor every instance of illicit financial transactions, and whose own integrity (in distinctly non-ideal circumstances) might also be compromised through far-too-intimate links to the corporations they are supposed to monitor. The example of Pinochet and Washington's Riggs Bank is a case in point. This bank, which went out of its way to attract Pinochet's multi-million dollar "investments," and to keep them secret, was supposed to be regulated by the Office of the Comptroller of the Currency. But the lead regulator himself ended up taking an executive position at the bank. That may have had something to do with the very lax oversight of the bank's activities. See, e.g., Timothy O'Brien, "At Riggs Bank, a Tangled Path Led to Scandal," *New York Times*, Jul. 19, 2004, at https://nytimes.com/2004/07/19/us/at-riggs-bank-a-tangled-path-led-to-scandal.html.

4.8 The Exile Proposal

known to do so, cannot expect a happy end if he loses political power due to a palace or military coup, for example. In such circumstances, losing power may very well mean also losing one's life. And so the prospect of a safe exile – away from ruthless competitors and compatriots eager to violently avenge corruption – may very well seem attractive in comparison, even if it involves surrendering a great deal of opulence.

Now, what links this proposal to our collectivist frameworks? With regard to the collective property framework, at least, the answer should be obvious: the exile proposal seeks to salvage as much of the people's property as possible, even in truly dire circumstances. But the collective integrity framework also supports – and refines – this proposal in at least four ways. First, this proposal exemplifies the sort of trenchant creativity that – as I have emphasized repeatedly in previous chapters – integrity requires when confronting difficult circumstances. Instead of liberal democracies accepting as fait accompli a vast gap between their commitments and their conduct, collective integrity requires that liberal democracies do their very best to honor these commitments – even when doing so involves quite heterodox tactics.

Second, the integrity framework refines the exile proposal, by specifying further how powerful democracies should go about offering exile to relevant dictators. For one thing, although a secure exile for a former dictator may very well involve something like a witness protection program – a hidden existence, perhaps even a new identity – the demands of public honesty that I have been associating with collective integrity mean that the offer of exile should itself be public rather than secret, and that the rationale grounding it should be made public as well. In other words, when offering exile, affluent democracies should not pretend that the offer's recipients are in any way better than they actually are. Rather, affluent democracies should openly proclaim that they are offering exile to unsavory characters out of a forward-looking concern with the needs of the people who have been suffering under them. Furthermore, once the authorities in an affluent democracy are satisfied that a dictator seeking exile has actually disclosed all of the funds he has held within this democracy's jurisdiction, the relevant democracy ought to publicly commit to transfer all of these funds to the relevant foreign people, once this people enjoys a sufficiently representative government that is sufficiently stable. In particular, just as an affluent democracy ought not appeal to uncertainty about the consequences of its past loans to impoverished countries as a justification for why these loans should be paid back in full, so an affluent democracy ought not invoke uncertainty about the origins of some of the funds a dictator holds under its jurisdiction as an excuse for keeping any portion of these funds.

Notice, moreover, that although the integrity framework insists on the intrinsic significance of public honesty, this is a case where intrinsic and instrumental considerations actually align to a significant extent. This is because an affluent democracy that publicly commits itself to offering a secure exile to dictators on the terms noted above is bound to have greater credibility, as far as dictators are concerned, than would fellow authoritarians who make a similar offer. A safe haven proposed by one dictator to another – even if offered publicly – may become much less safe if the host is toppled or if his whims simply change. But an exile that is publicly offered by a stable democracy, as an official policy backed by a transparent legislative procedure, is less likely to be fickle.[52]

With this point in mind, we can consider another way in which collective integrity informs the idea of conditional exile for dictators. Such an exile deal clearly involves various costs for affluent democracies. An affluent democracy proceeding with a deal of this sort would not only have to relinquish any dictator-held funds deposited in its banks. It would also have to take up the financial, diplomatic, and public relations costs associated with offering a safe home to some extremely – perhaps even universally – unpopular individuals. But

---

[52] IR scholarship offers some empirical backing for this contention, pointing, for example, to how an independent judiciary (absent in autocracies by definition) facilitates credible commitments. This scholarship also gives us reason to distinguish between democracies' ability to make credible commitments when facing dictators implicated in atrocities, as compared to dictators implicated in "mere" corruption. On the first issue, see Michael Findley and Joseph Young, "Terrorism, Democracy, and Credible Commitments," *International Studies Quarterly* 55 (2011): 357–378. On the second, see, e.g., Abel Escriba-Folch and Daniel Krcmaric, "Dictators in Exile: Explaining the Destinations of Ex-Rulers," *Journal of Politics* 79 (2017): 560–575, as well as Krcmaric, *The Justice Dilemma* (unpublished book manuscript). One more point that is worth mentioning here concerns another comparative advantage of established democracies as exile destinations: even those established democracies that are fairly minor international players (think, for instance, of Scandinavian countries) are unlikely to be the target of constant pressures from powerful democracies demanding that former dictators be extradited to them. In contrast, powerful democracies are likely to have few qualms about exerting similar pressures on many autocratic governments.

4.8 The Exile Proposal

what matters more from an integrity perspective is that these costs are still trivial for an affluent democracy to bear in comparison to the costs that an impoverished society saddled with odious debt will continue to endure if the dictatorship ruling it were to endure as well. Therefore, an affluent democracy that has an identity-grounding commitment to treat vulnerable others decently will accept, rather than balk at, the costs involved in an exile proposal of the kind outlined here.

Finally, just as with a variety of other policy issues discussed so far in this book, here too the collective integrity framework captures an important intuition as to how a liberal democracy's particular history might amplify its moral duties. To see this point, imagine a now-affluent democracy that was previously a poor authoritarian nation, in a manner not too different from, say, South Korea.[53] Suppose further that a crucial part of this society's past poverty had to do with odious debt traps that originated with a severely repressive regime, and that the memory of this regime (and the struggle to overcome it) is still very much alive in collective consciousness. It is intuitive to think that an affluent democracy with this particular historical identity has an especially weighty and stringent duty to pursue creative strategies – such as exile deals with dictators – in order to support the efforts by present-day impoverished societies to escape their own odious debt spirals. The collective integrity framework can easily make sense of this powerful intuition.

I should hasten to concede that, notwithstanding the support and specifications I just offered, many further details can and should be added to the exile proposal. For one thing, this proposal will clearly make more sense the more there is reason to think that a credible democratic opposition can succeed a dictator who goes into exile: in cases where the only likely alternative to one corrupt strongman is another such strongman, democracies should plainly have limited enthusiasm for extending exile offers.[54]

---

[53] See the World Bank overview of South Korea, at http://worldbank.org/en/country/korea/overview (last updated in April 2018).

[54] Along similar lines, it is also important to assess how likely it is that the existing power structure surrounding a dictator will crumble in his absence. In cases featuring Kuran-style collective action problems, of the sort emphasized in Chapter 3, one may hope that with the dictator gone, many of his underlings will be able to stop falsifying their preferences, and to support – or at least not actively "spoil" – a democratic transition. Where this is not the case, the

Moreover, even when a credible democratic opposition does exist, the proposal would have to be fine-tuned to take into account particular incentives on the dictators' part. The question of incentives associated with their families, and particularly with their offspring, is one example. Dictators are often concerned not only with the fate of their families in general (as I pointed out in the previous chapter), but also with their children's educational prospects in particular. Dictators therefore have a clear incentive to ensure that their children have access to the educational opportunities available in affluent democracies – opportunities that cannot be equaled in any fellow autocracy where they might seek exile.[55] It might therefore be appropriate for affluent democracies to make such access conditional on the kind of exile deal discussed here, at least absent special circumstances.[56]

Another example has to do with the fact that the proposal as I described it will predictably push dictators to seek exile in those democracies that hold the smallest portion of their illicit funds. One way to anticipate this problem might be for the authorities in any prospective host democracy to commit the dictator to a public disclosure of all of the assets he holds in any democratic country, with the hope of publicly shaming other democracies into action as well.[57]

Yet another problem may be posed by dictators who clearly feel confident that their rule can survive for many years, and who are accordingly reluctant to even consider the exile deal. At least in some instances, there might be a case for incentivizing such dictators to make the deal by offering to legalize a small percentage of their illicit holdings

---

prospective host may have to entertain exile offers to multiple members of the existing regime – hardly an enticing prospect.

[55] On just how common Western education is for dictators' children, see Thomas Gift and Daniel Krcmaric, "Who Democratizes? Western-Educated Leaders and Regime Transitions," *Journal of Conflict Resolution* 61 (2017): 671–701.

[56] That is, unless the children of a corrupt strongman manage to prove that they have taken no part in his wrongdoing and that their admission and tuition have nothing to do with his political or economic clout.

[57] The more extensive the disclosure that the potential host democracy requires, the harder it is for this democracy to verify the data provided by the dictator seeking exile. In circumstances where this is clearly a problem, it may be sensible to incorporate further clauses into the exile deal – for example, a clause stipulating that if, at any point following the deal, credible sources emerge that indicate specific funds that the relevant dictator has failed to disclose, the deal will be cancelled, and the former dictator (and his family) will be expelled.

in exchange for full disclosure and forfeiture of the remainder.[58] This legalized fraction may then serve, for example, as an above-board endowment that would fund the costs of ensuring the (former) dictator's safety in exile.[59]

These are the kinds of specific design concerns that would have to be worked out in order for the proposal I have been outlining here to be complete. But I hope that the sketch offered in the preceding pages already suffices to make clear why we have strong reasons, concerning both collective property and collective integrity, to seriously contemplate exile deals as a possible mechanism for structural change, in cases where more familiar policy options clearly fall short.

Before moving on, I should stress that deals of this sort – and other policy mechanisms I have been considering here – are of course non-ideal. We should not be delighted with official bargains that formally legalize, for example, even a portion of the proceeds of massive crimes. But in reflecting on justified policies in such cases, we must keep front and center the sad fact that the very nature of the relevant problems makes it impossible to satisfy all of our moral values without any kind of remainder. We must compromise on our values to some extent when dealing with tragic situations of this sort. The challenge is to do so in a limited and coherent way.

Two Final Objections

In the course of this chapter, I have sought to show that ideas regarding collective integrity and collective property can deliver compelling recommendations regarding odious debt problems, capturing many firm moral intuitions about such problems, while also providing

---

[58] Where there are credible fears that a given dictator will engage in further repression in order to improve his bargaining position – and the portion of the illicit funds that will be legalized – it might be sensible to make the exile offer a "one-off" – announcing it publicly, but also making clear that the dictator can only "take it or leave it," rather than engage in any protracted negotiations.

[59] Presumably with the stipulation that once the dictator-in-exile dies, or decides for any reason to live in another country, this endowment would then revert back to the people of his country. Moreover, at least in cases where the host democracy is especially affluent, and the dictator's country of origin is especially poor, one may also consider the idea of the host democracy committing to transfer, to the nation of origin, a sum equivalent to that portion of the proceeds of theft that had to be legalized to incentivize the dictator to make the deal.

guidance where our intuitions are less certain. Before concluding, I want to consider two last objections to the guidance I have offered.

The first objection holds that the account I presented here pays insufficient attention to the normative differences between private and public lenders. It is one thing to argue that a democratic government ought to refrain from lending funds to certain non-democratic regimes. But it is another thing altogether to argue that a democratic government ought to prohibit private firms based within its jurisdiction from lending to these regimes. Such a prohibition interferes with these private creditors' exercise of their property rights, and this interference may be unjustified independently of how governments ought to behave as public creditors.

One problem with this objection is that it misconceives the relationship between political regulation and private property rights, in a way that the collective property framework usefully brings out. This framework, I argued in Chapter 2, alerts us to the fact that private property rights are a political creation, and are always exercised within the parameters set by this regulation. Therefore, when there are compelling moral reasons for certain forms of political regulation, as there are in the case before us, these reasons cannot be trumped by appealing to private property rights: one cannot invoke such rights as fundamental constraints on political decision-making. Moreover, it is especially unconvincing to appeal to property rights as a justification for allowing private creditors to lend to odious regimes, insofar as such lending itself violates property rights – namely, as I have argued above, the property rights of the people who live under these regimes.

Joining these collective property points, the collective integrity framework suggests one more problem with the objection. As I stressed in Chapter 1, it is a failure of collective integrity for a democratic government to officially recognize a certain action or practice as profoundly wrong, and accordingly commit all public agencies to steer clear of this wrong, while taking no policy stance at all regarding the behavior of private agents. Although one can give numerous domestic examples by way of illustration, the international example prominent in the opening chapter – that of US divestment from South Africa's apartheid regime – seems especially on point here. A key part of what made the Comprehensive Anti-Apartheid Act passed by the US Congress truly comprehensive was not only the fact that it explicitly prohibited loans to the apartheid regime, but that it prohibited private actors from making such loans.[60] If this were not the case – if private actors were allowed to continue lending to the regime – this would have been an example of what I called in Chapter 1 the hypocrisy of distance: an example of a government implausibly shirking responsibility for the behavior of other agents whose conduct clearly falls under its purview. So including private lenders in the reach of the Anti-Apartheid Act was what integrity required. And what was true for this past law is true for similar laws that ought to be enacted in the present and the future.

With these points in mind, we can turn to the other objection. According to this objection, my position with regard to sovereign lending and borrowing (and perhaps even with regard to multiple other policy areas discussed so far in this book) is too demanding of affluent democracies to be feasible. The costs that my position requires of affluent democracies to bear are simply too great. In particular, in order for any normative position to have a real chance of getting a "foot in the door" in the world of the actual public policy, it would be far better to present affluent democracies with moral claims that are far more modest in the sacrifices they require.

There are at least three points that one can make in response to this objection. First, "getting a foot in the door," starting with the most minimal requirements, is only one way to try to convince agents to undertake reform. Another way is what social psychologists call the "door-in-the-face"[61] technique, where one starts with much more demanding requirements, and, on the basis of these requirements, pushes even reluctant agents to comply at least with bare-bones minimal standards ("if you do not live up to all that you ought to do, the *least* you can do is . . . "). Accordingly, we may think that it is not only philosophically appropriate to present affluent democracies with the

---

[60] See US *Comprehensive Anti-Apartheid Act* (1986), Sec. 305 (a): "No national of the United States may make or approve any loan or other extension of credit, directly or indirectly, to the Government of South Africa or to any corporation, partnership, or other organization which is owned or controlled by the Government of South Africa." Public Law 99-440, at www.gpo.gov/fdsys/pkg/STATUTE-100/pdf/STATUTE-100-Pg1086.pdf.

[61] For the classic experiment see R. B. Cialdini, J. E. Vincent, S. K. Lewis, J. Catalan, D. Wheeler, and B. L. Darby, "Reciprocal Concessions Procedure for Inducing Compliance: The Door-in-the-Face Technique," *Journal of Personality and Social Psychology* 31 (1975): 206–215. See also Cialdini's *Influence: Science and Practice*, 5th ed. (New York: Harper Collins, 2009).

full list of their moral duties, but, at least in some contexts, also practically useful.

Second, from a normative standpoint, it is essential to remember that the real alternative to affluent democracies undertaking sacrifices is not a world in which no one has to make sacrifices. Rather, the real alternative is a world in which the distribution of sacrifices is heavily skewed against the world's poorest. Moreover, it is worth stressing that this is true not only with regard to the relatively direct costs of customary sovereign borrowing practices. For poor countries, there can be considerable political and economic costs involved even in the process of trying to justify deviations from the status quo. A fragile democratic government in a poor country may try, for example, to ascertain which portion of the country's external debt might be odious. But it may very well encounter a combination of logistical obstacles due to poor record keeping, economic obstacles arising from the costs of a comprehensive audit, and political obstacles as powerful actors (such as the military and the security services) refuse to disclose information about their past dealings.[62] These are all hurdles that would be either non-existent or trivial in many established affluent democracies. And this difference provides yet another reason for shifting many more of the burdens associated with the practice of sovereign borrowing onto the affluent.

Third, very much related, once we are aware of the need to engage in this burden shifting, we should come to see even the most demanding policy proposals discussed above as much more reasonable. Thus, for example, the idea of affluent countries compensating poor nations for loans that private creditors made to repressive regimes in the past may initially seem too demanding. This is partly because creditors who made these loans were not doing anything illegal at the time – and so imposing duties of compensation directly on them may seem unfair in a way. On the other hand, if affluent democracies funded such compensation through measures such as tax contributions, taxpayers may claim that this policy too is unfair. It is not obvious that there is any perfect solution to moral dilemmas of this sort. But it does seem reasonable to say that, however the exact distribution of burdens is to be worked out, affluent democracies' governments and the major private creditors based in their jurisdictions should find a way to settle the bill

---

[62] Ecuador in the mid-2000s illustrated the last problem in particular. See Lienau, *Rethinking Sovereign Debt*, 216.

between them. Otherwise, it is the poor who will – once again – be left to pay.

Conclusion

If my claims in this chapter have been cogent, then ideas associated with the people's integrity and property can guide our thinking about policies related to odious debt, even in more difficult cases where our moral values may seem at least somewhat indeterminate, and potentially in conflict with one another.

In the next, final chapter of this book, I deploy the collective integrity and the collective property frameworks to address conflicts of a different sort. Here I shall be concerned less with conflicting values, and more with conflicting priorities. I will be focusing, in other words, on policy issues where it is fairly clear what, in principle, ought to be done, but it is imperative to ask what ought to be done first. The integrity and property frameworks, I now turn to argue, can be of help on this score as well.

5 | Policy Priorities for a Divided People: Israel as a Case Study

"I still define myself as an Israeli patriot, but the increasingly deteriorating Israel, that is turning its back on humanistic values and human rights, cannot be my spiritual homeland . . . culture in Israel has long been as poisoned as the extremist strands of Islam. From kindergarten till old age we feed our sons with a charge of hatred, suspicion, and contempt towards the alien and different, and especially towards the Arabs . . .

" . . . The victory march of religious nationalism is both impressive and terrifying. Thousands of people with higher education flee Israel every year . . . to distant but more normal countries. I envy them. But I am too old to experience an emigrant's trauma yet again, and so I prefer to stay as a migrant inside my own country." Sami Michael[1]

"What do you want me to do about it today?" John F. Kennedy[2]

This final chapter has two main aims. First, having discussed the divide between the people and its leaders (Chapter 3), and the divide between the people and outsiders (Chapter 4), here I wish to show how the integrity and property frameworks can help us think about internal divides *within* the people. In particular, I wish to use the two collectivist frameworks to advance our thinking about cases where minority

---

[1] One of Israel's most prominent novelists, Michael has been serving since 2001 as the President of the Association for Civil Rights in Israel, a position previously held by four senior jurists, including one (retired) Supreme Court justice and one (retired) Supreme Court chief justice. The quoted remarks appeared in a widely cited keynote lecture Michael gave at the 2012 International Conference of the Israeli Studies Association. See, e.g., Revital Hovel, "Sami Michael: Israel Is the Most Racist Country in the Developed World," *Haaretz*, Jun. 26, 2012, at http://haaretz.co.il/news/education/1.1740434 (Hebrew). All translations from Hebrew are my own.

[2] According to his former aide Walter Rostow, this was President Kennedy's common response when "an idea was presented to him." See, e.g., Walter Rostow and Elspeth Rostow, "Letter to the Mayor of Austin," *Proceedings of the American Philosophical Society* 136 (1992): 355–357.

groups are formal members of the political community, but where their actual place in this community is fraught with controversy. Moreover, I try to show that the proper resolution of such controversies can have important implications for outsiders who do not formally belong to the people, but who have urgent moral claims vis-à-vis the people, whether pertaining to its acts or omissions.

My second aim in this chapter is to take up what I believe is a key lacuna in philosophical discussions of public policy: the question of policy priorities. Far too often, philosophers seem to think that, once a list of morally justified policies has been laid out, public policy poses no further philosophical challenges: it now is the job of someone else – economists, political scientists, lawyers – to say how these policies can all be realized. This prevalent view, however, ignores the fact that policy priorities also have to be assigned – especially in all-too-common circumstances where a government has scarce political capital at its disposal.

The lack of philosophical attention to scarce political capital is striking given how common it is for philosophers to worry about whether government can afford the economic price of certain reforms. *That* worry, as I noted in Chapter 4, is often thought to be philosophically salient, even in cases featuring extremely affluent governments facing highly circumscribed economic costs. But if we take the economic costs of certain policy reforms so seriously, there is no reason to ignore the cost in political capital attached to any attempt at major policy changes. And once we are attentive to the constraints associated with this sort of capital, then we should also be attentive to the question of policy priorities, especially in circumstances where such capital is in particularly short supply. In a political environment where virtually any major reform advanced by a government risks its very survival, no government, no matter how astute and morally determined, is going to realize all of the policy goals that it has compelling moral reasons to pursue. In such circumstances, then, it is especially important to try to identify which policies ought to be at the top of the government agenda.

Now, to be fair to the philosophical mainstream, it is extremely hard, if not outright impossible, to give a systematic all-things-considered answer to this question, even when the details of a particular political environment are all taken into account. There is a staggering variety of factors bearing on the assignment of all-things-considered government priorities. Nonetheless, it is worthwhile for philosophers reflecting on public policy to try to identify, and to systematize, less obvious moral considerations that should also play a role in the setting of such priorities. I hope to show here that the integrity and property frameworks can advance this task.

The two aims I have just outlined – the exploration of divides internal to "the people," and the exploration of policy priorities in light of scarce political capital – are independent of one another. But I believe that these two aims can be fruitfully combined, by focusing on an example of a specific society in which both scarce political capital and internal divisions are clearly politically salient. The specific example on which I will focus is that of Israel. A key reason for this choice is the fact that Israel is not only one of the most politically charged societies in the Western world, but is also one of the most internally divided. Moreover, insofar as political theorists pay sustained attention to the country's politics, their focus tends to rest exclusively on Israel's territorial conflicts – first and foremost on the Israeli-Palestinian conflict.[3] Yet far less philosophical attention has been given to Israel's internal divisions, despite these divisions' normative significance, and despite the fact that they relate to Israel's territorial conflicts in important ways.

Furthermore, exploring how ideas regarding the people's integrity and property might bear on Israeli policy priorities seems appropriate, given the acute scarcity of political capital that any government in Israel can deploy to pursue its agenda. This scarcity, in turn, is most directly a result of the complex coalitions that any prime minister has to assemble in Israel's multi-party system. These coalitions frequently face the danger of collapse when a significant reform is offered in almost any policy area: the larger the reform, the greater is the likelihood that it will be opposed by some of the parties that are essential to the government coalition. This point is especially pertinent for understanding the de facto veto power that comparatively small right-wing and ultra-orthodox[4] parties have held in many governments: even with a relatively modest number of seats, these parties have often been able

---

[3] For a very small sample out of a very large pool, see Tamar Meisels, "Can Corrective Justice Ground Claims to Territory?", *Journal of Political Philosophy* 11 (2003): 65–88; Meisels, *Territorial Rights* (New York: Springer, 2009); Chaim Gans, *A Just Zionism: On the Morality of the Jewish State* (Oxford: Oxford University Press, 2008); Anna Stilz, "Settlement, Expulsion and Return," *Politics, Philosophy & Economics* 16 (2017): 351–374.

[4] The ultra-orthodox in Israel commonly refer to themselves and are referred to by other Israelis as *haredim* – a plural of *hared*, best translated as "anxious" (to do

Policy Priorities for a Divided People 193

to threaten government survival due to the fact that their leaving the government would deprive the coalition of its majority in parliament, triggering a new election.

A vivid illustration of this kind of disproportional power came in early 2017, when the leader of an extreme right-wing party, with only eight seats in Israel's 120-member parliament (Knesset), effectively forced Prime Minister Binyamin Netanyahu to pass a law that Netanyahu himself had vehemently opposed for a long period. The law officially confiscates certain Palestinian lands in the West Bank and thus retroactively "legitimates" what have long been, by the lights of Israel's own law, illegal Jewish settlements.[5] At the time of writing, the fate of this disturbing piece of legislation is subject to the decision of the Israeli Supreme Court, and Netanyahu himself, while seeking "credit" for this law with the ring-wing electorate, has simultaneously made clear to extremely critical foreign officials that he hopes the court will strike the law down.[6]

I mention this specific law partly in order to make another important framing remark regarding the plan of this chapter. A law that would never be applied to Israel's Jewish citizens, and which confiscates, without any kind of democratic participation by Palestinians, what Israel's own legal system has recognized as the property of the Palestinian people, obviously fails moral tests that are central to both the property and the integrity frameworks. But it seems to me that the moral failure of laws of this kind is so obvious, that focusing directly on such laws is not a useful way of bringing out the distinctiveness of these frameworks. That is why, although I will discuss here some of the most pernicious dynamics of the Israeli-Palestinian conflict, I will approach

---

God's bidding). I will refer to the community as "ultra-orthodox" simply to preserve a terminology more familiar to readers outside of Israel.

[5] See Yehonatan Liss, "Knesset Approves Law Confiscating Palestinian Lands," *Haaretz*, Feb. 7, 2017, at http://haaretz.co.il/news/politi/1.3630778 (Hebrew). All translations are mine unless noted otherwise. See also Ian Fisher, "Israel Passes Provocative Law to Retroactively Legalize Settlements," *New York Times*, Feb. 6, 2017, at https://nytimes.com/2017/02/06/world/middleeast/israel-settlement-law-palestinians-west-bank.html

[6] Barak Ravid, "The Israeli Response to Foreign Criticism of the Confiscation Law: The High Court Might Strike it Down," *Haaretz*, Feb. 7, 2017, at http://haaretz.co.il/news/politics/.premium-1.3658137 (Hebrew); see also Shai Nir, "Regulation – Till the Judges Decide: The High Court Continues to Freeze the 'Regulation Law'," *Davar Rishon*, Dec. 5, 2017, at http://davar1.co.il/97796/ (Hebrew).

these dynamics in a more indirect manner. In the course of this chapter, I will note various processes related to the conflict that are widely condemned, such as the significant growth of violence (including even recurring lynching) between Israel's Jewish majority and the one-fifth of the country's citizens who are Palestinian.[7] Yet although the property and integrity frameworks can join the rejection of such blatant wrongs, I intend to show that they can do more than that.

With this aim in mind, I proceed as follows. I begin with basic background about injustices concerning two minorities in Israel – the little-known Druze community, and the better-known ultra-orthodox community (5.1, 5.2). I then show how collective integrity considerations provide distinctive grounds for prioritizing reforms of these injustices (5.3). In 5.4, I advance a further, more instrumental argument for this priority: using collective integrity as well as collective property ideas, I explain why prioritizing reforms related to the Druze and the ultra-orthodox might very well be a useful gradualist strategy for advancing positive change in the context of the Israeli-Palestinian conflict. In 5.5, I use the integrity framework to discuss issues related to Israel's refugee policy. In the conclusion, I briefly discuss, through the integrity lens, how prevalent demographic, political, and economic dynamics shape the prospects for progressive civic engagement in Israel going forward.

5.1 The Druze in Israel: A First Look

We can start with the case of the Druze minority. The Druze are a small, close-knit sect that arose out of the Ismailiyah movement in Islam and split

---

[7] In 2012, for example, Israel's current President (and then Knesset speaker) Reuven Rivlin noted upon visiting an Arab victim of lynching in Jerusalem that "racist violence is a strategic threat. We ought not hide this . . . This writing has long been on the wall, and the letters are burning in a fire that might burn us all. And we – the government, the Knesset, the education system – are responsible. More and more youth think that hatred and racist violence are luxuries. Till now we looked the other way, we said that these [perpetrators] are marginal, that it will pass, we paid lip service. But it is now time for us to stop covering up." See Arik Bender, "Rivlin Visited the Lynch Victim: "An Outrageous Act," *NRG*, Aug. 23, 2012, at http://nrg.co.il/online/1/ART2/397/878.html (Hebrew); see also Netanel Katz, "Rivlin to the Injured: Apologetic and Angry," Channel 7, Aug. 23, 2012, at http://inn.co.il/News/News.aspx/243043 (Hebrew). See also (more recently) Nehemya Shtresler, "The End of the Third Temple," *Haaretz*, Aug. 28, 2018, at https://haaretz.co.il/opinions/.premium-1.6420900 (Hebrew).

5.1 The Druze in Israel: A First Look

off mainstream Islam in the eleventh century. The Druze are Arab by language, culture, and custom. Yet they only marry other Druze, and almost always live in villages with an overwhelming Druze majority. These facts, combined with their distinct beliefs and the secrecy surrounding their religious practices, have long distinguished the Druze identity from that of other Arabs. The Druze are concentrated primarily in Syria, Lebanon, Jordan, and Israel. As of 2015, there were slightly fewer than 140,000 Druze in Israel.[8]

As is the case with the Druze in the three other countries, Israeli Druze do not harbor national ambitions of their own and are content with religious autonomy, which the state provides. Survey data has long suggested that Israeli Druze identify themselves first and foremost as Druze (in terms of their religion), secondarily as Arab (in terms of their culture), and thirdly as Israeli (in terms of citizenship).[9] Notably, however, very few Israeli Druze strongly identify as Palestinians, thus setting them apart from the vast majority of Israel's Arab citizens, who do identify themselves in this way.[10]

The Druze minority comprises less than 2 percent of Israel's population. Yet the normative significance of the relationship between this minority and Israel's Jewish majority vastly exceeds the Druze's modest numbers. The reason is that this relationship makes vivid one of the country's deepest and most existential questions – who can genuinely be a member of its political community. This question comes to the fore in the Druze context because, since 1956 (eight years after Israel's independence), Druze men have been drafted into the Israeli Defense Forces. Moreover, although their service is mandatory, Druze motivation for service in the Israeli military has traditionally been high – in some periods surpassing the motivation of the Jewish majority.[11] Through the years, the Druze have successfully struggled – against prejudice – to be eligible for service in all military units, including the

---

[8] See Central Bureau of Statistics, "Press Release: The Druze Population of Israel," Apr. 20, 2016, at http://cbs.gov.il/reader/newhodaot/hodaa_template.html?hodaa=201611119 (Hebrew).

[9] See Rabah Halabi, "Invention of a Nation: The Druze in Israel," *Journal of Asian and African Studies* 49 (2014): 267–281. Although the trend may be changing, not least as a response to informal discrimination, more on which below.

[10] See, e.g., Nisan Mordechai, "The Druze in Israel: Questions of Identity, Citizenship, and Patriotism," *The Middle East Journal* 64 (2010): 575–596.

[11] See, e.g., Ilana Kaufman, "Ethnic Affirmation or Ethnic Manipulation: The Case of the Druze in Israel," *Nationalism and Ethnic Politics* 9 (2004): 53–82.

most prestigious. This is primarily because employment in the defense forces has been the dominant professional route for Druze men, and their main chance of social mobility in Israel.[12]

The need for such mobility, in turn, is made all the more acute by the fact that public infrastructure in Druze towns and villages, as well as socio-economic opportunity for the Druze, is consistently inferior in comparison to the infrastructure and opportunities enjoyed by Israel's Jewish population. The eleven Druze municipalities in which the vast majority of Israel's Druze citizens live provide a clear illustration. In 2014, Israel's Central Bureau of Statistics (CBS) placed nine of these municipalities at either the third or the second lowest decile of the country's socio-economic scale, factoring education, employment, infrastructure, land uses, housing and transportation (the other two municipalities were ranked in the fourth-lowest decile).[13] According to CBS data, the average employee salary in each of these eleven municipalities ranged from about two-thirds to less than three-quarters of the average salary in the country as a whole.[14]

These grim statistics are accompanied – and reinforced – by informal social discrimination. Jewish Israelis typically hold the Druze in high regard for their military service, and concede that the Druze have

---

[12] See, for example, the detailed account in Part 1 of Ronald Krebs's *Fighting for Rights* (Ithaca, NY: Cornell University Press, 2006). Recent estimates place the proportion of Druze men in Israel's standing army (career soldiers) at almost four times their proportion in the country's population (see Yair Kraus, "The Battalion Commander Who Went to Battle over the Young Druze," *NRG*, Nov. 27, 2013, at http://nrg.co.il/online/54/ART2/525/462.html [Hebrew]). Druze women do not serve in the military, and their chances of social mobility are hindered by Druze gender norms, though these seem to be changing in recent years. See, e.g., Naomi Weiner-Levy, "Patriarchs or Feminists? Relations between Fathers and Trailblazing Daughters in Druze Society," *Journal of Family Communication* 11 (2011): 126–147.

[13] See CBS data (all in Hebrew) concerning the eleven settlements at https://old.cbs.gov.il/webpub/pub/text_page.html?publ=58&CYear=2014&CMonth=1

[14] See sources in the previous note. It should be acknowledged that in late 2013, the government adopted a resolution to direct 209 million shekels (roughly 55 million dollars) to four Druze villages in the Golan Heights, adjacent to Syria. It is hard to say whether this decision was only due to fears related to the Syrian civil war or to a genuine desire to improve the condition of these villages. Whether these funds will be joined by more sustained investment, and what will be their long-term effects, is still unclear. See Eli Ashkenazi, "While Assad Is Mired in Civil War, Israel Will Invest 209 Million Shekels in the Golan Druze," *Haaretz*, Dec. 22, 2013, at https://haaretz.co.il/news/education/1.2195995 (Hebrew).

important claims to society's resources and recognition. Yet in civilian life it is nonetheless common for Jews to fail to draw any meaningful distinction between the Druze and Israel's Arab Palestinian citizens, whom most Jews do not see as entitled to anything like the same consideration. As the Druze scholar Rabah Halabi notes, "since Arabs are considered the enemy by the Jews and are largely rejected, the Druze try to shed this identity in their encounters with Jews, in order to be accepted."[15] But this attempt is always fraught with difficulty. In one of Halabi's studies, an interviewee offers a telling anecdote, referring to his last day of service in the Israeli military:

> On the day I was to be released, I was in uniform and was on my way to the base, and a religious (Jewish) guy sat down next to me and started to talk with me. He said that you Druze help us, and we need to love you and blah blah etc. . . On my way back home after I'd turned in my uniform, some other Jewish guy sat next to me. I was so tired that I fell asleep and I guess my head was resting on him or something, for a second, and he looks at me and calls me a dirty Arab.[16]

Informal social dynamics of this kind, combined with socio-economic marginalization, generate predictable alienation and resentment on the part of the Druze and decreasing support for the continuation of obligatory military service.[17] "A good Druze," as one sardonic reporter put it, "is a Druze who proudly serves in the IDF, signs up for a Jewish party, and is silent in the face of the systematic neglect of his town."[18]

5.2 The Ultra-Orthodox

Having introduced the case of the Druze, let us now turn to Israel's ultra-orthodox minority. In late 2016, a survey by Israel's Central Bureau of Statistics found that 14 percent of the country's Jewish population identifies itself as ultra-orthodox.[19] Demographers agree

---

[15] Halabi, "Invention of a Nation, "275.
[16] Halabi, "Invention of a Nation," 276.   [17] I say more on this trend below.
[18] Dan Tamir, "The Druze Society – Outlines of an Ethnic Group Undergoing Change," *Haaretz*, Dec. 4, 2009, at http://haaretz.co.il/misc/1.1293299 (Hebrew).
[19] See Central Bureau of Statistics, "The Social Survey of 2009," May 16, 2010, at https://old.cbs.gov.il/webpub/pub/text_page.html?publ=58&CYear=2014&C Month=1. Less subjective measurements of the ultra-orthodox are controversial, given the different, and conflicting, definitions that may be used.

that the share of the ultra-orthodox in the country's Jewish population is growing. In 2006, for example, more than a quarter of the babies born to Jewish families in Israel were born to ultra-orthodox families.[20] In 2009, the CBS estimated that the average ultra-orthodox woman in Israel gives birth to 6.5 children,[21] a vastly higher birth rate than that of the Jewish population as a whole, which is estimated at roughly 2.80.[22]

These demographic trends amplify the normative weight of the relationship between the ultra-orthodox minority and the broader population. This relationship can be understood as the opposite of the Druze situation. If in the Druze case the issue has to do with state imposition of extremely significant burdens without corresponding benefits, in the case of the ultra-orthodox minority the concern is the opposite. This minority is overwhelmingly reliant on resources and services generated by the broader society, yet contributes markedly little to the broader society's undertakings.

The ultra-orthodox system of religious study is a key case in point. Since Israel's founding, ultra-orthodox parties in the Knesset have sought – with considerable success – to ensure generous state funding for institutions of religious study.[23] This funding begins already at the K-12 level, where an ultra-orthodox schooling system exists in parallel to secular public schools. Only one of the most famous worries about this system is the absence of almost any topics of study that could prepare its pupils for participation in the modern economy. Past attempts by Israel's ministry of education to enforce core curricula in the ultra-orthodox system have been thwarted repeatedly by ultra-orthodox politicians. Consequently, even basic competence in English

---

See Yair Etinger, "How Many Ultra-Orthodox Live in Israel – It Depends on Which Statistician You Ask," *Haaretz*, Apr. 21, 2014, at http://haaretz.co.il/news/education/1.1171794 (Hebrew).

[20] See Uzi Rebhun and Gilad Malach, *Demographic Trends in Israel* (Jerusalem: Metzilah Center, 2008), at http://lib.ruppin.ac.il/multimedia_library/PDF/29091.pdf, 29.

[21] Quoted in Lee Cahaner, Maya Choshen, and Gilad Malach, *Yearbook of Ultra-Orthodox Society in Israel 2017* (Jerusalem: Israeli Democracy Institute, 2017), 14.

[22] Rebhun and Malach, *Demographic Trends in Israel*, 28.

[23] And this success only keeps increasing. See for example Tzvi Zarhiya, "The Largest Yeshivot Budget Ever Has Been Approved," *The Marker*, Nov. 20, 2016, at http://themarker.com/news/1.3127609 (Hebrew); Arik Bander, "A Third Record in a Year for the Yeshivot Budget," *Maariv*, Mar. 3, 2017, at http://maariv.co.il/news/politics/Article-576687 (Hebrew).

5.2 The Ultra-Orthodox

or math is not a part of ultra-orthodox education, let alone any subject in the sciences, in civics, or in world history.[24] Thus the vast majority of the graduates of this – publicly funded – system are woefully ill-prepared to either join Israel's labor market or acquire college-level education that will enhance their viability in this market.[25] That is one reason (alongside the norms pervasive in much of the ultra-orthodox society) why the majority of these graduates pursue further biblical studies as their adult vocation.[26]

The result is a significant burden on public resources, in two ways. First, these graduates' continued studies are supported not by any market forces but by state budgets (again secured by ultra-orthodox parties).[27] Second, very much related, over the course of their lives the

---

[24] According to an NGO working with individuals who leave the ultra-orthodox world for secular life, "an ultra-orthodox Yeshiva pupil reaches the age of 18 with knowledge in math equivalent to that of a fourth grader; he has no knowledge of English, sciences, history, geography, literature, civics, biology, or economics; he lacks the professional, academic, and social skills needed in the new world of the modern state of Israel." Quoted in Mordechai Kremnitzer, Yael Cohen-Rimer, and Roi Konfino, "Who Should Fund the Society of Pupils" (op. ed.), *The Israeli Democracy Institute* Dec. 15, 2008, at https://idi.org.il/articles/7867 (Hebrew).

[25] Strikingly, a small internal minority within the ultra-orthodox community has recently started to protest this state of affairs. This minority drew some media attention when hundreds of ultra-orthodox parents demanded an "alternative" ultra-orthodox educational route, where basic competence in English and math will actually be provided. Further attention arose as fifty former yeshiva pupils, who have left the ultra-orthodox world to secular life, filed a lawsuit against the state, alleging that in failing to enforce core curricula requirements, the state has failed its duty to provide them with basic education. Even more strikingly, the state's official response was to threaten to sue these pupils' parents and their *yeshivot* as the main "culpable" parties. The lawsuit was dismissed on technical grounds. See "lawsuit demanding compensation for not studying core curricula dismissed," Aharon Rabinovitz, *Haaretz*, Aug. 11, 2017, at https://haaretz.co.il/news/1.4344134 (Hebrew); Yair Etinger, "Hundreds of Haredi Parents Are Demanding the Establishment of an Alternative Educational Route – with Core Curricula," *Haaretz,* Jul. 29, 2016, at https://haaretz.co.il/news/education/.premium-1.3022139 (Hebrew); see also Susan Hattis Rolef, "Think About It: Yotzim Beshe'ela' – Those Who Drop the Religious Way of Life," *Jerusalem Post*, Jan. 12, 2014, at https://jpost.com/Opinion/Columnists/Think-about-it-Yotzim-Besheela-Those-who-drop-the-religious-way-of-life-337953.

[26] This fact regarding *avrechim* (married yeshiva students) is connected to the scope of state support. See, e.g., Shahar Ilan, "Following the Budget Increases – a Record in the Number of Avrechim Funded by the State – 75,000," *Calcalist*, Mar. 5, 2017, at https://calcalist.co.il/local/articles/0,7340,L3709009,00.html (Hebrew).

[27] See notes above.

majority of graduates of the ultra-orthodox school system who pursue biblical studies as a vocation are overwhelmingly likely to benefit from the public welfare system far more than they contribute to it, because they do not seek any employment. The ultra-orthodox norm is that the wives of the men who dedicate themselves to biblical study become the providers for the family. Thus the head economist of the Israeli Treasury estimated in 2015 that only 45 percent of ultra-orthodox men were employed,[28] compared to 90 percent of non-ultra-orthodox Jewish men.[29] The employment of ultra-orthodox women, in turn, does not make up for this sizable gap, partly because of the extraordinarily high birth-rate in ultra-orthodox families, and partly because of strict gender norms in the ultra-orthodox community requiring women to bear virtually exclusive responsibility for child-rearing. In 2014, for example, of the 70 percent of ultra-orthodox women who were employed, only 10 percent held a full-time job, and almost half earned less than the minimum wage.[30] Such statistics explain why the ultra-orthodox community is heavily – and many would say voluntarily – reliant on the public welfare system.

However, while this public support is a topic of recurrent consternation for many secular Jews, the divide between them and the ultra-orthodox is most visible, and most combustible, in the context of military service. For decades, ultra-orthodox leaders have been determined to prevent any conscription of their community,[31] despite the fact that these leaders have been more than content to see secular Jews conscripted.[32]

[28] Quoted in Mandi Gruzman, "Ultra-Orthodox 2015," at http://nrg.co.il/online/1/ART2/726/986.html (Hebrew).
[29] See Neta Moshe, "Data Regarding Ultra-Orthodox Employment," *Knesset Research Center*, Mar. 14, 2016, at https://fs.knesset.gov.il/globaldocs/MMM/4e572e2a-f5ce-e511-80d6-0015 5d0204d4/2_4e572e2a-f5ce-e511-80d6-0015 5d0204d4_11_10402.pdf (Hebrew).
[30] See "Employment of Ultra-Orthodox Women in Israel – 2014," *Knesset Research Center*, at http://knesset.gov.il/committees/heb/material/data/maa mad2014-05-12.docx (Hebrew).
[31] For the latest example see Yehonatan Liss, "The New Conscription Law Approved: Criminal Sanctions Will Be Postponed and Implementation Procedures Lengthened," *Haaretz*, Nov. 16, 2015, at http://haaretz.co.il/news/politi/1.2777453 (Hebrew).
[32] In 2012, for example, five in every six ultra-orthodox men did not serve in the military, as compared to only one in every eight non-ultra-orthodox Jewish men. See, e.g., Amos Harel, "A Sharp Decline in Exemptions Given to the Secular, the Majority of Exemptions Given to Ultra-Orthodox," *Haaretz*, Jul. 11, 2012, at www.haaretz.co.il/news/education/1.1753240 (Hebrew).

5.2 The Ultra-Orthodox

This determination, moreover, shows no sign of ebbing – quite the contrary. Following the 2015 elections, for example, the ultra-orthodox parties in the Knesset conditioned their joining the new government coalition on the effective removal of any criminal sanctions against ultra-orthodox who do not serve in the military. Their demands were met with new legislation enacted in 2016. This legislation, in turn, was challenged in the Supreme Court, which eventually struck down the new legislation and – much as it had done in multiple occasions during previous decades – instructed the government to make amendments to ensure that the law does not conflict with basic norms of equal citizenship. Yet, much as they had done in previous decades, the ultra-orthodox parties did not relent, and in March 2018 threatened to withdraw from the coalition and trigger a new election unless new regulations were adopted which would make conscription of the ultra-orthodox all but impossible. The dissolution of the government was only narrowly avoided, with the coalition partners essentially agreeing to disagree until after the next elections.[33]

I will say more below about the trenchant ultra-orthodox opposition to conscription. But already at this point it should be clear that, due to this opposition, the ultra-orthodox situation with regard to military service is a diametric opposite of the Druze case: the Druze shoulder all of the burdens associated with military service, yet receive limited benefits from the state. The ultra-orthodox shoulder none of these burdens, yet receive extraordinary benefits.

Confronted with these facts, many political philosophers are likely to respond with a certain impatience. Such philosophers will be quick to agree that the problems I have been describing are morally alarming. But, they will say, the moral wrongs here are so clear, that they call for no sustained philosophical reflection. Of course the Druze ought not to suffer the kinds of discrimination that I have just described. Of course the ultra-orthodox ought not to enjoy the special state support I have just described in the absence of any contribution to the broader society. There is no philosophical puzzle here: plainly, the facts I have just outlined ought to be changed.

---

[33] See, e.g., Haim Levinson, Yehonantan Liss, and Aharon Abaramovich, "Coalition Partners Reach a Compromise to Prevent Elections," *Haaretz*, Mar. 13, 2018, at https://haaretz.co.il/news/politi/LIVE-1.5896534 (Hebrew). See also Yagil Levy, "The Bluff of Ultra-Orthodox Conscription," *Haaretz*, Jun. 30, 2018, at https://haaretz.co.il/opinions/.premium-1.6221192.

What this objection misses, however, is the fact that all elected governments have to decide which particular changes they are going to prioritize during their mandate. This point is especially true, moreover, in a case such as Israel, where, as I have been emphasizing, the survival prospects of virtually any government are imperiled by the country's multi-party political system. In such circumstances, it is extremely important not only to consider which states of affairs are wrong, and therefore ought to be reformed. It is also essential – to reiterate my earlier remarks – to ask which reforms a government should prioritize when allocating its extremely scarce political capital. My aim in the next section is to start showing how the historical elements of the collective integrity framework can help us tackle this question.

5.3 The Priority Problem and Integrity as an Amplifier

In previous chapters, I used the historical elements of the integrity framework to argue that the presence of a particular history can have an amplifying function with regard to some of a liberal democracy's moral duties. A particular history, I have argued, makes certain duties incumbent upon a given democracy especially weighty and stringent, in a way that sets this particular democracy apart from other democracies that lack the relevant history. But if a particular history amplifies the weight and stringency of some of a liberal democracy's moral duties, then this history also provides an important reason to prioritize fulfillment of the relevant duties over other moral duties. I now turn to elaborate two ways in which this "historical priority" argument bears on reforms focused on the minorities I just discussed – first the Druze, and then the ultra-orthodox.

5.3.1 Israeli Identity, Military Service, and Druze Sacrifice

One way in which the historical priority argument affects the Israeli cases outlined above has to do with the special significance of military service in Israeli society. As many scholars have noted, Israel is unique among democratic countries in the sheer scope and longevity of military presence in collective affairs.[34] It is therefore unsurprising that,

---

[34] Israel has consequently been a central case study for scholars from different disciplines studying the relationship between armed forces and society. See, e.g.,

5.3 The Priority Problem and Integrity as an Amplifier

since the country's founding, the ethos of military service and sacrifice has been central to Israeli collective identity, and to how many individual citizens situate themselves vis-à-vis the collective. As one Israeli scholar put it at the turn of the millennium, military service

> has traditionally been the primary rite of passage initiating one into full membership in the Zionist civil religion ... [t]he type of unit in which one (or members of one's group) serves, and even the proportion of causalities suffered by the members of one's group, are seen to be proof of one's commitment and centrality of the group in the mainstream of society ... In essence *it is the "ownership" of military casualties that provides the most dramatic claim on centrality in Israeli society.*[35]

To be sure, the standing of the military, and the status of military sacrifice in Israel, has been far from constant since Israel's independence. For one thing, refusal to serve in the military – even for mundane professional reasons, or simply due to a lack of willingness to bear the risks and burdens involved in such service – does not carry anything like the same stigmatizing effect in the Israel of recent decades as it did in the state's early years.[36] Nonetheless, it is still the case that military service is a focal point of collective identity to a degree that is unparalleled in any other democratic country. This focal point is still evident in any major area of social life, from the mainstream secular education system,[37] to the numerous monuments commemorating those who have made the ultimate

---

Eyal Ben-Ari and Edna Lomsky-Feder, "Introduction: Cultural Constructions of War and the Military in Israel," in Eyal Ben-Ari and Edna Lomsky-Feder (ed.), *The Military and Militarism in Israeli Society* (Albany, NY: State University of New York Press, 2000).

[35] Myron Aronoff, "Wars as Catalysts of Social and Political Change," in Ben-Ari and Lomsky-Feder, *The Military and Militarism in Israeli Society*, 37–53, at 42.

[36] The causes of this shift in social norms are in some ways deep and complex. Arguably, one key cause here are neo-liberal economic reforms (on which I say more at the end of this chapter). Since the 1980s, these reforms undermined the intensely collectivist spirit that animated the early years of the state, when the Labor party was still hegemonic and still explicitly advanced a comprehensive socialist ethos. Another key cause is the widespread loss of confidence in political and military elites following the trauma of the Yom Kipur War in 1973, and the sense that many of Israel's following wars and skirmishes – most prominently the 1982 war in Lebanon – were ones that could have been avoided, unlike pre-1973 wars. See, e.g., Udi Lebel, "Civil Society versus Military Sovereignty," *Armed Forces & Society* 34 (2007): 67–89.

[37] See, e.g., Mirta Furman, "Army and War: Collective Narratives of Early Childhood in Contemporary Israel," in Ben-Ari and Lomsky-Feder, *The Military and Militarism in Israeli Society*, 141–168.

sacrifice during their service. These monuments, in turn, are so numerous that some have argued they represent nothing less than a "national obsession."[38] Memorialization of military dead

> ... is such a central leitmotif in Israeli political culture that it has evolved into national cult. . . . There are vast numbers of war memorials and shrines in Israel and as many rites of commemoration held at them and at the thirty-nine military cemeteries throughout the country . . . the immediacy and constancy of death in war and due to acts of terror has facilitated the primary salience of the memorialization of the victims of war in Israel.[39]

I am emphasizing the special salience of military service and sacrifice in Israeli collective identity for a simple reason. If we follow the preceding chapters' claims about the historical elements of collective integrity, then an Israeli government's moral reasons to end the unjust distribution of burdens and benefits associated with military service go beyond the "normal" moral reasons, which would apply to any liberal democracy, irrespective of its history. Alongside these universal reasons, we need the account of liberal integrity – one founded upon, but not reducible to, universal liberal values – in order to see why a society whose identity is so heavily permeated with the ethos of military service has an especially stringent and weighty moral duty to end unjust differential treatment associated with such service.

We can further spell out this amplifying function of the integrity framework – and evince further contributions of the framework – by noting the marked absence of the Druze from the symbols and rituals of Israeli collective identity. Despite the pivotal role that military sacrifice has played in Israeli collective memory since the inception of the state, and despite the range of monuments and rituals dedicated to Israel's fallen soldiers, commemoration for Druze sacrifice for the country has been conspicuously lacking.[40] What might we say about this state of affairs?

---

[38] See, e.g., Alex Weingrod, "Dry Bones: Nationalism and Symbolism in Contemporary Israel," *Anthropology Today* 11 (1995): 7–12; Meira Weiss, "Bereavement, Commemoration, and Collective Identity in Contemporary Israeli Society," *Anthropological Quarterly* 70 (1997): 91–101.

[39] Aronoff, *Wars as Catalysts*, 43.

[40] For a rare exception see Yair Kraus, "Remembering Zidan," *NRG*, Sep. 24, 2015, at http://nrg.co.il/online/1/ART2/727/043.html (Hebrew). It should be acknowledged that the Druze belief in reincarnation inhibits certain forms of

One thought, which follows naturally from the integrity reasoning I just presented, is that the dearth of commemoration of Druze sacrifice is especially morally troubling in a society where military service has had a unique impact on claims of collective belonging. Any society that fails, because of morally irrelevant features such as ethnicity, race, or religion, to adequately honor those who died to protect it, is guilty of a profound moral failure. But a society whose collective identity pivots in many ways on military sacrifice is guilty of an especially acute failure. This is one reason why addressing the symbolic gap of Druze commemoration ought to be a priority for any Israeli government.

Another, very much related, thought is that the gap here is far from "merely" symbolic. At least in Israel, what is at stake in commemoration of military sacrifice is nothing less than the fundamental question of who can be part of "the people." More specifically, the question here is ultimately whether Israeli society, speaking with one voice, can demand that the Druze risk their lives in defense of the collective, while effectively denying the Druze entry into this collective. This is not a question that Jewish Israelis are often – or ever – keen to ask. But this is nonetheless a question that must be answered, even if Israeli society is keen to behave as if it does not exist. Such collective self-deception does not, in the end, change the fact that the Druze have, for decades now, been legally obligated to put their lives at risk for a people to which they cannot belong. All this, notwithstanding the Druze's modest numbers, amounts to a massive failure of collective integrity – one whose remedy ought to be at the top, rather than the bottom, of the government priority ladder.

5.3.2 The Ultra-Orthodox and Israel's Collective Project

With these points in mind, let us now return to ultra-orthodox attitudes regarding military service. Once we examine these attitudes a bit more closely, we can evince another way in which the integrity framework,

---

commemoration of fallen Druze soldiers (see, e.g., Marwan Dwairy, "The Psychosocial Function of Reincarnation among Druze in Israel," *Culture, Medicine and Psychiatry* 30 [2006]: 29–53). Yet just as collective integrity requires trenchant creativity in finding solutions to much more macro-level problems of "high politics," as I argued in previous chapters, so one could easily argue that trenchant creativity is important here on the part of the state, in seeking forms of commemoration that would align with the Druze's particular religious sensitivities.

and its historical elements in particular, amplify the moral significance of service-related reforms.

Outsiders asked to consider the attitudes of the ultra-orthodox in Israel regarding military service may be led toward an intuitive but crucial mistake. The mistake is to assume that ultra-orthodox opposition to military service is akin to the religious pacifism of self-secluding communities found in various other countries. Israel's ultra-orthodox, however, are not akin to, say, the Amish or the Quakers in the United States.[41] Unlike these religious communities, Israel's ultra-orthodox do not view themselves as pacifists, nor do they advocate pacifism more generally.[42] Their arguments as to why they should not serve in the military have a different basis.

More specifically, two arguments have been underlying the long-lasting ultra-orthodox opposition to participation in military service. One is that the ultra-orthodox do their part to defend the state through religious study. But the other, and in many ways more telling, argument is that the very existence of the state is bound up with religious study in a deeper sense. On the ultra-orthodox view, exempting a significant portion of the population from military service, and allowing it to devote itself exclusively to Jewish religious study (at the state's expense), is necessary because such study is the very root of Jewish existence.

An especially famous example of this ultra-orthodox line was a meeting between Israel's first prime minister, David Ben Gurion, and the most important religious authority of the ultra-orthodox community in the state's early years, Avrohom Yeshaya Karelitz (popularly known by the name of his magnum opus, Chazon Ish). Ben Gurion sought the meeting, which took place in October 1952, to find a basis

---

[41] For one thing, as should be clear by this point, unlike the Amish, Israel's ultra-orthodox do not seek to be as independent of state support as possible – quite the contrary.

[42] A vivid and recurring illustration of this point is ultra-orthodox violence against rare members of their own community who choose to serve in the military. See, e.g., Nir Hason, "Again: A Soldier Was Attacked in a Haredi Neighbourhood in Jerusalem," *Haaretz*, Aug. 8, 2013, at http://haaretz.co.il/news/law/1.2093013 (Hebrew); Mandi Gruzman, "Not Just at the Stronghold of Extremism: Ultra-Orthodox Soldiers Attacked in a Central Synagogue," *NRG*, Nov. 3, 2016, at http://nrg.co.il/online/11/ART2/845/386.html (Hebrew). See also
Binyamin Neuberger, "The Refusal to Serve in the Military – The Case of the Amish," *Ma'arachot* 2014, No. 455, 48–51 (Hebrew).

5.3 The Priority Problem and Integrity as an Amplifier

for fruitful coexistence between the secular majority and the ultra-orthodox minority. Ben Gurion's aide recorded the exchange:

Ben Gurion began and said: "I came to talk to you about one topic, how will religious and non-religious Jews live together in this country, without us exploding from the inside? Jews come here from many countries, in the hundreds and in the thousands, with different traditions, out of different cultures, and with different worldviews. The state faces external danger, the Arabs still want to destroy us, and we have to make the most of everything that is common to all parts of the people. And there is a fundamental problem: these are Jews and these as well, and how shall they live together?"

Chazon Ish answered through a Talmudic tale: "If two camels meet in a path, one carrying a heavy burden and the other without a burden, the latter must give the right of way to the former. We the religious Jews are like the burdened camel – we carry the burden of a great many commandments [*mitzvot*]. You have to give us the right of way."

Ben Gurion responded: "And this camel carries no burden of commandments? (tapping his own shoulder) And what is being done by the boys that you so resist, who sit in the borders guarding you, is that not a commandment [*mitzvah*]?"

Chazon Ish said: "They exist because we study the Torah."

Ben Gurion said: "If these boys would not be guarding you, the enemies would have slaughtered you."

Chazon Ish said: "On the contrary. Thanks to our studying of the Torah, they can live and work and guard."

Ben Gurion said: "I do not belittle the Torah, but if there will not be living people, who will study the Torah?"

Chazon Ish said: "The Torah is the tree of life, the source of life."[43]

This theological conception of the polity's collective project has endured all the way from the 1950s to the present: it still dominates ultra-orthodox discourse whenever policy debates arise regarding conscription, or denial of state funding for ultra-orthodox institutions of religious study that ignore core curriculum requirements.[44]

This conception, in turn, must be borne in mind when considering both the shape of morally necessary reforms relating to ultra-orthodox

---

[43] Quoted in David Melamed, "Which Cart is Fuller: The Secular or the Ultra-Orthodox," *NRG*, Aug. 26, 2013, at http://nrg.co.il/online/11/ART2/502/494.html (Hebrew). Ben Gurion slipped here: the ultra-orthodox never protested against or "resisted" military service in general – only calls to conscript their own.

[44] See references above.

military service, and the priority that any Israeli government ought to assign to such reforms. If the ultra-orthodox refused to serve in the military on pacifist grounds, then justified policies would be those that would match the ultra-orthodox's special prerogatives with the prerogatives of other pacifists (whether individuals or communities). But given the ultra-orthodox view, the issue here is not the highly limited one of if and how a democratic society should accommodate pacifist commitments. Rather, the much more fundamental issue here – which ought to be a top priority for any morally viable Israeli government – is determining *what Israeli society is about*: what is it that, at the most basic level, the collective project that is Israel is meant to accomplish?

The reason why it is so natural for the ultra-orthodox to arrogate to themselves the "right" not to serve in the military, and to have religious study as an extremely widespread, publicly funded "occupation," is their very particular answer to this question: they see the project of Jewish religious study as the only fundamental collective project that Israeli society can permissibly pursue. This answer, however, not only fails to offer any other members of Israeli society a vision of its collective undertakings that they can be expected to share. It also fails to match the most basic elements of Zionism as a historical movement. The Zionist movement, since its inception in the late nineteenth century, sought precisely to liberate Jewish life from an exclusive focus on religious study. In fact, the decidedly secular roots of the movement are a key part of the reason why it was treated as heresy in the midst of Eastern Europe's traditional Jewish communities. The basic Zionist aspiration was to create a state in which Jews could be engaged in the full plethora of modern economic and social activities, extending far beyond the synagogue.[45]

Unsurprisingly, the ultra-orthodox could never accept this secular ambition. In the words of Menachem Friedman, one of the leading scholars of the ultra-orthodox in Israel: "All groups and strands that identify as ultra-orthodox share the view of Zionism as a nationalist secular ideology ... which conflicts with the essence of Judaism ... [On the ultra-orthodox view] [t]he Zionist ideal of establishing a national secular entity in the Land of Israel is heresy, a denial of the foundations

---

[45] See, e.g., Moshe Berent, *A Nation like All the Nations: Towards the Establishment of an Israeli Republic* (New Rochelle, New York: Israel Academic Press, 2015).

5.3 The Priority Problem and Integrity as an Amplifier

of Jewish existence."[46] The ultra-orthodox community is "unable to recognize the right to exist of a Jewish identity that is not committed to Jewish religious law."[47] Understood in this historical light, disputes about conscription of the ultra-orthodox, as well as about state support of ultra-orthodox religious study, can be seen as ultimately existential: these debates bear on the very reason for why there should be such a thing as the State of Israel.

Another way to bring out just what is at stake in such disputes is to note the stance that the ultra-orthodox have explicitly adopted, since Israel's independence, toward the state's claim to authority over its citizens. The ultra-orthodox have never tried to hide the fact that they do not recognize this authority. Since Israel's earliest years, the ultra-orthodox have explicitly characterized cooperation with state institutions as a pragmatic strategy, not an indication of any kind of ideological reconciliation with secular Jews or acceptance of the state's moral authority.[48] That, indeed, is a key reason why it seems obvious to the ultra-orthodox, that whenever the needs of religious study demand certain resources from the secular majority, these ought to be provided. And it is equally obvious that whenever there arise conflicts in any area of social life between religious and secular norms, the former always ought to prevail. Secular Jewish existence, after all, is devoid of meaning; only strict observance of Jewish religious study and religious law has value – indeed, without such observance there is no reason at all for Jews to live.

The result of all this is a situation that is arguably just as disturbing as the Druze case. While the Druze are required by law to risk their lives for the people without being genuinely allowed to claim membership in the people, ultra-orthodox Jews fight to ensure that secular members of the people risk their lives for them, so they can pursue "the people's true calling" with public support. The integrity framework, in turn, not only provides a forceful way of capturing why these facts are morally abnormal. More distinctively, this framework also highlights the crucial moral need to make reform of this state of affairs a public policy priority.

---

[46] See Menachem Friedman, *The Ultra-Orthodox Society: Sources, Trends, and Processes* (The Jerusalem Institute for Israel Studies: Jerusalem, 1991), 8 (Hebrew).
[47] Friedman, *The Ultra-Orthodox Society*, 188.
[48] See Friedman, *The Ultra-Orthodox Society*, passim.

Before moving to the next stage of our inquiry, I want to make three more remarks with regard to this priority. First, if the integrity framework I have been developing throughout this book is compelling, then it should lead us to think that so long as conscription exists in Israel, obliging the ultra-orthodox to serve as well (or at least to perform alternative national service) ought to be a central public policy goal, even if the practical gains from such a policy turn out to be limited. From an integrity perspective, there would be considerable moral value in imposing equal legal demands on the ultra-orthodox, even if, for example, the military can very well manage its tasks without them. Independently of such pragmatic calculations, the integrity framework highlights the independent significance of preventing a minority in society from unilaterally imposing a theologically driven vision of the people's collective project, on a majority expected to provide lives and resources to further this project.

Second, very much related, the demand of the integrity framework to reform the distribution of burdens and benefits pertaining to the ultra-orthodox is also a demand for government steadfastness. Since Israel's founding, no government has ever made a sustained attempt either to enforce conscription of the ultra-orthodox or to abolish state support for ultra-orthodox schools that ignore core curriculum requirements. Additionally, whenever the idea of conscripting the ultra-orthodox receives serious attention, ultra-orthodox leaders threaten that all ultra-orthodox men called to serve will riot in masses and/or go to prison.[49] The societal costs of either of these responses would be considerable. And that is partly why the threat of these costs materializing – despite the uncertainty about how genuine the threat really is – has been effective. The integrity framework insists, however, that despite these potential costs, reform ought to happen. At minimum, the government ought to force the ultra-orthodox community to choose between the abolition of state support for its educational system and a meaningful form of national service, if not simply conscription. If such a forced choice will trigger sustained and costly protests from the

---

[49] For one example out of many, see the explicit threat by Meir Porush, Vice Minister of Education, that ultra-orthodox Jews will "rebel" if conscripted. See Michal Levy, "Porush: Ultra-Orthodox Jews Will Declare a Rebellion," Channel 7, Apr. 27, 2016 at http://inn.co.il/News/News.aspx/320968 (Hebrew).

ultra-orthodox, that is simply a price that Israeli society must be willing to pay for the sake of collective integrity.

The final observation I want to make here is that this reasoning generates moral duties incumbent not only on politicians but also on voters. One may hope that ministers and prime ministers would be determined enough to impose burdens on Israel's ultra-orthodox population that are equivalent to those that the state requires of its secular Jewish majority. But realistically the reforms that would be necessary to achieve this will not happen unless the secular electorate consistently supports politicians who can be trusted to oppose the power of the ultra-orthodox parties, and unless the electorate punishes those who promise to engage in the necessary reform but never deliver.[50] This is one way in which the many secular Israelis who live in the country and are too politically apathetic to exercise their right to vote are guilty of neglecting the polity's collective project.[51] The integrity of the Israeli polity requires more of them.

5.4 The Druze, the Ultra-Orthodox, and the Conflict: A Gradual Strategy for Change

In the last section, I relied on the collective integrity framework to offer some initial grounds for prioritizing reforms related to the Druze and the ultra-orthodox. In this section, I wish to further support this priority through arguments associated with the collective integrity as well as the collective property framework.

The main thought driving these arguments is that in order to offer a persuasive moral case for making specific policy issues a government priority, it is important to see how progress with regard to these particular

---

[50] For some of the latest ignored promises in this context see Shahar Ilan, "The Next Secular Party Is Already on Its Way," *Calcalist*, Jan. 29, 2017, at http://calcalist.co.il/local/articles/0,7340,L-3706663,00.html (Hebrew).

[51] The decline in voting rates in Israel has been evident since the early 2000s, when voting rates consistently dropped below 70 percent (although the 2015 elections drew out 72 percent of the electorate). This decline is often attributed to a combination of political apathy and voter fatigue. The latter is primarily the result of the fact that the multi-party system generates new elections in very quick succession (for instance, six national elections were held between 2001 and 2015). On the especially high rate of voter abstention within the secular population see, for example, The Gutman Center at the Israeli Democracy Institute. "Who Doesn't Vote?" Feb. 26, 2015, at https://idi.org.il/articles/3535 (Hebrew).

issues can have an impact on other policy domains, including ones whose moral and practical significance is widely acknowledged. It is this kind of impact that I wish to trace here. More specifically, I want to show how policy reforms related to the Druze and the ultra-orthodox cases might yield important – even if only circumscribed and gradual – progress regarding the Israeli-Palestinian conflict.

This may seem like an overly modest aspiration. But normative reflection on a prolonged violent conflict is a manifestly non-ideal affair. And in a manifestly non-ideal context, there is considerable value to the pursuit of pragmatic, gradualist strategies for positive political change.[52] In turn, one way to pursue such a gradualist strategy in the case of the Israeli-Palestinian conflict is to focus on a moral value at the heart of the integrity framework that has clear implications for this conflict, but whose role in Israeli society is increasingly marginalized. This is the very basic value of the rule of law. Some of the conflict's most pernicious dynamics stem from the reluctance of consecutive Israeli governments to enforce Israel's own law vis-à-vis Jewish citizens in key contexts where such enforcement would mean protecting Palestinian rights. The reluctance of consecutive governments to enforce Israel's own law against the settler movement, so as to protect Palestinian property claims, is arguably the most significant example.[53] It is therefore worthwhile, even from the perspective of the conflict, to consider how reforms pertaining to the Druze and ultra-orthodox might help to bolster the country's rule of law.

In turn, when assessing this question, it is important to bear in mind that while Israel does maintain a recognizable system of rule of law, it is a system that is seriously fragile and incomplete. The rule of law is fragile, insofar as the basic norm of respect for the law is coming under increasing attack, especially from theologically motivated Jews – whether settler or ultra-orthodox – who see adherence to what they interpret as divine commands to be far more significant than adherence to secular law.[54] And the rule of law is woefully incomplete, insofar as

---

[52] This gradualist approach has much in common with what Hanna Lerner calls an "incrementalist" approach to the politics of divided societies, although Lerner's main focus is specifically on the forging of a constitution. See Hanna Lerner, *Making Constitutions in Deeply Divided Societies* (Cambridge: Cambridge University Press, 2011).

[53] Recall the confiscation law mentioned in the introduction.

[54] One may add here the increasingly explicit assault on the legal system by Prime Minister Netanyahu, an assault that continues to intensify as his personal legal predicaments deepen (see for example Bret Stephens, "Time for Netanyahu to

5.4 The Druze, the Ultra-Orthodox, and the Conflict

it often seems to give (at best) a subordinate place to the rights and interests of non-Jews.

Now, it may seem tempting to oppose this "ethnocratic" legal system simply through direct appeals to the equality of all human beings.[55] Yet unfortunately, in the current political climate, such cosmopolitan appeals are extremely unlikely to be effective. In a reality in which Palestinians – both within Israel and in the Palestinian territories – are seen by many as a mortal enemy bent on the destruction of the Jewish state, simply insisting on their basic moral equality does not hold much promise for improvement on the ground.[56] A more indirect strategy, focused on cases such as those of the Druze and the ultra-orthodox, might be more promising. In what follows, I want to develop some examples of such a strategy. Once again, I start with the Druze (5.4.1), and then turn to the ultra-orthodox (5.4.2).

5.4.1 The Rule of Law, Equality before the Law, and the Jewish National Fund

In stark contrast to the perception of Israel's Palestinian citizens, no one in Israel – not even the most ardent right-wing politicians – perceives the Druze as enemies. Therefore, a focus on the Druze's equal claims to membership in society is much more likely to spur positive legal reforms, which may ultimately extend far beyond the Druze community, to apply to Palestinians both inside Israel and in the Palestinian territories.

Go," *New York Times*, March 1, 2019). I plan to say more in future work on how the integrity framework firmly opposes such conduct.

[55] I borrow the term "ethnocracy" from Oren Yiftachel. See, e.g., Oren Yiftachel and Michaly D. Segal, "Jews and Druze in Israel: State Control and Ethnic Resistance," *Ethnic and Racial Studies* 21 (1998): 476–506.

[56] As Ronald Krebs put it, "in the mid-1990s, when many were still hopeful that the Oslo process would bear fruit, Israel's Jewish citizens showed little inclination to include the Arab minority symbolically, socially, institutionally, or even economically, and politically. A large majority believed that the state should show preference for Jewish over Arab citizens, opposed any modification in the major national symbols, and was unwilling to live in a religiously mixed neighbourhood. Half treated 'Israeli' as synonymous with 'Jewish.' Substantial minorities thought that only Jews should hold civil service jobs and favored the expropriation of Arab land to further Jewish development. Such views have only hardened and grown more extreme since the outbreak of the second intifada" (Krebs, *Fighting for Rights,* 109). These views, in turn, have only hardened further in the decade that has passed since Krebs's remarks.

A specific example will help to make this gradual strategy a bit more concrete, and will also allow us to see how the collective property framework can inform our reflections here. At the root of this example lies a particular institution: *Keren Kayemet Leyisrael*, known in English as the Jewish National Fund (JNF). Since the story of the JNF involves a fair amount of administrative detail, and since it ties together several themes of collective integrity and collective property in an especially forceful way, it is worth spelling out at some length.

The JNF was founded in 1901 as a private company owned by the World Zionist Organization. Its aim was to raise donations from Jews worldwide, in order to purchase territory in the Holy Land and prepare it for Zionist settlement. Between 1901 and Israel's establishment in 1948, the JNF had acquired slightly more than 942 square kilometers of land – roughly 4 percent of the new state's territory. Between 1949 and 1953, however, the government of the young state made the JNF the owner of sizable lands from which Palestinians had fled or were driven away during Israel's war of independence.[57] This governmental decision, which more than tripled the JNF's holdings, was explicitly motivated by the thought that state authorities had to manage public property with equal concern for all of the country's citizens, including its non-Jewish citizens. In contrast, since the JNF's goal was to develop land for Jews only, making it the owner of sizable lands would ensure that these lands will be used exclusively by Jews.[58] This rationale received formal expression when, in 1961, the JNF – by now a company under Israeli law – signed a "charter" with the state. The charter tasked a governmental body with the management of JNF lands, but made clear that decisions about these lands would be made in accordance with the JNF's incorporation documents – meaning that, even though they are to be managed by the state, JNF lands could still be sold only to Jews.[59] One senior Knesset member justified this charter as follows:

---

[57] Arnon Golan, "The Transfer to Jewish Control of Abandoned Arab Land during the War of Independence," in S. I. Troen and N. Lucas (eds.), *Israel, The First Decade of Independence* (Albany: State University of New York Press, 1995): 403–440.

[58] See Michal Oren-Nordheim, "Land in Public Hands Forever?" *Studies in the Geography of Israel* 16 (2003): 146–180. (Hebrew)

[59] See the charter text at http://kkl.org.il/?catid=%7BDFF37A9A-254F-4764-B2 C8-7A5EEF5D6043%7D (Hebrew).

5.4 The Druze, the Ultra-Orthodox, and the Conflict 215

We want something that is hard to define. We want it to be clear that the land of Israel belongs to the Jewish people. "The Jewish people" is a broader concept than the people who reside in Zion, since the Jewish people is present all over the world. On the other hand, every law we enact is made for the good of all those who reside in the state, and all those who reside in the state also include individuals who do not belong to the Jewish people ... we are giving a legal dress to the JNF's regulations ... [60]

The collective property framework directly explains why this rationale was both misleading, and profoundly morally misguided. In particular, the idea of deep public ownership that I associated with this framework in Chapter 2 explains why transferring public lands from the state to the JNF cannot legitimate managing these lands in a way that only accounts for Jews' interests. The idea of deep public ownership alerts us to a simple fact: the state can always reclaim – in the name of the sovereign body politic as a whole, including Jews and non-Jews alike – the very property that it has transferred to the JNF. But if it was the state's decision, as a representative of the sovereign body politic, to vest certain rights of ownership in the JNF, and if the state could revoke these rights, then it makes no moral sense for the state to allow itself – when managing the JNF's lands – to engage in blatant discrimination that it would avoid if the relevant lands were simply to remain formally designated as state property. Morally speaking, at least, discrimination associated with state property cannot be justified by blurring the public nature of this property through a hybrid entity such as the JNF. Ultimately, such "justification" is merely an accounting gimmick: it may alter the formal balance sheets, but it cannot alter the fundamental moral calculus.

The collective integrity framework, in turn, reinforces the very same point. In previous chapters, I argued that the value of collective integrity rules out certain forms of governmental hypocrisy. Among these forms was what I called the "hypocrisy of distance," which features a government attempting to shirk moral responsibility for profound political wrongs by casting these wrongs as the responsibility of other agents, despite the fact that the government itself is clearly in a position to alter the behavior and/or power of these actors. This kind of hypocrisy is obviously present in the case before us, since the government transferred

---

[60] Zerach Varheftig, in *The Chronicles of the Knesset*, Meeting 138 of the Fourth Knesset, Jul. 19, 1960, p. 1920 (Hebrew).

public lands to the JNF precisely in order to – artificially – distance itself from responsibility for discriminatory provisions related to these lands.

This blatant moral failure, in turn, has in many ways persisted into the present. As of 2014, the JNF still owned about 13 percent of the total land in Israel, and roughly 40 percent of the land outside the largely empty Negev desert,[61] yet the governmental body managing the JNF's lands (currently the Israeli Land Authority – ILA) is still formally prohibited from selling these lands to non-Jews. Traditionally, this state of affairs has been "resolved" through a dubious legal compromise: whenever a non-Jewish person would win a bid to purchase land owned by the JNF, the ILA would swap this land with the JNF in exchange for other land. This compromise was always destined to be unstable, partly because of its implications for third parties: individuals or companies who have been leasing public lands would suddenly find (typically without consultation or even notification) that the JNF, rather than the state, is their lessor – a change with significant implications. In light of such concerns, the ILA's legal counsel brought the land-swap compromise to a halt in 2004. Thus the ILA had to actually enforce JNF restrictions, preventing non-Jews from purchasing JNF lands it was managing.[62] But the story did not end there: non-governmental organizations working for minority rights in Israel responded by filing a lawsuit, asking Israel's Supreme Court to prohibit the ILA from upholding the JNF's "Jewish clause." The JNF insisted to the court that it is accountable to the Jewish people, rather than to Israel's citizens.[63] The state, in contrast, conceded in 2008 that the Jewish clause is discriminatory, asking only

---

[61] Moshe Lichtman, "Land Shortage in the Center of the Country? The JNF Has 2.4 Million Dunams," *Globes*, Mar. 18, 2014, at http://globes.co.il/news/article.aspx?did=1000925264 (Hebrew).

[62] Hadas Shefer, "The Rabbis' Letter" – The ILA version," *Calcalist*, Jan. 3, 2011, at http://calcalist.co.il/real_estate/articles/0,7340,L-3469421,00.html (Hebrew).

[63] "The JNF," read the response, "is not the trustee of the general public in Israel. Its loyalty is given to the Jewish people in the Diaspora and in the state of Israel . . . The JNF, in relation to being an owner of land, is not a public body that works for the benefit of all citizens of the state. The loyalty of the JNF is given to the Jewish people and only to them is the JNF obligated. The JNF, as the owner of the JNF land, does not have a duty to practice equality towards all citizens of the state." Quoted, e.g., in The Association for Civil Rights in Israel (ACRI), "Cancel the Land Swaps between the State and the JNF," Jan. 10, 2016, at https://acri.org.il/he/36846 (Hebrew).

that the court provide it with an opportunity to reach a settlement with the JNF while the land-swapping policy continues.[64] But in 2015 the state re-affirmed the "temporary" land-swap arrangement,[65] and currently no alternative arrangement is in sight.

This status quo is morally indefensible in at least two ways. First, so long as the land swaps between the state and the JNF persist, a sizable portion of the country's land will remain unavailable to its non-Jewish citizens: swaps only mean reshuffling the precise plots of land that are unavailable in this way.[66] Second, the land-swap compromise does nothing to remove the profound symbolic affront involved in formally barring non-Jewish citizens from a great many land purchases.

This affront, in turn, is especially vivid in the case of the Druze minority. The fact that the Druze are obliged by the Israeli legal system to risk their lives in defense of "the people," but that the very same legal system formally, at least, prohibits them from acquiring the land of "the people," represents at once a disturbing conception of this property and an utmost failure of collective integrity.

What ought to be the solution? For one thing, as many of the JNF's critics had argued, this institution has become obsolete with the establishment of the state. Accordingly, the JNF simply ought to be abolished, and its lands transferred to the state's direct control.[67] Moreover, insofar as the state wishes to privilege any sector of the population in terms of access to publicly owned land, the relevant criterion ought not to be ethnic, but rather contribution to the collective civic project through some form of national service. In virtue of

[64] Shefer, *The Rabbis' Letter*.
[65] ACRI, *Cancel the Land Swaps*. I am grateful to Oren Yiftachel and Alexandre Kedar for discussion of the current state of affairs regarding the land-swap policy.
[66] This point is especially important in light of the fact that the main plots of land that the JNF receives as part of the land swaps are in the Galilee and Negev desert, where the main housing needs are those of non-Jewish citizens.
[67] This claim was made already a few years after Israel's independence. See Michal Oren-Nordheim, *The Crystallization of Settlement Land Policy in the State of Israel from Its Establishment and during the First Years of the Israel Lands Administration (1948–1965)* (PhD dissertation, Hebrew University of Jerusalem, 1999), Chapter 9 (Hebrew). The same claim has been repeated many times since. Thus, for example, Eitan Kabel, a long-serving Member of the Knesset, pointed out in 2015, "The JNF ought to have been abolished long ago. But no one has the courage to do it." Quoted in Roni Zinger, "I Don't Know Why the JNF Is Needed – Get Back to Me on That," *Calcalist*, Oct. 21, 2015, at http://calcalist.co.il/local/articles/0,7340,L-3671499,00.html (Hebrew).

their military service, the Druze would clearly fulfill the service requirement for any privileges associated with public land.[68]

Now, I am aware that some readers may be puzzled as to the relevance of all this to the Israeli-Palestinian conflict. Upon reflection, however, the answer should be fairly clear. While the Druze suffer from the fact that they cannot purchase land owned by the JNF, they are not the only non-Jews who suffer in this way. The much larger population of Palestinian Israelis suffer from this problem as well. Unlike the Druze, Israel's Palestinian citizens neither want nor are called to serve in the military. But if, through the Druze example, the norm were established that some form of contribution to the people's collective projects entitles individuals to privileges with regard to the purchase of public land, regardless of their ethnicity, then Palestinian Israelis could qualify for these privileges as well through forms of national service other than military service – be it through community work in public education, the public health system, community policing, or other alternatives.

In turn, by involving Palestinians in civic endeavors shared with the Jewish majority, such policies will help combat the self-reinforcing prejudice in Israeli society, which dehumanizes Palestinians, regards them as necessarily uninterested in any joint civic efforts, and as necessarily hostile toward Jewish existence in the Middle East. Moreover, the very same policies, insofar as they would generate important legal entitlements for Israel's Palestinian citizens, would help in combating the all-too-prevalent

---

[68] This solution, in line with the integrity framework, once again involves a principled stance, in at least two respects. First, abolishing the JNF, or at least its "Jewish clause," would be of considerable moral significance even if the matter were primarily symbolic: formal changes would be needed to the regulations surrounding JNF lands even if, through some legal gymnastics, their everyday implications for Israel's non-Jewish citizens would be minimal. Second, the demand to end the discrimination surrounding JNF lands is principled insofar as, just as with the aforementioned reforms regarding the ultra-orthodox, it requires steadfastness. Any attempt to abolish the JNF, or even simply remove the "Jewish clause" from its incorporation documents, is likely to trigger fierce resistance, both from politicians who have used the JNF as a key source of political patronage, and from right-wing politicians who wish to detach the JNF entirely from the state so that it can manage "its own property" explicitly with an eye toward the interests of Jews only, without any burdens imposed by the state's egalitarian commitments. (See, e.g., Lilach Waisman, "The Knesset Committee Will Expedite a Law Proposal Preventing the Leasing of JNF Lands to Arabs," *Globes*, Jul. 10, 2007, at http://globes.co.il/news/article.aspx?did=1000230371 (Hebrew); see also Zinger, "I Don't Know Why the JNF Is Needed.")

5.4 The Druze, the Ultra-Orthodox, and the Conflict 219

tendency in Israeli society to view its legal system as "relevant" exclusively for Jews. All of these developments, insofar as they might actually be incentivized through legal reform that begins with the Druze, can only have positive effects on the way in which Israel's Jewish majority manages its territorial conflict with the Palestinians, both inside Israel and in the Palestinian territories.

The significance of this point, moreover, only becomes more manifest the more Israel's law formally acquires Jewish rather than Israeli dimensions. In November 2017, for instance, a special Knesset Committee, convened to advance a basic law titled "Israel as the Nation-State of the Jewish People," made extensive efforts to include in the law a clause that would allow, for the first time in the country's history, the establishment of settlements officially designated as meant "for Jews only." This initiative was thwarted only after the committee's legal staff asserted that such a law would have no parallel in "any other constitution, anywhere in the world."[69] The final version of the bill, which was approved by the Knesset in the summer of 2018, deprives Arabic of its historical standing as an official language in the country, on par with Hebrew (merely designating Arabic as a language with "special status"), while also refraining, in direct contrast with Israel's Declaration of Independence, from any explicit commitment to upholding the equality of all of the country's citizens, Jews and non-Jews alike.[70]

This particular bill is especially pertinent for our purposes, given that the large-scale social protest at its approval featured – for the first time in the country's history – a central role for the Druze community.[71] The

---

[69] Yeohantan Liss, "The Nation-State Committee Discussed a Clause That Would Allow the Establishment of Jews-Only Settlements," *Haaretz*, Nov. 28, 2017, at https://haaretz.co.il/news/politi/.premium-1.4633166.

[70] See, e.g., "Israel Passes 'National Home' Law, Drawing Ire of Arabs," *New York Times*, Jul. 18, 2018. See also Ronald Lauder, "Israel, This Is Not Who We Are," *New York Times*, Aug. 13, 2018, at https://nytimes.com/2018/08/13/opinion/israel-ronald-lauder-nation-state-law.html; Judi Meltz, "In Protest of the Nationality Law: The Jewish Agency Reaffirmed the Principles of the Declaration of Independence," *Haaretz*, Oct. 25, 2018, at https://haaretz.co.il/news/education/.premium-1.6592315 (Hebrew). Israel's declaration of independence explicitly guarantees "full and equal citizenship" to "the Arab inhabitants of the State of Israel." See https://knesset.gov.il/docs/eng/megilat_eng.htm.

[71] Immediately upon the bill's passage, current Knesset member and former head of the military's personnel branch, Elazar Shtern, commented: "This law is

community's leaders took to the stage in a massive rally at the heart of Tel Aviv, announcing that "having fought for the country, we will fight for its character," and explicitly threatening to reconsider their decades-long support of Druze conscription.[72] The results were immediate. Whereas certain politicians sought to dismiss protests from other Arab citizens, and in some cases even to point to these protests as evidence of the law's "necessity,"[73] no politician was able to dismiss the Druze community's protests with anything like the same ease. In fact, even extreme right-wing politicians found themselves with little choice but to apologize to the community.[74] Key Knesset members who voted in favor of the bill effectively sought to retract their vote, and voiced public support of multiple lawsuits submitted to the Supreme Court demanding that the court strike the law down.[75]

It is of course an open question whether the unprecedented presence of the Druze at the heart of Israeli public discourse will fade just as suddenly as it has emerged. Similarly, it is an open question whether Israel's Supreme Court – which, at the time of writing, has agreed to consider the appeals against the bill – will strike it down. Whether or

   a finger in the eye of our Druze and Bedouin brethren who serve alongside us in the military and defense forces . . . this [bill] will turn even soldiers who fight and die for this country into enemies." Quoted in Moran Azulay, "Nationality Law Approved," *Ynet*, Jul. 19, 2018, at https://ynet.co.il/articles/0,7340,L-5312599,00.html (Hebrew).
[72] See, e.g., Mark Weiss, "Israel's Divisive Nationality Law Incites Political Backlash," *Irish Times*, Aug. 8, 2018, at https://irishtimes.com/news/world/middle-east/israel-s-divisive-nationality-law-incites-political-backlash-1.3590022; Daoud Kuttab, "Nationality Law Makes Israel's Druze Second-Class Citizens," *Al-Monitor*, Jul. 31, 2018, https://al-monitor.com/pulse/originals/2018/07/israel-nationality-law-anger-druze-protest.html; Hassan Shaalan and Itamar Eichner, "Druze Leaders to Continue Protests over Nationality Law," *Ynet*, Aug. 2, 2018, at https://ynetnews.com/articles/0,7340,L-5321301,00.html.
[73] See, e.g., "Netanyahu: The Attack on the Nationality Law Proves How Low the Left Has Sunk," *Haaretz*, Jul. 27, 2018, at https://haaretz.co.il/news/politi/1.6318504 (Hebrew).
[74] See, e.g., Raoul Wootliff, "Bennett: Government Must 'Heal Wound' Caused to Druze by Nation-State Law," *Times of Israel*, Jul. 25, 2018, at https://timesofisrael.com/bennett-government-must-heal-wound-caused-to-druze-by-nation-state-law/.
[75] See, e.g., David Israel, "Kahlon, Bennett, Regret Parts of Nationality Law, Promise Amendments," *Jewish Press*, Jul. 26, 2018, at http://jewishpress.com/news/israel/the-knesset/kahlon-bennett-regret-parts-of-nationality-law-promise-amendments/2018/07/26/.

5.4 The Druze, the Ultra-Orthodox, and the Conflict

not the court is courageous enough to do this, however, this episode provides ample illustration of how demands to remedy the injustices suffered by the Druze could be strategically significant in improving the lot of other non-Jews subject to Israeli law. The thought, then, is that legal reforms that initially focus on the Druze, and that give them a place in Israeli society that is far more commensurate with their sacrifices, may ultimately lead more Jewish Israelis to question the dangerous notion that Israel's legal system is ultimately meant to serve Jews only.[76] And this questioning, in turn, is essential for any long-term hope of a peaceful solution to the Israeli-Palestinian conflict.

5.4.2 Religion and the Conflict

The ideas expressed in the last subsection with regard to the Druze have fairly close parallels with regard to the ultra-orthodox. Just as reforms seeking the genuine equality of the Druze before Israeli law may help in curbing the law's ethnic elements, so will reforms ensuring the genuine equality of the ultra-orthodox before the law will help to curb its theological elements. In both cases, reforms that begin with Israel's internal minorities might make Israeli law into more Israeli and less Jewish law. And this shift, once again, can only have a positive impact on the shape of the Israeli-Palestinian conflict. If nothing else, this is because such a shift could help counteract the conflict's alarming transformation – evident since the early 2000s – from a territorial into a religious dispute.

The scale and significance of this shift is not sufficiently well-known outside of Israel, and so it is worth elaborating. On the Palestinian side, the main manifestation (and cause) of the conflict's theological elements is the ascendance of the religious Hamas to a position of political leadership, at the expense of the traditionally secular PLO – especially since Hamas's victory in the 2006

---

[76] Insofar as the current government has played a key role in spreading this reprehensible notion, it is quite unlikely that it will be the source of such reforms. If these reforms ever came about, it is overwhelmingly likely that they will come about because of the efforts of far less morally obtuse governments than the ones that have been presiding over the country since 2009.

Palestinian elections.[77] On the Israeli side, the conflict is assuming an increasingly religious emphasis due to the continued political growth of the settler movement, with repercussions for all three branches of government,[78] and even for the traditionally secular military.[79] Thus, for example, Yagil Levy, a prominent scholar of the Israeli military, has documented in detail what he calls the military's striking "religionization" process.[80] This process is partly due to the efforts of leading rabbis in the settler movement to increase the settler presence in the military, and to inculcate in Jewish soldiers the idea that their core task is to protect the religious settlement project – even if this means disobeying the secular government's authority when it comes to evacuating illegal settlements. Levy writes:

In 2009, for the first time in the country's history, soldiers in uniform . . . raised protest signs, in this case against the dismantling of illegal settlements . . . the IDF punished the soldiers. In late 2009, in an unprecedented move, the Ministry of Defense retracted *Har Bracha Yeshiva's* status as a hesder yeshiva [a yeshiva that combines Torah studies and military service] *after its head openly and publicly encouraged soldiers to disobey orders to dismantle Jewish settlements.* Other threats to refuse to carry out orders to demolish settlements have been heard clearly since then. The IDF thus reformulated its position, stating that it preferred that the army not be on the front lines of dismantling outposts and that police units should do the job, although the police are incapable of doing so alone.

Whether the military and its political supervisors admit it or not, it is safe to assume that a central consideration in refraining from dismantling illegal

---

[77] Whether Hamas's current isolation will change its approach remains to be seen. See, e.g., Ian Fisher and Majd Al Waheidi, "New Hamas Charter Would Name 'Occupiers,' Not 'Jews,' as the Enemy," *New York Times,* Mar. 9, 2017, at https://nytimes.com/2017/03/09/world/middleeast/hamas-gaza-israel-jews.html.

[78] With regard to the judiciary in particular, see Sharon Pulwer, "Israel Taps Four New Supreme Court Justices, Shifting Balance of Power to the Right," *Haaretz* (English edition), Feb. 23, 2017, at http://haaretz.com/israel-news/.premium-1.773328; see also Aluf Benn, "With Supreme Court Picks, Netanyahu's Government Launches Anti-Constitutional Revolution," *Haaretz* (English edition), Feb. 23, 2017, at http://haaretz.com/israel-news/.premium-1.773379.

[79] This is true as well as for Israeli society more generally. See, e.g., Yoav Peled and Orit Herman Peled, *The Religionization of Israeli Society* (London: Routledge, 2018).

[80] See, e.g., Yagil Levy, "Religious Authorities in the Military and Civilian Control: The Case of the Israeli Defense Forces," *Politics & Society* 44 (2016): 305–332.

5.4 The Druze, the Ultra-Orthodox, and the Conflict

settlements ... despite the Israeli pledge to the United States, is the simple understanding that doing so would open the military to massive refusals from religious soldiers.[81]

A further vivid example of the military's "religionization" process occurred in July 2014 when, in preparation for a major military operation in Gaza, a senior IDF officer, Ofer Vinter, issued a message to his division that included the following statement:

> History chose us to be at the forefront of the battle against the terrorist Gaza enemy, which is cursing and swearing at the Lord of Israel ... I look above and call with you "Hear, O Israel: the Lord our God, the Lord is one." Lord make our way successful, for we are going to stand and fight for your people against an enemy cursing your name.[82]

Statements of this kind are profoundly disturbing. One does not need to endorse the teachings of Carl Schmitt to think that a violent conflict in which both sides claim to be fighting in the name of God is far more likely to be long and bloody, and far less likely to be resolved peacefully, than a conflict not rooted in theological underpinnings. One way to resist such narratives of theistically driven wars is, of course, to sanction those who propagate them, in any official state role. But another way is to insist, wherever and whenever this is necessary, on a firm separation between the Israeli state on the one hand – including both its civic and military undertakings – and, on the other hand, Jewish religion and ethnicity.

In turn, once we see just how necessary such a separation really is, it should also be easier to see why upholding the supremacy of Israel's law over the theological demands of its ultra-orthodox community has implications that extend far beyond this community. If, through

---

[81] Levy, "Religious Authorities in the Military," 312.
[82] Gili Cohen, "Head of Givati Battalion to Commanders: 'Lord of Israel, We Are Fighting against an Enemy Cursing Your Name'," *Haaretz*, Jul. 11, 2014, at http://haaretz.co.il/news/politics/1.2373864 (Hebrew). See also Israel Cohen, "God's Army or the People's Army," *Haaretz*, Aug. 14, 2018, at https://haaretz.co.il/opinions/.premium-1.6382699 (Hebrew). One wonders to what extent ordinary Jewish citizens who heard of these remarks remembered that there might very well be Druze soldiers in the unit that was urged to "fight in God's name." Moreover, in line with what I said earlier, one wonders whether such a possibility would be livelier in the minds of ordinary Jewish citizens had Druze military sacrifice been recognized by Israeli society to the degree that it ought to be.

confrontation with the ultra-orthodox, it would be established that the country's law is neither equivalent nor subordinate to Jewish theological aims – if the law were to be repeatedly and firmly enforced, for instance, against ultra-orthodox leaders who call for rebellion and riots against the secular majority's will – this would only help in quashing the idea that Israeli law can ever be used to pursue some supposedly "divinely ordained" land. Combating this dangerous idea will help to take the focus of the Israeli-Palestinian conflict from the extremist notion that fanatics on both sides have been propagating: that the land is more sacred than the people who walk on it. And battling this fanatic notion is one of the keys to a peaceful resolution of the Israeli-Palestinian conflict.

5.5 Refugees

Equipped with these claims regarding the Israeli-Palestinian conflict, I now want to turn to another context in which outsiders have had urgent moral claims vis-à-vis Israeli society. This context features refugees who have been seeking to gain entry, or permission to stay, in Israel. In this case as well, I want to suggest that collective integrity's amplifying function can help us think about public policy priorities. Moreover, while this contribution is eminently practical, it also involves theoretical dividends.

Let me start with the theoretical issue, which has to do with a classic complaint against integrity arguments. This complaint holds that a focus on integrity invariably pushes agents to give excessive attention to their own purity, at the expense of others' practical needs: integrity leads agents to avoid compromising their own clean hands, even if doing so may be of tremendous practical help to others. Thus for instance, the classic examples that Bernard Williams offered for integrity at work – the reluctance of a pacifist chemist to take a job in a chemical weapons factory even if doing so would be for the good of the world, or the compunction of an innocent bystander asked to shoot one person in order that the lives of many others will be spared[83] – have struck Williams's critics, especially of the consequentialist sort, as

---

[83] Bernard Williams, "A Critique of Utilitarianism," in Williams and J. J. C. Smart, *Utilitarianism – For and Against* (Cambridge: Cambridge University Press, 1973), 97–99.

proving integrity's self-indulgence. Robert Goodin's impatience with "the dandy who prates on about his integrity while others are suffering needlessly"[84] sharply illustrates this self-absorption charge against integrity arguments.

The claims of earlier chapters, especially regarding connections between integrity and decent treatment of vulnerable others, should already make clear that I think this objection fails. But we can deploy the case of a refugee crisis to make this failure even clearer. To see how, imagine a liberal democracy whose collective identity is constituted to a significant degree by its being a refugee society. Its founding documents, its education system, even the names of its streets, make ubiquitous references to its establishment by refugees. The society's pride in its economic and scientific progress, for example, is inseparable from the refugee experience, given the prevalent conviction that the refugee background of so many citizens has made such progress especially difficult to achieve. Now imagine that a refugee crisis erupts in a neighboring country. I take it to be a widely shared conviction that all reasonably affluent liberal democracies have a duty to step in to offer support to the refugees (even if the extent of this duty and its precise details are likely to be a matter of dispute).[85] But we can nonetheless draw a fairly direct connection between the integrity framework and the following thought: whatever is the "standard" duty of an affluent liberal democracy with regard to refugees who are in clearly dire straits, this duty is especially salient in the case of a liberal democracy whose collective identity is oriented to a significant extent around the experience of refugee life.

More precisely, following the reasoning outlined in previous sections, we can say that a liberal democracy with this kind of identity has an especially stringent and weighty duty to help refugees. It would be especially wrong for this liberal democracy to refuse to help the refugees, as compared to other liberal democracies that lack its constitutive refugee history. And this particular liberal democracy ought to be willing to make greater sacrifices for the sake of refugees – for instance, admitting more refugees at a greater pace than other liberal democracies that lack a refugee identity. The reason, it seems safe to say, is that for this particular liberal democracy to behave otherwise

---

[84] Goodin, *Utilitarianism as a Public Philosophy*, 69.
[85] This conviction can be shared even by those known in global justice debates as "statists." See, e.g., Michael Blake, "Immigration, Jurisdiction, and Exclusion," *Philosophy and Public Affairs* 41 (2013): 103–130.

would be to turn its back not only on the refugees but also, in some sense, on itself – to betray its own integrity. But if all this is true, then the polity's integrity, with the particular history underlying it, amplifies rather than diminishes the weight of others' needs in its practical decision-making. And if this is right, then the charge that integrity arguments necessarily push agents to make self-absorbed practical decisions is wrong.

This theoretical point, in turn, has clear practical implications for the case of Israel and its responses to refugee crises. After all, there are few political communities in the world whose collective identity is as suffused with refugee history as is the case with Israel. Every single aspect of a collective "refugee identity" I described above can be found in Israeli society, not least due to the continuous, and ubiquitous, presence of the holocaust in Israeli collective consciousness.[86] This fact in turn suggests that whatever duty reasonably affluent countries have in general to aid refugees who are in clearly dire straits, the duty of Israeli society to extend such aid is especially weighty and stringent.[87]

---

[86] Consider, for instance, the following remarks from Avraham Burg, former speaker of the Knesset: "The list of Shoah [Holocaust] manifestations in daily life is long. Listen to every word spoken and you find countless Shoah references. The Shoah pervades the media and the public life, literature, music, art, education. These overt manifestations hide the Shoah's deepest influence. Israel's security policy, the fears and paranoia, feelings of guilt and belonging, are products of the Shoah ... Sixty years after his suicide in Berlin, Hitler's hand still touches us ... Israel naturalizes the Shoah victims who were dead even before we were born, embracing them into the bosom of the third State of Israel ... [T]herefore our dead do not rest in peace. They are busy, present, always a part of our sad lives." Avraham Burg, *The Holocaust Is Over, We Must Rise from Its Ashes* (New York: Palgrave Macmillan, 2008), 23–24.

[87] In this context, it is worth pointing out that while the state goes to great lengths to honor gentiles who risked their lives to save Jews throughout the Holocaust, these honors have long pivoted on basic universal values – or, as Yad Vashem calls them, simply "human values" (see, e.g., Yad Vashem, "My Brother's Keeper: The Project of Recognizing the Righteous Among the Nations," at https://yadvashem.org/yv/he/exhibitions/righteous/milestone04.asp) (Hebrew). That, surely, is the only plausible way to think about the issue. The "righteous among nations" ought to be honored not because they recognized any supposed unique claim that Jews qua Jews had to be treated in certain ways, which would not apply to non-Jews in similar trouble. Rather, the "righteous among the nations" ought to be honored because, accepting ultimate personal risks, they helped *fellow human beings* who were suffering predicaments rarely thought possible before – simply out of recognition of the moral weight of shared humanity.

5.5 Refugees

This rationale has received expression in actual political debate in Israel. One especially vivid example occurred in September 2015, at the height of the Syrian refugee crisis. The Leader of the Opposition at the time, Yitzhak Herzog, urged Prime Minister Netanyahu to admit Syrian refugees to Israel using the following terms:

> I call on the Israeli government to take initiative to receive refugees from the fighting in Syria alongside the humanitarian measures that are already being pursued. Jews cannot remain indifferent when hundreds of thousands of refugees are seeking safe harbor . . . for years, I have been warning about the horrible crisis that is ongoing in Syria and about the refugees' grave condition. And the world is silent. Recently the Druze in Syria have also been subject to severe risks to their very lives. And still, horrible silence. Our people experienced firsthand the silence of the world, and cannot be indifferent in the face of the rampant murders and massacres taking place in Syria.[88]

Herzog was joined by members of other parties, including a Jewish religious member of a centrist party and a Druze member of the ruling right-wing Likud party, who similarly argued in Holocaust-laden terms: "It is inconceivable for a people that went through an experience seventy years ago to ignore this [crisis]. This cannot happen."[89] Later on, as Prime Minister Netanyahu claimed that Israel is "too small" and "lacks demographic depth" to absorb the refugees, and Netanyahu's allies criticized Herzog's humanitarian pleas as "populist," Herzog responded: "You have forgotten what is it like to be Jewish. Refugees. Persecuted. The Prime Minister of the Jewish People does not close the heart and the gate when human beings are running for their lives away from their persecutors, with their babies in their hands."[90]

Parallel disputes occurred in the public sphere. Days after Herzog's statements, fans of one of Israel's largest soccer clubs, Maccabi Tel

---

[88] Quoted in Barak Ravid, Yehonatan Liss, and Gilli Cohen, "Herzog Calls on the Government to Receive Refugees from the Syrian Civil War," *Haaretz*, Sep. 5, 2015, at http://haaretz.co.il/news/politics/1.2724593 (Hebrew).

[89] Barak Ravid and Yehonatan Liss, "Netanyahu Rejects Herzog's Call to Receive Refugees: "Israel Is a Small State without Demographic Depth," *Haaretz*, Sep. 6, 2015, at https://haaretz.co.il/news/politics/.premium-1.2725006 (Hebrew).

[90] Quoted in Arik Bender and Dana Somberg, "Israel Is a Small Country That Should Block Infiltrators," *Maariv*, Sep. 6, 2015, at http://maariv.co.il/news/politics/Article-496687 (Hebrew).

Aviv, lifted signs in English reading "Refugees not welcomed." Fans of the local rivals, Hapoel Tel Aviv, generally known as a left-leaning club, lifted opposing banners reading "Who here isn't a refugee?"[91]

Unsurprisingly, given Israel's current political climate, the call to allow Syrian refugees into the country did not prevail. Nor has there been any positive change in the precarious legal status of African refugees who (especially between 2007 and 2012) have made their way to Israel from Sudan and Eritrea. Though they are protected from deportation in line with international conventions to which Israel has been a signatory, racist incitement against them, including by senior politicians, is ubiquitous, to an extent that has even triggered official protests from the heads of Yad Vashem, the main state authority overseeing the commemoration of the Holocaust.[92] Moreover, the government is pursuing almost any possible measure – at times in contravention of Supreme Court rulings – to push them to leave. All this despite the fact that, contrary to government rhetoric, they pose at most limited security risks, and their numbers (currently less than forty thousand) remain very modest as a portion of the country's overall population.[93] At the time of writing, their prospects of enjoying a stable, safe haven in Israel are slim, with the government oscillating between attempts to force more of them to leave as a way of placating domestic right-wing pressures, and allowing more refugees to stay, in line with international obligations.[94] In general, one can say that this

---

[91] See "'Who Isn't a Migrant Here' Says Banner at Israeli Soccer Game," *Times of Israel*, at http://timesofisrael.com/who-isnt-a-migrant-here-says-banner-at-israeli-soccer-game/, Sep. 13, 2015 (although the title of this article mistranslates the banner welcoming refugees).

[92] See "Press Release: The Response of the Heads of Yad Vashem," *Yad Vashem*, May 29, 2012, at http://yadvashem.org/he/press-release/29-may-2012-12-43 (Hebrew).

[93] Asaf Golan, "Israel Has Few Refugees, a Drop in the Ocean Compared to Europe," *NRG*, Aug. 25, 2015, at http://nrg.co.il/online/1/ART2/720/116.html (Hebrew); for April 2018 figures, see Israel's Population and Immigration Authority, "Data on Foreigners in Israel," at https://gov.il/BlobFolder/reports/foreign_workers_stats_0118/he/%D7%A8%D7%91%D7%A2%D7%95%D7%9F%201.pdf (Hebrew).

[94] See, e.g., "Netanyahu Is Zigzagging: Freezing the Agreement on Asylum Seekers," *Calcalist*, Apr. 2, 2018 at https://calcalist.co.il/local/articles/0,7340,L-3735429,00.html (Hebrew); see also Li Yaron, "After Removing Their Protection, the State Has Announced: We Will Expel Hundreds of Congolese Citizens," *Haaretz*, Oct. 9, 2018, at https://haaretz.co.il/news/politics/1.6545531 (Hebrew).

oscillation is a serious moral failure. But one can also say, more specifically, that it is a particularly abject failure of collective integrity.

5.6 Looking to the Future

In this final chapter, I used the example of Israeli society to argue that ideas regarding the people's property and integrity, although rooted in a conception of the people as a unitary agent, can inform our thinking about deep ethnic and religious divisions internal to the people. In the process of developing this claim, I also sought to show how the collective property and collective integrity frameworks can contribute to our thinking about the policy priorities that form an inevitable background to real-world politics. Finally, as in previous chapters, I tried to show how, under manifestly non-ideal conditions, the two frameworks yield strategies for positive political change.

It might be appropriate to close by discussing the status of the hope for such change in Israel. While the arguments I presented here reflect the belief that such hope still exists, it is also highly uncertain, insofar as it rests predominantly with Israel's Jewish secular sector. For one thing, the demographic trends emphasized above mean that the share of this sector in the country's population is diminishing. Moreover, the economic condition of the secular middle class is deteriorating. Israel's intense neo-liberalization, manifest since the 1980s in everything from diminishing public education, through dramatic reduction of public sector employment, to the privatization of health care, has seriously undermined the social safety net previously enjoyed by the middle class.[95] This neo-liberal process, combined with an exponential growth in living costs (especially housing costs) relative to the middle class's purchasing power, make it difficult even for many members of the Jewish secular majority – including well-educated young adults – to make ends meet.[96]

---

[95] See, e.g., Guy Ben-Porat, Yagil Levy, Shlomo Mizrahi, Arye Naor, and Erez Tzfadia, *Israel Since 1980* (New York: Cambridge University Press, 2008).

[96] The spike in housing costs in particular is often captured in Israel through reference to the number of monthly salaries needed to buy an apartment, where, despite different possible metrics, Israel is consistently in the worst position among OECD countries. See, e.g., Hadas Shefer, "A Global Comparison: 126 Salaries for an Apartment in Israel, Twice than Britain," *Calcalist*, Aug. 14, 2013, at http://calcalist.co.il/real_estate/articles/0,7340,L-3609995,00.html (Hebrew).

This problem, in turn, is compounded by the widespread sense that the economic priorities of consecutive governments have been skewed against the secular middle class, because both their ideological agenda and their political calculations push them to prioritize instead the interests of the settler movement and the ultra-orthodox minority. Thus, for example, at the height of the social protests that engulfed Israel in the summer of 2011, triggered primarily by the country's housing crisis, Israel's equivalent of "Saturday Night Live" captured the secular middle-class mindset with a skit in which Prime Minister Netanyahu was portrayed guaranteeing the protesters a "complete transformation of our priorities": instead of having the "settlers at the top, the ultra-orthodox second, and everyone else at the bottom," the prime minister announced, "we will have the ultra-orthodox first, the settlers second, and *then* everyone else at the bottom."[97] While it is likely that few in Israel's right laughed, for many young progressives feeling the combined brunt of profoundly un-equal military service (including reserve duty), high taxes, low salaries, and escalating living costs, this skit was a pithy summary of a painful reality. Nor has this reality changed in any fundamental way in the years since the protests.

The combined result of all of these dynamics is evident in survey data indicating that almost 40 percent of Israel adults are considering leaving the country.[98] Of course, just how seriously this portion of the population is "considering" leaving the country is another matter. But even if only a very small portion of these potential emigrants actually end up leaving, a very large share of them – especially among young progressives – can be predicted to withdraw further and further away from Israel's civic struggles. As demographic changes and failed progressive protests accumulate, things might very well get worse. And they might get worst still as right-wing "siege mentality" intensifies, defending the most blatant forms of discrimination and violence against non-Jews, fueling and being fueled by a rise in alienation and animosity on the part of Israel's Palestinian citizens.

---

[97] See *Eretz Nehedret*, ["*A Wonderful Country*"], Protest Special, at http://mako.co.il/mako-vod-keshet/eretz_nehederet-s8/VOD-b519856e13ea131006.htm (Hebrew).

[98] See Sivan Kligenbale and Shani Shilo, "Why Almost 40% of Israelis Are Considering Leaving," *Haaretz*, Dec. 14, 2012, at http://haaretz.co.il/magazine/1.1884838 (Hebrew).

5.6 Looking to the Future

Faced with such trends, many members of the country's shrinking progressive camp might very well respond with apathy and resignation to a society in which they are becoming more and more of a minority, and to a politics that constantly moves further away from their liberal values. And, at some stage, there may come a time in which it will no longer be reasonable to issue moral criticism of such apathy and resignation. At that point, in line with the integrity warning of Chapter 1, the country's liberal citizens may very well be warranted in feeling such profound alienation from their society that the reason for its existence – and the reason for why they ought to make sacrifices for its existence – will elude them.

A preview of this stark scenario came in August 2012, when intense debates in Israel about Iran's nuclear project were temporarily disrupted by widespread media reports of the lynching of three Arab citizens in Jerusalem by a large group of young Jews.[99] Jewish journalist Jackie Levy responded by dedicating a column to violence and racism in the mundane aspects of daily life, taking as an example, the behavior of two Jewish train conductors that he and his children witnessed when using Jerusalem's light train. After reporting on one conductor's mistreatment of an elderly man, Levy described the other conductor's confrontation with an Arab citizen who did not validate his train ticket:

"What does it mean to 'validate?'"
"It means that you are coming with me to the police right now."
"But I bought a ticket."
"I don't care. A fine or the police."
"Excuse me, then I'll get off here."
"You're not getting off anywhere."

The passenger . . . did not even manage to make it to the next stop. Within moments insane violence erupted. The two conductors pounced at him. They tried to block his way, and when they failed, started hitting him and smashed him on the train platform . . .

That night we could not sleep. Here we received a big lesson in civics, lots of food for thought and mainly reasons for worry. I should stress that both the children and I were very impressed with the passenger public that did not

---

[99] The main perpetrator of the lynching, a teenager, was sentenced to eight months in prison. See Avishai Glikman, "Prison Sentences for Those Involved in the Attempted Lynch in the Center of Jerusalem," Channel 10/Nana News, at http://news.nana10.co.il/Article/?ArticleID=989866 (Hebrew).

keep quiet, that came to the aid of the victims and told the conductors exactly what it thinks of them. And yet, the last sentence that the conductor said, a moment before everything became a jumble, was, and I quote: "so, you're in favor of the Arab . . ."[100]

Levy ended his column by tying this "mundane" event to the much more publicly discussed lynching that occurred in Jerusalem, reaching a dramatic conclusion:

Less than two days later at the center of Jerusalem tens of Jewish teenagers pounced at three Arabs and beat them to a pulp. In this case almost no one raised a finger and no one can claim innocence. It turns out that this people has gone through a process, and is now fully ready for lynching. The hearts have been prepared . . . the list of the guilty is as long as the road to Tel Aviv. Guilty are the parents of these lost boys. Guilty are everyone who neglected the education system . . . Guilty are the religious educators who inspired the despicable slogan "A Jew is a soul, an Arab is an S.O. . . ." Guilty is every teacher, every rabbi, every intellectual, whose public utterances are contaminated with violence and xenophobia . . . guilty is everyone who has cultivated common street violence – Jewish and Arab – and thought that they will only gain from doing so . . .

Guilty is everyone who basked in the purity of their hands, and who forgot that we too have weak publics. And that after all is the teaching of the weak: moral superiority means nothing to him. Moral superiority is a luxury of enervated elites. The weak one wants a simple victory, violent and bloody. The weak one wants the same moral exemption he thinks the Arabs have managed to achieve. *Guilty is anyone who thinks that the most urgent thing today is to speak for or against attacking Iran. For if Jerusalem can lynch, why is it even important, whether we will be here or not.*"[101]

Israel's progressive citizens as a whole may not yet share this sentiment. But without fundamental political transformations – starting with gradual changes of the kind I sought to elaborate here – that sentiment may not be too far off.

---

[100] Jackie Levy, "Disrespectful Thugs," *Israel Hayom*, Aug. 24, 2012, at www.israelhayom.co.il/article/45463 (Hebrew).
[101] Levy, *Disrespectful Thugs*.

Conclusion

Having started this book with one *Yes, Prime Minister* episode, it may be fitting to end it with another. In an earlier episode, "The Official Visit," Jim Hacker is still far from the lofty heights of Number Ten Downing Street. He has only recently been appointed minister for administrative affairs, and is facing a looming diplomatic crisis. The new leader of the fictional African nation Burunda, Colonel Selim Mohammed, arrives in the UK, having just installed himself as president following a military coup. Burunda has considerable oil supplies that will come on line in a few years' time, and President Mohammed is visiting in order to place a large contract with the British government for offshore drilling equipment. Hacker seeks to combine these geopolitical benefits with electoral gains by insisting that the Burundan president be officially greeted by the Queen in Scotland – more specifically, in three marginal Scottish constituencies (swing seats), where offshore drilling equipment is to be found and where by-elections will soon be held. Hacker's plan backfires, however, once President Mohammed shares with the British a draft of his speech. Alongside what Hacker dubs "all the usual drivel" ("happy to be here, thanks for the gracious welcome, ties between our two countries, bonds of shared experience, happy and fruitful cooperation in the future"), the draft contains the following proclamation:

Burundans feel a special affinity with the Celtic peoples in their struggle for freedom. We, too, had to fight to break free from the chains of British colonialism. We bid you to recall your former greatness, to remember William Wallace, Robert the Bruce, Banockburn . . . The people of Burunda urge the Scots and the Irish to rise up against English oppression, cast off the imperialist yoke, and join the fellowship of free nations.[1]

---

[1] Johnathan Lynn and Anthony Jay, *The Complete Yes Minister* (London: BBC Books, 1989), 48.

Upon reading the draft, Hacker and Sir Humphrey seek an urgent meeting with the new Burundan president, who, upon landing in the UK, turns out to be Hacker's old classmate, formerly known as Charlie Umtali. The meeting, described in Hacker's diary, begins in earnest when the new president responds to Hacker's congratulations on becoming head of state:

"Thank you," he said. "Though it wasn't difficult. I didn't have to do any of the boring things like fighting elections." He paused and then added casually "Or by-elections," and smiled amiably at us . . . "Jim, of course I'm delighted to see you, but is this purely a social visit . . .? Because I do have to put the finishing touches to my speech . . ." I tried to make him realize that the bit about colonialist oppression was slightly – well, *profoundly* embarrassing. I asked him if he couldn't just snip out the whole chunk about the Scots and the Irish. Charlie responded by saying "This is something I feel very deeply to be true. Surely the British don't believe in suppressing the truth?" A neat move . . .

. . . after quite a pause: "[W]hile you're here, Jim, may I sound you out on a proposal I was going to make to the prime minister at our talks?" I nodded. He told us that his little change of government in Burunda had alarmed some of the investors in their oil industry . . . So he wants some investment from Britain to tide him over. At last we were talking turkey. I asked how much. He said fifty million pounds. Sir Humphrey looked concerned. He wrote me a little note. "Ask him on what terms." So I asked. "Repayment of the capital not to start before ten years. And interest free." Humphrey chocked into his coffee. So I pointed out that fifty million was a lot of money . . . I got another note from Humphrey, which pointed out that, if interest ran at ten percent on average, and if the loan was interest free for ten years, he was in effect asking for a free gift of fifty million pounds.

Cautiously, I put this point to Charlie. He . . . explained that it was all to our advantage, because they would use the loan to buy oil rigs built on the Clyde. I could see the truth of this, but I got another frantic, and, by now, almost illegible note from Humphrey, saying that Charlie wants us to give him fifty million pounds so that <u>he</u> can buy <u>our</u> oil rigs with <u>our</u> money (his underlinings, I may say). We couldn't go on passing notes to each other like naughty schoolboys . . . Sir Humphrey demanded a private word with me, so we went and stood in the corridor . . . Humphrey said we'd never get the money back, and therefore he could not recommend it to the Treasury, and the Treasury would never recommend it to Cabinet. "You are proposing . . . to buy your way out of a political entanglement with fifty million pounds of public money." I said that this is diplomacy. He said it was corruption.[2]

---

[2] Lynn and Jay, *The Complete Yes Minister*, 51–54.

Conclusion 235

Hacker finds a way out of his quagmire by seizing on Sir Humphrey's own narrow self-interest, threatening to withhold Humphrey's next official honor unless he cooperates. Thus united, Hacker and Sir Humphrey convince themselves – with each other's help – that the only result of avoiding investment in Burunda would be Soviet investment in the country. Buoyed by this reasoning, Humphrey further proposes they appeal to the government's "third world obligations" to justify the deal, although it is plain that neither he nor Hacker really assign these obligations any weight, nor are they truly concerned (more specifically) with how the loan they are going to recommend will actually impact the people who live under Burunda's new military leader. This leader gets his desired loan, and omits the "embarrassing" remarks about British colonialism from his speech in exchange.[3]

There are several reasons why this episode provides a fitting coda for the inquiries of this book. First, and most obviously, there are the topics that the episode explicitly puts center stage. Morally dubious loans propping up authoritarians, corruption and the abuse of public funds, classic political calculations concerning electoral survival – all of these issues have featured prominently throughout this book. Second, there are the episode's secondary themes: self-seeking rationalizations; the predictable appeals to moral excuses associated with how other governments are likely to behave in the international realm; the weight of history and desire to sweep "inconvenient" historical truths under the rug; hypocritical invocations of the needs of the world's vulnerable. All of these themes as well have played an important role in my arguments.

However, perhaps the most important reason to conclude with this episode is that it reminds us yet again just how natural it is to explore all of these significant moral issues by focusing on the behavior of individual political actors. In this book, by contrast, I pursued a different, much more collectivist tack: I reflected on many of the issues highlighted in "The Official Visit" – and on a range of other political problems – by developing two frameworks that focus directly on the people as a collective agent.

In one sense, this collectivist choice took me down well-traversed paths. Political actors routinely appeal to "the will of the people" to justify revolutions and vilify opponents. Political theorists routinely examine different aspects of the agency, voice, and normative standing

---

[3] Lynn and Jay, *The Complete Yes Minister*, 54.

of "the people." And key legal documents of the modern world – from numerous constitutions to core treaties of international law – invoke "the sovereignty of the people" as a fundamental principle. Yet, notwithstanding this ubiquitous presence of "the people" in modern political thought and practice, this book tried to show that the idea of the people still remains under-theorized.

Confronting this gap, I have argued that rich theoretical and practical dividends follow once we think systematically about the sovereign people in a liberal democracy as an agent with its own integrity. Parallel dividends, I suggested, follow from systematic thinking about the sovereign people as an owner of public property. I sought to demonstrate how these two collectivist frameworks, taken together, can advance our thinking about multiple real-world policy problems that revolve not around the unity of "the people," but rather around intense friction and division – between the people and its leaders, between the people and outsiders, and between different ethnic and religious groups within the people.

However, rather than recap the specific arguments I have made with regard to each of these divisions, I want to end by suggesting several areas of future research that I believe follow from these arguments. One such area has to do with links between the collectivist ideas of the preceding pages and the more common, individual-level discussions of political ethics. In particular, although my collectivist analysis of corruption and integrity sought to depart from the standard focus on individual political actors, it is also important to see how collective and individual integrity arguments can enrich one another. How, at the end of the day, does the integrity of individual politicians – or their lack of integrity – relate to the integrity of liberal democracy? Should we, for instance, praise individual political actors who espouse unconditional moral commitments, and therefore seem to be paragons of individual integrity, even if their steadfast adherence to these commitments prevents them from climbing up to positions of real power where they can better protect the integrity of a liberal democracy's identity-grounding institutions? If we are troubled by this cost, must we simply accept a world in which – as Minister Hacker pointedly observes to Sir Humphrey – "Every man has his price?"[4] And if so, should we feel more sympathy toward the real politician who – just like the fictional

---

[4] Lynn and Jay, *The Complete Yes Minister*, 54.

Hacker – virtually always prioritizes short-term electoral success over "doing the right thing?" And how should such sympathy, in turn, affect our moral analysis of governments who often have good reason to fear that "doing the right thing" may threaten their electoral survival?

A different set of questions that follows from the inquiries of this book concerns further policy issues that ideas about collective integrity and property can illuminate. One important example here is the case of legislative and regulatory capture in affluent democracies. Although this is a familiar topic in some respects (especially for political theorists in the United States), much more remains to be said about the full implications and severity of legislative and regulatory capture. In turn, one natural way to understand this capture is to see it, in Rawls's apt phrase, as "selling the public trust."[5] How should we conceptualize such a – recurrent – sale? Can this sale become so blatant so as to undermine the duty of those it harms to "play by the rules" of the political system? And what, more generally, are the most morally appropriate strategies for combating this sale? There is reason to hope that ideas regarding the people's integrity and property can help us tackle such questions in a way that yields both philosophical and practical dividends.

Alongside these specific issues, the preceding pages suggest three broader topics that warrant further investigation. The first topic is the complex normative links between domestic and global politics. Over the last generation, analytical political philosophy has studied these links first and foremost through the prism of perfect justice. The recurring question has been whether ideal visions of perfect justice used to assess a society's internal arrangements should also apply to the world at large. In this book, by contrast, I tried to show the value of theorizing the relationship between domestic and global politics in a way that is oriented around manifestly non-ideal problems. But I have not, of course, even come close to exhausting the relevant inquiries here. Thus for example, I noted, as part of my development of collective integrity ideas, the relationship between collective integrity revolving around the law of a liberal democracy and the duty to obey the law. But I have said very little about how a liberal democracy's global conduct might undermine its own citizens' general duty to obey the law within its own

---

[5] Quoted in Samuel Freeman, *Justice and the Social Contract: Essays in Rawlsian Political Philosophy* (Oxford: Oxford University Press, 2006), 326.

borders. The practical significance of this topic can hardly be over-stated; I hope to be able to shed more light on it in the future.[6]

A second broad theme associated with some of the key claims of this book has to do with duties of civic engagement. Throughout the book, I have argued that individual citizens in a liberal democracy have important moral duties to engage in active efforts to advance liberal-democratic values, especially through the legal system. But at several points in the preceding chapters, I also noted distressing circumstances where the moral failures of legal institutions, and the deeply morally flawed views held by a majority in society, are so entrenched that individuals could conceivably see themselves as released from these civic duties. Contemporary political theory, however, lacks a sustained account of when that release happens. Moreover – to take an adjacent but perhaps more dramatic issue – contemporary political theory lacks a sustained account of when we should stop seeing ordinary individual citizens as culpable for certain collective institutional and social failures, and start seeing them as victims of these failures. This normative shift may be salient, for example, in countries whose fragile democratic institutions are giving way to renewed authoritarianism. There is a stage where ordinary citizens are (arguably) culpable if they do not make efforts to protect democratic institutions against authoritarian tendencies. Yet once these institutions have been eroded to an extent that allows a regime to credibly threaten dissenters' most basic liberties and interests, we may have to view ordinary citizens less as accomplices of the regime and more as its victims. How to understand this normative transition is a fundamental question about the political responsibilities of individual citizens, to which we currently lack good answers.

The final, most general area for future inquiry has to do with my attempt, throughout this book, to incorporate circumstances of real-world political decision-making into normative frameworks. Though I would like to believe that the preceding pages represent some progress on this score, a great deal of work remains here too. At the most basic level, this is because normative political theory still lacks a systematic basis for deciding which features of real-world politics to incorporate into its inquiries. To take one example, normative political theory still

---

[6] For an initial effort in this direction, see my "Injustice abroad, authority at home? Democracy, systemic effects, and global wrongs," *American Journal of Political Science* 62 (2018): 72–83.

lacks a systematic basis for deciding which, if any, of the feasibility concerns that are ubiquitous in political life should be seen as fundamental constraints for normative purposes. Another example is morally dangerous views that are ubiquitous in actual policy debates: are there circumstances where political theorists should try to develop "incompletely theorized" agreements with the proponents of such views? When should political theorists actually scrutinize these views, seeking to expose their flaws? And when should political theorists simply ignore morally repugnant views, no matter how popular? This is another set of meta-theoretical questions concerning real-world politics, about which we lack sustained answers. Any normative theorist interested in real-world politics, and anyone interested in the normative role of the people in politics, should take these questions seriously.

Index

Aboriginal peoples, territorial rights of, 95
Ackerman, Bruce, 32
Agent-principal theory, corruption and, 114–115
Alfonsin, Raul, 139
Ali, Muhammad, 65
Alienation, integrity and, 23–24, 40
Amish, 206
Amnesties
　overview, 103, 134–137, 153
　consequentialism and, 135–137
　effect on authoritarian regimes, 138–142
　equal rights and, 145–146
　exclusion of moral claims in prosecution of officials versus, 145
　"kangaroo trials" of officials versus, 144–145
　leniency toward authoritarianism and, 143
　"peace versus justice" dilemma, 134, 137
　plea-bargains and, 141–142
　political divides regarding, 16
　preference falsification and, 139–140
　revocation of, 149–152
　　authoritarian means, amnesty imposed by, 149
　　collective integrity framework offering solutions to problems of, 150–152
　　democratic means, amnesty imposed by, 149–150
　　"kangaroo trials" of officials following, 151–152
　rule of law and, 145–146
　theft of public property and, 142–146
　truth commissions and, 146–148 (*See also* Truth commissions)
Apartheid, 20–21, 38–39, 42, 43, 45, 48
Argentina, democratic transition in, 139
Arneson, Richard, 72

Barry, Christian, 159, 168–169
Belgium, "vulture funds" and, 167–168
Belkovsky, Stanislav, 41
Ben Gurion, David, 206–207
Bob Jones University, 88–90
Bodily rights, 81–82
Bolsonaro, Jair, 110–111
Brazil
　corruption in, 110–112
　immunity of government officials in, 16
Bribery, 37–38
British Petroleum (BP), 11
Buchanan, Allen, 42, 53, 75
Burg, Avraham, 226
Burkina Faso
　corruption in, 70–71
　reappropriation in, 101
　theft of public property in, 70–71, 74, 101
Bush, George H. W., 126
Bush, George W., 89

Calheiros, Renan, 118–119
Cambodia, sovereign debt in, 161
Canada, territorial rights in, 93
Carnation Revolution, 152
Carter, Stephen, 25, 48, 128
Catalans, 95–96

Index

Ceaușescu, Nicolae, 151–152
Chazon Ish, 206–207
Chile, democratic transitions in, 143–144
China, lack of public honesty in, 50
Chirac, Jacques, 107
Churchill, Winston, 61–62
Civic engagement, duties of, 32, 64, 115, 238
Clinton, Bill, 122
Cohen, G. A., 72
Collective agency, 10–11, 15, 27–28, 235–236
Collective integrity. *See* Integrity
Collectivist frameworks
 consequentialism versus, 6–7
 ethics and, 236–237
 functions of, 14
 fundamental democratic convictions and, 8
 individualism versus, 235–236
 of integrity, 4–5 (*See also* Integrity)
 law in liberal democracy and, 7
 multiple moral judgments and, 7
 of property, 5–6 (*See also* Property)
Colombia, FARC peace referendum, 118
Community Driven Development Projects, 9–10
Compaoré, Blaise, 70–71, 101
Congo, Democratic Republic of, sovereign debt in, 166
Congo-Brazzaville, sovereign debt in, 166–167
Consequentialism
 amnesties and, 135–137
 collectivist frameworks versus, 6–7
Constructive engagement, 21, 46–47
Copyrights, 82
Corruption
 overview, 235
 agent-principal theory and, 114–115
 in Brazil, 110–112
 defined, 102–103
 exclusion of moral claims in prosecution of, 145
 executive immunity in cases of
  overview, 109–112
  collective integrity framework offering solution to problems of, 113–119
 collective property framework offering solution to problems of, 112–113
 referenda and, 112–119
 "kangaroo trials" of officials for, 144–145
 prosecution as unifying strategy, 143–144
 in South Korea, 116

Decency
 collective integrity and, 57–60
 global integrity test and, 58
 integrity and, 25–26
 "the Nazi's integrity," 51–52
 toward people in dire need, 57–58
 personal integrity and, 51–53
 toward vulnerable persons, 53–57
  blatant exploitation, 54
  in dispute resolution, 55
  drowning child example, 54, 56
  identity-grounding commitments and, 55–56
  integrity and, 55–57
  sacrifice and, 56–57
  self-seeking rationalizations and, 55
Deception, integrity and, 26
Deep public ownership model
 overview, 72–73, 101
 challenges to, 101
 copyrights and, 82
 eminent domain and, 83
 heterodox nature of, 72–73
 libertarianism and, 84, 90–91
 popular sovereignty over property, 79–80, 81–82
 private conduct versus public policy, 90, 91–93
 private property and, 83–84
 racism and, 85–91
 redistribution of wealth and, 84–85
 in single world state, 97
 social equality and, 85–91
 strengths of, 101
 taxation and, 80
 territorial rights and, 93–98
 theft of public property and, 82–83
 unilateral privatization and, 83

De Frank, Tom, 128
Democracy, intertwining with liberalism, 22
Democratic boundary problem, 8
Democratic transitions
　amnesties in (*See* Amnesties)
　in Argentina, 139
　in Chile, 143–144
Distance, hypocrisy of, 44–45, 215–216
Domestic and global politics, normative links between, 237–238
Donegal International, 166
Dresden bombing (1945), 62
Druze in Israel. *See* Israel
Dworkin, Ronald, 12, 28, 30, 71–72, 81–82

Ecuador, sovereign debt in, 163–164
Egypt, sovereign debt in, 163–164
Elster, Jon, 18
Eminent domain, 83
Equal rights
　amnesties and, 145–146
　executive immunity, objections to based on, 105
　integrity and
　　failure of, 29–30
　　as identity-grounding commitment, 28–29, 38–39
　　legal institutions and, 29
　　necessity of, 28–29
　in Israel, 212–213, 217
　pardons, objections to based on, 122–123
Equatorial Guinea, theft of public property in, 141
Eritrea, refugees from, 228–229
Ethics, collectivist frameworks and, 236–237
Ethnic and religious divisions
　overview, 153, 189
　in Israel
　　overview, 17
　　collective integrity framework offering solutions to problems of, 209–211, 229
　　collective property framework offering solutions to problems of, 211, 229
　　Druze and (*See* Israel)
　　future trends, 229–232
　　ultra-orthodox and (*See* Israel)
　political divides regarding, 17
Executive immunity
　overview, 102–103, 153
　alternative institutional procedures, 108–109
　corruption, in cases of
　　overview, 109–112
　　collective integrity framework offering solution to problems of, 113–119
　　collective property framework offering solution to problems of, 112–113
　　referenda and, 112–119
　effective governance as justification for, 104–105
　in France, 104
　objections to
　　equal rights, based on, 105
　　extension of immunity beyond term of office, based on, 105–107
　　more stringent standards for officials, need for, 105
　　opportunistic lawsuits, minimal danger of, 108
　political divides regarding, 15–16
　in Portugal, 104
Exile agreements, sovereign debt and
　overview, 179–180, 185
　cancellation of, 184
　collective integrity framework and, 181–183
　collective property framework and, 181
　credible democratic opposition, necessity of, 183
　incentives regarding, 184–185
　International Relations scholarship and, 182
　as less-than-ideal solution, 185

Fanaticism, 60–61, 137–138
Federalist Papers, 120
Ferrante, Elena, 109
FG Capital Management, 166
Ford, Gerald, 102, 128–134
France, executive immunity in, 104

Index

Franco, Francisco, 146
Fried, Barbara, 76
Friedman, Menachem, 208–209

Garcia Marquez, Gabriel, 179
Garsten, Bryan, 80
Germany, lack of public honesty in, 49–50
Global and domestic politics, normative links between, 237–238
Global integrity test, 34, 42–43, 58
Goodin, Robert, 4–5, 68, 225
Gormley, Ken, 129
Group agency. *See* Collective agency
Guatemala, truth commission in, 147
Gulf of Mexico oil spill (2010), 11

Haiti, natural disasters in, 57
Halabi, Rabah, 197
Hamas, 221–222
Hamilton, Alexander, 120
Herzog, Yitzhak, 227
Hitler, Adolf, 61
Holocaust, 226, 227
Honore, Tony, 71
Hughes, Langston, 65
Human trafficking, 45–46
Hussein, Saddam, 160–161
Hypocrisy, integrity and, 44–48
  apartheid, 45
  human trafficking, 45–46
  "hypocrisy of distance," 44–45, 215–216
  "hypocrisy of self-seeking rationalizations," 46–48
  public honesty compared, 48
  racism, 44
  women's rights, 45

Identity-grounding commitments
  equal rights as, 28–29, 38–39
  people in dire need, and decency toward, 57–58
  vulnerable persons, and decency toward, 55–56
Identity intuition, 21–22
Immunity of government officials. *See* Executive immunity
Individualism

collective integrity framework versus, 66–67
collectivist frameworks versus, 235–236
Integrity
  overview, 22–23
  actual practices and, 30–31
  alienation and, 23–24, 40
  amnesties, collective integrity framework offering solutions to problems of, 150–152
  bribery and, 37–38
  collective agency and, 27–28
  collectivist framework of, 4–5
  as consisting in fidelity to projects and commitments, 4, 23–25
  contested liberal identity and, 62–65
  decency and, 25–26 (*See also* Decency)
  deception and, 26
  equal rights and
    failure of, 29–30
    as identity-grounding commitment, 28–29, 38–39
    legal institutions and, 29
    necessity of, 28–29
  ethnic and religious divisions, collective integrity framework offering solutions to problems of
    overview, 211, 229
    Israel, military service in, 209–211
  executive immunity, collective integrity framework offering solution to problems of, 113–119
  in extremis, 60–62
  fanaticism versus, 60–61, 137–138
  in global action, 36–40
  in global context, 33–36
  global integrity test, 34, 42–43, 58
  hypocrisy and, 44–48
    apartheid, 45
    human trafficking, 45–46
    "hypocrisy of distance," 44–45, 215–216
    "hypocrisy of self-seeking rationalizations," 46–48
    public honesty compared, 48
    racism, 44
    women's rights, 45

Integrity (cont.)
  identity intuition and, 21–22
  of liberal polity, 27–28
  liberal values and, 26–27, 34–36
  moral wrongs and, 31
  natural resources trade with dictatorships and, 40–43
  "the Nazi's integrity," 51–52
  objections to collective framework of
    illiberal polities versus, 68–69
    individualism versus, 66–67
    moral judgment as separate from, 67–68
  pardons, collective integrity framework offering solution to problems of, 129–130
  personal integrity, 51–53
  popular sovereignty and, 27–28
  property as subset of, 8
  psychological fragmentation and, 23–24
  public honesty and, 48–50
  purposefulness and, 24–25
  refugees, collective integrity framework and, 224–227
  rule of law and, 32
  sacrifice and, 25, 32–33
  sovereign debt, collective integrity framework offering solutions to problems of
    overview, 157
    authoritarian governments, loans to, 161–164, 235
    constitutional and international protections compared, 177–178
    exile agreements, 181–183
    future loans, 171–172
    private versus public lenders, 186–187
    reputational calculations, 164–166
    vulnerable agents, debts of, 164–168
    "vulture funds," 166–168
  torture and, 39
  truthfulness and, 26
  in World War II, 61–62
International Criminal Court (ICC), 180
International Monetary Fund, 168, 169
Iran, theft of public property in, 141

Iran-Contra scandal, 126
Iraq, sovereign debt in, 160–161
Israel
  Central Bureau of Statistics (CBS), 196, 197–198
  confiscation of Palestinian lands in, 193–194
  conflict with Palestinians
    Druze situation, relevance of, 212, 213, 218–219, 221
    ultra-orthodox situation, relevance of, 221, 223–224
  Druze in
    overview, 194
    conflict with Palestinians, relevance to, 212, 213, 218–219, 221
    demographics of, 194–195
    discrimination against, 196–197
    "Israel as the Nation-State of the Jewish People" (basic law), impact of, 219–221
    in Israeli Defense Forces, 195–196
    lack of commemoration of military service, 204–205
    property rights of, 217–218
    self-identity of, 195
    socioeconomic status of, 196
    ultra-orthodox compared, 198, 201, 209
  economic situation, deterioration of, 229–232
  equal rights in, 212–213, 217
  ethnic and religious divisions in
    overview, 17
    collective integrity framework offering solutions to problems of, 209–211, 229
    collective property framework offering solutions to problems of, 211, 229
    future trends, 229–232
  Hapoel Tel Aviv (soccer club), 227–228
  housing costs in, 230
  "Israel as the Nation-State of the Jewish People" (basic law), 219–221
  Israeli Defense Forces, 195–196

Israeli Land Authority (ILA), 216–217
Jewish National Fund (JNF), 214–217
  abolition proposed, 217–218
  collective integrity framework offering solutions to problems of, 215–216
  collective property framework offering solutions to problems of, 215
  equal rights and, 217
Maccabi Tel Aviv (soccer club), 227–228
military service
  collective integrity framework and, 209–211
  Druze and, 195–196
  importance of, 202–204
  lack of commemoration of Druze in, 204–205
  "religionization" and, 222–223
  ultra-orthodox, opposition of, 200, 201, 205–211
political capital in, 192–193
political divides in, 192
racist violence in, 194, 231–232
refugees in
  overview, 224
  collective integrity framework and, 224–227
  from Eritrea, 228–229
  Holocaust compared, 226, 227
  from Sudan, 228–229
  from Syria, 227, 228
"religionization" in, 222–223
rule of law in, 212–213
shrinking progressive camp in, 229–232
territorial rights in, 98
ultra-orthodox in
  overview, 194
  conflict with Palestinians, relevance to, 221, 223–224
  demographics of, 197–198
  Druze compared, 198, 201, 209
  education of, 198–200
  employment of, 198–200
  military service, opposition to, 200, 201, 205–211
  relationship with general population, 198
  religious study versus secular society, 198–200, 208–211
  use of term, 192–193
  voting rates in, 212
  Yad Vashem, 228
  Zionism and, 208–209

Jamaica, sovereign debt in, 163–164
Jewish National Fund (JNF), 214–217
  abolition proposed, 217–218
  collective integrity framework offering solutions to problems of, 215–216
  collective property framework offering solutions to problems of, 215
  equal rights and, 217
Joint action, 11

Kabel, Eitan, 218
Karelitz, Avrohom Yeshaya (Chazon Ish), 206–207
Kennedy, Edward, 128
Kennedy, John F., 190
King, Martin Luther, 65
Krebs, Ronald, 214
Kuran, Timur, 139–140, 183–184

Lazarus, Emma, 63–64
Legislative capture, 237
Lepora, Chiara, 68
Lerner, Hanna, 212–213
Levy, Jackie, 231–232
Levy, Yagil, 222–223
Liberalism, intertwining with democracy, 22
Liberal nationalism, 31–32
Libertarianism
  deep public ownership model and, 84, 90–91
  property and, 75–76
Lienau, Odette, 164–165
List, Christian, 10, 37, 69
Louis XIV (France), 124
Luban, David, 158
Lula da Silva, Luiz Inacio, 110–111

246   *Index*

Marcos, Ferdinand, 160
Massie, Robert, 20
McCarthy, Joseph, 53
Mcfall, Lynn, 52
Michael, Sami, 190
Millennium Development Goals, 169
Minority groups
    ethnic and religious divisions (*See*
        Ethnic and religious divisions)
    territorial rights of, 94
Modi, Narendra, 141
Moore, Kathleen, 123–124
Moral framework, 12–14
    multiple moral intuitions, unification
        of, 12–13
    special efforts in, 14
    values, unification of, 12

Nal, Lon, 161
Natural resources trade with
    dictatorships, 40–43
"The Nazi's integrity," 51–52
Netanyahu, Binyamin, 193, 224, 227,
    230
New York Times, 128–129
Nicaragua
    Sandinista government, 155,
        157–158
    sovereign debt in, 155, 157–159, 175
Nixon, Richard, 120, 126–127,
    128–134, 146
NML Capital, 166–167
Normative political theory, 17–19
    character of rhetoric and, 19
    domestic and global politics, links
        between, 237–238
    real-world political decision-making
        incorporation of, 238–239
    uncertainty and, 17–19
Norway, cancellation of sovereign debt
    by, 163–164
Nozick, Robert, 81

Odebrecht, 110

Pacifism, 206
Palestinians
    confiscation of lands by Israel,
        193–194
    conflict with Israel

        Druze situation, relevance of, 212,
            213, 218–219, 221
        ultra-orthodox situation, relevance
            of, 221, 223–224
    Hamas, 221–222
    territorial rights of, 98
Pardons
    overview, 103, 119–120, 153
    collective integrity framework
        offering solution to problems of,
        129–130
    collective property framework
        offering solution to problems of,
        130–131
    of former elected officials, 127–134
    justifications for
        indigent persons without access to
            legal services, 122
        mercy as, 120
        unjust laws, 121
    monarchs, sovereignty of, 123–125
    objections to
        equal rights, based on, 122–123
        legal reform as preferred remedy,
            121
        not waiting until conclusion of
            legal process, based on, 121
        publicly funded legal services as
            preferred remedy, 122
        voiding of unjust laws as preferred
            remedy, 121–122
    political divides regarding, 16
    as presidential prerogative, 123–127
    in United States, 125, 126–127,
        128–134
"Paris Club," 167–168
Park Geun-hye, 116
Paul, Rand, 86
"Peace versus justice" dilemma, 134,
    137
"The people"
    collective agency and, 10–11, 27–28,
        235–236
    political divides within, 190–191
    popular sovereignty, 8–9, 27–28, 236
Peru, sovereign debt in, 163–164,
    166–167
Petrobras, 110
Pettit, Philip, 10, 37, 69
Philippines

Index 247

sovereign debt in, 160
theft of public property in, 141
Pinochet, Augusto, 135–136, 143–144, 145, 180
Plea-bargains, 141–142
Pogge, Thomas, 176–177
Policy priorities, 191–192
Political capital, 191–193
Political divides, 15–17
  amnesties and, 16
  collective agency versus, 15
  ethnic and religious divisions, 17
  immunity of government officials and, 15–16
  incrementalist approach to, 212–213
  in Israel, 192
  pardons and, 16
  within the people, 190–191
  sovereign debt and, 16–17
Political realism, 6–7
Popular sovereignty, 8–9, 27–28, 236. *See also* Integrity; Property
Portugal
  Carnation Revolution, 152
  executive immunity in, 104
  "kangaroo trials" in, 152
Preference falsification, 139–140
Pre-political property, 78–79
Privacy rights, 91–92
Private aggregation model, 76–79
Private property
  deep public ownership model and, 83–84
  harmful uses of, 87
  requirement of, 75
  unilateral privatization, 83
Property
  overview, 72–73, 101
  accounting for
    challenges in, 76–79
    collectivist requirement, 74–75, 77
    deep public ownership model as, 99–101
    moral framework requirement, 75
    private property requirement, 75
  bodily rights versus, 81–82
  collective property rights, 74
  collectivist framework of, 5–6
  convention, property rights as, 99–101
  deep public ownership model (*See* Deep public ownership model)
  derivative, property rights as, 99
  enforcement of property rights, 73–74
  ethnic and religious divisions, collective property framework offering solutions to problems of, 211, 229
  executive immunity, collective property framework offering solution to problems of, 112–113
  incidents of property rights, 73–74
  libertarianism and, 75–76
  pardons, collective property framework offering solution to problems of, 130–131
  pre-political property, 78–79
  private aggregation model, 76–79
  private property
    deep public ownership model and, 83–84
    harmful uses of, 87
    requirement of, 75
    unilateral privatization, 83
  proprietary rights construed, 81
  reappropriation of, 101
  scholarly neglect of public property, 71–72
  in single world state, 97
  sovereign debt, collective property framework offering solutions to problems of
    overview, 157, 159
    constitutional and international protections compared, 177–178
    exile agreements, 181
    future loans, 171–172
    presumptions regarding, 159–160
    private versus public lenders, 186
  as subset of integrity, 8
  taxation and, 76–77, 78–79
  territorial rights and, 93–98
  theft of public property (*See* Theft of public property)
Proudhon, Pierre-Joseph, 71
Psychological fragmentation, integrity and, 23–24
Public honesty, integrity and, 48–50

Purposefulness, integrity and, 24–25
Putin, Vladimir, 41

Quakers, 206

Racism
  apartheid, 20–21, 38–39, 42, 43, 45, 48
  deep public ownership model and, 85–91
  hypocrisy and, 44
  Israel, racist violence in, 194, 231–232
  in United States, 63, 65
Rawls, John, 6, 14, 29, 35–36, 51, 67, 71–72, 84, 85, 93–94, 237
Raz, Joseph, 66
Reagan, Ronald, 21, 46–47, 126
Redistribution of wealth, 84–85
Referenda, 112–119
Refugees in Israel
  overview, 224
  collective integrity framework and, 224–227
  from Eritrea, 228–229
  Holocaust compared, 226, 227
  from Sudan, 228–229
  from Syria, 227, 228
Regulatory capture, 237
Religious divisions. *See* Ethnic and religious divisions
Rich, Mark, 122
Riggs Banks, 180
Risk versus uncertainty, 17–18
Rivlin, Reuven, 194
Roemer, John, 72
Romania
  "kangaroo trials" in, 151–152
  sovereign debt owed to, 166
Rose-Ackerman, Susan, 103
Rothstein, Bo, 114–115
Rousseau, Jean-Jacques, 69, 79–80, 113, 119, 120
Rousseff, Dilma, 110, 111
Rubenfeld, Jed, 25
Rule of law
  amnesties and, 145–146
  integrity and, 32
  in Israel, 212–213
Russia
  natural resources trade with, 41
  theft of public property in, 74, 141

Sack, Alexander, 158
Sacrifice
  integrity and, 25, 32–33
  vulnerable persons, and decency toward, 56–57
Salazar, António de Oliveira, 152
Saudi Arabia, natural resources trade with, 41–42
Schmitt, Carl, 223
Self-seeking rationalizations
  overview, 235
  hypocrisy of, 46–48
  vulnerable persons, and decency toward, 55
Sen, Amartya, 72
Shafter, Jonathan, 177–178
Shielding government officials from liability. *See* Executive immunity
Shklar, Judith, 44
Shribman, David, 129
Shtern, Elazar, 220
Sierra Leone, sovereign debt in, 163–164
Sikkink, Kathryn, 135–136, 137, 151–152
Singer, Peter, 54
Slavery, 27–28
Somoza Debayle, Anastasio, 155
Somoza family, 155, 157–159
South Africa
  apartheid in, 20–21, 38–39, 42, 43, 45, 48
  constructive engagement with, 21, 46–47
  divestment from, 20–21, 38–39, 48
  sovereign debt in, 164–166
  theft of public property in, 74
  truth commission in, 147
  United States, relations with, 20–21, 38–39, 45, 48
South Carolina confederate flag controversy, 63
South Korea
  corruption in, 116
  theft of public property in, 74
Sovereign debt

Index 249

overview, 153, 154–155
alternatives to, 188–189
in Cambodia, 161
cancellation of, 163–164, 168–171
collective integrity framework
    offering solutions to problems of
    overview, 157
    authoritarian governments, loans
        to, 161–164, 235
    constitutional and international
        protections compared, 177–178
    exile agreements, 181–183
    future loans, 171–172
    private versus public lenders,
        186–187
    reputational calculations, 164–166
    vulnerable agents, debts of,
        164–168
    "vulture funds," 166–168
collective property framework
    offering solutions to problems of
    overview, 157, 159
    constitutional and international
        protections compared, 177–178
    exile agreements, 181
    future loans, 171
    presumptions regarding, 159–160
    private versus public lenders,
        186
in Congo-Brazzaville, 166–167
constitutional protections against
    abuse, 176–177
"democracy fund," 176–177
"democracy panel," 176–177
in Democratic Republic of Congo,
    166
in Ecuador, 163–164
in Egypt, 163–164
exile agreements
    overview, 179–180, 185
    cancellation of, 184
    collective integrity framework and,
        181–183
    collective property framework and,
        181
    credible democratic opposition,
        necessity of, 183
    incentives regarding, 184–185
    International Relations scholarship
        and, 182

as less-than-ideal solution, 185
form of government and, 156
future loans
    overview, 171
    collective integrity framework and,
        171–172
    collective property framework and,
        171
    private creditors, incentives of,
        172–176
inherited debt, 156–157
institutional design and, 176–178
international protections against
    abuse, 177
in Iraq, 160–161
in Jamaica, 163–164
in Nicaragua, 155, 157–159,
    175
Norway, cancellation by, 163–164
as "odious debt," 156
personal debt versus, 157–159
in Peru, 163–164, 166–167
in Philippines, 160
political divides regarding, 16–17
popular protests and, 173
private versus public lenders,
    186–188
Romania, owed to, 166
in Sierra Leone, 163–164
in South Africa, 164–166
in Zambia, 166
Sovereignty of the people, 8–9, 27–28,
    236. See also Integrity; Property
Soviet Union, collapse of, 139–140
Spain
    Catalans in, 95–96
    "pact of forgetting" in, 146–147
    territorial rights in, 95–96
"Spoilers" (of democratic transitions),
    147–148
Stalin, Josef, 61
Stanford Encyclopedia of Philosophy,
    72
Steadfastness, 48
Stilz, Anna, 9
Sudan, refugees from, 228–229
Supervenience, collective agency and,
    10
Syria, refugees from, 227, 228
System justification, 46

Taiwan, public honesty in, 50
Taxation
  disclosure of tax returns of
    politicians, 92–93
  property and, 76–77, 78–79
Territorial rights, 93–98
Theft of public property
  overview, 71, 235
  accounting for, 74
  amnesties and, 142–146
  in Burkina Faso, 70–71, 74, 101
  deep public ownership model and, 82–83
  defining, 79
  in Equatorial Guinea, 141
  in Iran, 141
  in Philippines, 141
  in Russia, 74, 141
  in South Africa, 74
  in South Korea, 74
Timerman, Hector, 167
Torture, 39
Trade in natural resources with dictatorships, 40–43
Truman, Harry, 18
Trump, Donald, 63–65, 87–88
Trump Management Corporation, 87–88
Truth commissions, 146–148
  backlash, danger of, 147–148
  in Guatemala, 147
  multiple policy options for, 147
  "pact of forgetting" versus, 146–147
  in South Africa, 147
  "spoilers" (of democratic transitions) and, 147–148
  third parties, use of, 148
Truthfulness, integrity and, 26
Tsai Ing-wen, 50

Ultra-orthodox in Israel. *See* Israel
Uncertainty
  normative political theory and, 17–19
  risk versus, 17–18
United Kingdom
  anti-gay laws in, 121–122
  Bomber Command, 62
  Brexit referendum, 118
  Debt Relief Act 2010, 167
  public honesty, lack of, 49–50
United States
  Amish in, 206
  Civil Rights Act, 86
  Comprehensive Anti-Apartheid Act, 20, 186–187
  copyrights in, 82
  disclosure of tax returns of politicians in, 92–93
  Fair Housing Act, 86–88
  Internal Revenue Service (IRS), 89
  Iran-Contra scandal, 126
  Library of Congress, 82
  Muslim ban, 63–65
  pardons in, 125, 126–127, 128–134
  public honesty, lack of, 49–50
  Quakers in, 206
  racism in, 63, 65
  slavery in, 27–28
  South Africa, relations with, 20–21, 38–39, 45, 48
  South Carolina confederate flag controversy, 63
  Watergate scandal, 120, 126–127, 128–134

"Veto players," 18–19
Vinter, Ofer, 223
Vulnerable persons, decency toward, 53–57
  blatant exploitation, 54
  in dispute resolution, 55
  drowning child example, 54, 56
  identity-grounding commitments and, 55–56
  integrity and, 55–57
  sacrifice and, 56–57
  self-seeking rationalizations and, 55
"Vulture funds," 166–168

Waldron, Jeremy, 37, 72
Wall Street Journal, 129
Watergate scandal, 120, 126–127, 128–134
Weinert, Richard, 159, 175

Wenar, Leif, 80, 170
Williams, Bernard, 4, 22–25, 224–225
Wisor, Scott, 173
Women's rights, hypocrisy and, 45
World Bank, 168, 169
World War II
   Dresden bombing, 62
   integrity in, 61–62

World Zionist Organization, 214

"Yes, Prime Minister" (television program), 1–6, 17, 77, 233–235, 236–237

Zambia, sovereign debt in, 166
Zionism, 208–209